The Making of a Mysti

M000195620

"*The Making of a Mystic in the Twenty-First Century* by Carol E. Parrish-Harra offers an excellent introduction to the path of mysticism by someone who has not only studied deeply but has had deep mystical experiences herself. As she writes: 'Our real heartfelt desire is to be in the Presence.' This book describes her quest to bring this heartfelt desire to realization. It is an inspiring work for travelers on the path."

—**Robert Powell PhD,** co-founder of the Sophia Foundation and author of *The Sophia Teachings, The Most Holy Trinosophia, The Mystery, Destiny, and Biography of Mary Magdalene,* and other works

"Carol Parrish-Harra is a dynamic, spiritual trailblazer and a real visionary. Her spiritual path is a living synthesis of multiple strands of living wisdom and her story is a document of great importance. As a modern Mystic she is a source of evolutionary inspiration and spiritual renewal, and I warmly recommend the book!"

—**Søren Hauge,** spiritual teacher, counsellor and author, www.sorenhauge.com

"*The Making of a Mystic in the Twenty-First Century* is what I would like all newcomers to the field of spiritual Esoterics and Mysticism to read. Carol Parrish-Harra gives easy-to-read descriptions of some essential Do's and Don'ts from her personal experience, and warns of several traps that can befall the advanced student. A gentle, but firm entry into this vast subject."

—**Archbishop Frank Bugge,** Australian Church of Antioch— Malabar Rite, author, *Numerology Reveals Your All*

"Carol Parrish-Harra offers a precise, practical wisdom contextualizing the emerging and evolving present with the past, while visioning our future destiny. This can change your life! In your heart is a Mystic seeking to reveal itself."

—**Daniel Dangaran D. Min.,** Bishop & Pastor of the Church of Antioch at Santa Fe

"Carol Parrish-Harra's latest book, *The Making of a Mystic in the Twenty-First Century*, speaks to the emptiness many people find in denominational Christianity. In doing so, she introduces the reader to the essence of the mystical path. Mysticism is by nature 'esoteric,' a term used to describe spiritual truths that are hidden, but which can be illuminated by following a mystical path. The author herself is a well-known and gifted person, and she reveals the steps on the path in the hope that you will find and follow your own mystical pathway."

—**Monsignor John W. Sweeley, Th.D.**, author of *Reincarnation for Christians*

"Over thirty years ago it was with some trepidation I attended my first intensive training with the Rev. Carol Parrish-Harra. I longed for inner activity, growth and mystical joy. There just had to be more to the life of Spirit than I had as yet experienced. For over twenty years I studied with and worked with now 'Bishop' Parrish-Harra. Read this book and you can share in the same experience. Many of the rather short and pithy observations she offers from page to page have hidden within them the esoteric experiences her mystery school stimulated, and also in an exoteric way. She is a true manager of learning for the spiritual seeker."

—**Bishop Bernie O. Finch, DC, DD,** Ascension Alliance

"I honor Carol Parrish-Harra's profound work, her deep knowledge of esotericism and her unrelenting service to the Hierarchy and Humanity. She is one of the finest representatives of the Great White Brotherhood and has delivered mightily on Their behalf through a long life dedicated to the dissemination of the highest spiritual values. The world esoteric community is greatly enriched by all she has done."

—**Michael D. Robbins, Ph.D.,** President, Seven Ray Institute and University of the Seven Rays

"The Making of a Mystic in the Twenty-First Century is the culmination of forty years' searching, finding and sharing insights into higher reality. Carol Parrish-Harra has inspired generations of students, and her new book—written in the straightforward, compelling style that is her hallmark—is a 'must-read' for all on the Path."

—**John F. Nash, Ph.D.,** author of *The Soul and Its Destiny* and *The Sacramental Church*

"The Making of a Mystic in the Twenty-First Century takes us to the very heart of experiencing Creator God. There is simplicity and fluidity in Carol E. Parrish-Harra's writing that encourages one to go further down the path of spiritual investigation. This 'how to' book is for the novice as well as the scholar. It paves the way for one to reach toward enlightenment. The author explains the unexplainable as only a true mystic can."

—**Most Rev. Patsy Grubbs. D.D.,** Presiding Bishop, Ascension Alliance Independent Catholic Church

"About the time that I had a mystic experience that revealed my life purpose as aiding the manifestation of the New Schools of Occult Meditation, I also heard the story of Carol Parrish-Harra and Sancta Sophia Seminary. I began to think of her as walking alongside of me as I brought Christ College of Trans-Himalayan Wisdom into manifestation. I share her vision of a new world religion that is both mystical and occult. This book is a joy to read because it is her personal journey and so much my/our journey."

—**Lawson Bracewell,** Christ College of Trans-Himalayan Wisdom

"Carol's spiritual journey is one that encompasses and envelopes many different perspectives from many different sources. She is insightful, thoughtful, knowledgeable, and she invites her readers to go with her to new places in the heart and mind."

—**Most Rev. Michael Adams,** Bishop, Community of Ascensionists

Other Books by Carol E. Parrish-Harra

The New Age Handbook on Death and Dying (1982, 2nd Ed. 1989)

Messengers of Hope (1983, 2nd Ed. 2001)

The Aquarian Rosary (1988)

The Gateway of Liberation and *Spiritual Laws*, with Mary Gray (1992)

New Dictionary of Spiritual Thought (1994, 2nd Ed. 2002)

Adventure in Meditation, Vol. I (1995)

Adventure in Meditation, Vol. II (1996)

Adventure in Meditation, Vol. III (1997)

Reflections (1997)

The Book of Ritual (1999)

ESP and the Bible, with Laurence Tunstall Heron (2003)

Sophia Sutras (2006)

Esoteric Secrets of Passion, Sex and Love (2011)

Remember to Remember, The Mayan Mysteries (2011)

The Making
of a
Mystic
in the
Twenty-First Century

CAROL E. PARRISH-HARRA

Blue Dolphin Publishing

Published by Blue Dolphin Publishing, Inc.
P. O. Box 8, Nevada City, CA 95959
Orders: 1 800 643-0765
Web: www.bluedolphinpublishing.com

ISBN: 978-1-57733-284-8 paperback
ISBN: 978-1-57733-461-3 e-book

Library of Congress Control Number: 2014947726

First Printing: August 2014

Cover painting: "The Mystic Within" by Cedar Carrier

Printed in the United States of America
5 4 3 2 1

Dedication

to
Charles Clayton Harra
whom I love,
he understood.

Acknowledgments

I acknowledge two most helpful individuals
in assisting me to make this work available:
Jesse Garnee and LaRhonda McBrayer
for countless details and support.

Seekers

PAUSE A MOMENT and contemplate the journey of a seeker of the Greater Light. It can be likened to an exciting quest. Personal progress toward self-mastery is accelerated by Wisdom herself. Nurtured by coincidences, and prompted by synchronicities, our discoveries are only limited by personal dedication. Progress comes with studies, experiments, and exercises that lead towards enlightenment.

Acknowledge Sophia

I, Wisdom, have created prudence,
And I possess knowledge and reason.
I love those who love me;
And those who seek me shall find me.

—Proverbs 8: 12-17

Table of Contents

Foreword

IN THIS EMINENTLY PRACTICAL and at times almost poetically articulated work, the author, Carol Parrish-Harra, reveals a deep inner wisdom gleaned from a lifetime of soul/spiritual explorations: from her earliest involvement with Christianity to esoteric Christianity to the knowledge gleaned from exploring the mysticism of the East.

We discover old and new metaphysical concepts, sociological, psychological insights as well as Hindi, Tibetan and Buddhist viewpoints carefully and thoughtfully interwoven and presented. East meets West on the stepping stones of her spiritual landscape. Ancient Wisdom traditions and teachings are revealed with candor and craft as we are introduced to what it means to profoundly engage the ever-unfolding dimensions of consciousness.

Students, teachers and seekers of the Inner Way and all who genuinely, seriously wish to access a perspective of the mystical pathway will be richly rewarded. This is a most valuable text which will guide, illumine and reveal some of the deeply spiritual, specific steps and stages of the soul's awakening. *The Making of a Mystic* offers insights intimate, subtle and spiritually significant. It will nourish the inquiry thoroughly, thoughtfully and provokingly, in these golden pages. It's a loving work of a lifetime.

Rev. LeRoy E. Zemke
Senior Pastor
Temple of the Living God of St. Petersburg, Inc.

Introduction

A MYSTIC BEARS WITNESS to worlds hidden within worlds, to truths unrevealed of which others merely dream. Secret sights and sounds animate their lives, adding dimension upon dimension.

I ask, "*What is my goal?* **Why** *am I sharing these thoughts that are so precious to me?*"

I answer my own question. "*Because they are treasures I have received from others who have gone before … teachers and others who have inspired me.*"

Imagine sitting beside me as I tell you what remarkable lives are possible … if chosen for this walk, and should you be so fortunate to have the Beings in the Higher World notice your efforts. They will see you, care for you, and test you. Some call it being "a disciple on a thread."

We feel alone, although we never are. A Holy One walks in the shadows close at hand. He or She oversees our steps and whispers actions that will train us to carry the *Mystery*, and to share it in time with others as they become available.

Some will hear and join the rich journey. Some will not. Some do not recognize the gift and will only come to the *Wisdom* at another time. Some will misuse the opportunity. It is not ours to judge but to give. Keep the heart open, even if some seem childish, for they are, "*the sons and daughters of the Most High.*"

Come sit as I share … *the making of a mystic.*

ONE

Off on an Adventure We Go

MYSTICISM RESIDES IN THE WORLD OF THE MUSE ... in a land of make-believe, magic and other-world realities waiting to be explored by those who seek them. The greatest work of the mystic is to be a living light. I hope there is a glimpse of that reality in this writing and you gain the fragrance of this joyful place. A wonderful phrase from ancient wisdom, "*You can enter into the Light, but you can never touch the flame,*" reminds us that to enter the Light and to carry the Light is the real "Work" in this world of confusing, false values.

Mysticism is the name given for the treasure hidden within each of us. To satisfy this longing *for something that seems just out of reach*, one must find a way to bring to fruition the divine seed that exists within. The longing begins without conscious understanding, but through this inner spark, we come to know our Oneness with the Creator and the Creation. The goal of human evolution is to become increasingly aware of and responsive to the calling that satisfies the empty space within each of us, the space that desires union with Creator and all others.

To find this Oneness, to live in the higher reality, we must work, worm, or fight through the mass of thought-forms that constantly invade and surround each of us. Our own mental activity creates thought-forms, while being bombarded by all the cultural thought-forms that surround us: media, advertising, patriots and fanatics—all vying for influence and harking their message, all charged with emotionalism, manipulation, and power.

1

In addition to these influences we have our own spiritual desire influencing us, as well as a blanket of thought-forms to work
through, and we do this by learning the value of silence. We must
get past our emotional nature, which, with all its charges and con-
tradictory instructions, clutters the higher frequencies. And then,
to work through old programming so we can "hear" the voice of the
Silent One, or "Solar Angel" as he/she is sometimes called.

The *One*, whom Christians know as Master Jesus, awakens and
inspires many on the inner journey, here referred to as "Esoteric
Christianity." Should the religions of the world be pictured as a
circle, each faith tradition would have an arc of the circle, with all
denominations and perspectives within it. Within this framework
of traditions no one could claim the entire circle, and each could
rightly claim a part of it. With this view, we learn that each religion
has an outer form and an inner expression, and that both one's
desire and their private spiritual practice deepen the experience
of Oneness with the Source. This penetration into the consciousness of the Source is the goal, for here we enter the space of *holy
consciousness, salvation, or enlightenment.*

Those dedicated to their quest are inner directed. They have
found that their great desire is to touch Eternal Truths and to experience the Loving Presence. Spiritual disciplines, when practiced,
prompt one to grow in consciousness—to feel with the heart of a
child (of the divine) and to care respectfully for others: "*Let the mind
that is in Christ Jesus be also in me.*" This results in finding God, newly
revealed, repeatedly, in the midst of our everyday personal journey.

There are a variety of paths to enlightenment. There are fast
ways and slow ways. There are masculine ways and feminine ways.
There is a human "being" and a human "doing." Think of the
masculine way as "doing' … those who give richly of themselves in
service: praying, helping, and offering. The human "being" resides
in the natural state of "just being," not particularly doing anything
specific, but carrying an enlightened presence into whatever space
one is in at any given time. The all-nurturing essence of mothering
is that of caring and loving in a feminine manner, even when done

by a male. Many country doctors in rural areas cared for everyone and sought to solve every problem with tenderness. By shifting from a personality with one style in a lifetime to another style in following lives, we learn the various conditions needed to align our heart and mind.

We may have a fast, instantaneous happening that provides an experience of *knowing* God in a deep and wondrous manner. We emerge a changed person. Or, we may have a long, slow journey of meditation and study, of service and helping others, with lots of experiences—large and small—woven together to knit that heart-mind balance we speak of as *the mystic.*

Near-death experiences, saintly visions, or apparitions have been recorded from time to time in the past, and are now once again being looked at with interest. That has not always been the case. There are interesting stories to guide us in *The Lives of Saints* and in the book *Cosmic Consciousness* by Richard C. Burke. His work is the classic for this type of writing in the twentieth century. Modern-day stories of *near-death* and *out-of-body experiences* are excellent examples of rapid shifts of awareness which often manifest as mystical experiences.

Likewise, teachers, saintly ones, gurus, books, and philosophical organizations all describe the many steps to be taken to "enlightenment" and attempt to describe this process. Their various stories illustrate the many persistent efforts they made to gain awareness on the path … and how they followed time-tested routines … until the daylight dawns for each individually.

Seeking Transformation

Usually our heart begins to seek transformation when we are filled with dissatisfaction with the way our life is unfolding. We suffer *divine discontent,* a knowing that our life is not what it could be. Our very nature cries for something more or different. Our quest begins as we find ourselves drawn to *the way, the truth and the light.* Eventually we do find that we are being drawn onto the path to the God-Self. We find a bonding of heart and mind, with flashes of inspiration—even wee flashes—occurring … and we do change.

All seekers take on trials. The average individual suffers much discouragement and has much need for hope in the dark periods when doubt grows between glimpses. Our nervous systems revolt against these earth-plane difficulties and we can easily become confused or mildly depressed. Sometimes something worse happens, much worse: the motors of our emotional life stop running. The emotions stall out, as it were, and cannot be forced any further, taking on no new emotional empathy or understanding. It is an old truth: we can only stomach so much and then we sicken. The great danger of our civilization is in this state of shock. It is not a mental breakdown, but emotional passiveness. It becomes impossible to care about everything—so we end up caring about nothing. A numbness that no tragedy can touch replaces the sense of outrage that motivates us to take action.

Many persons today are experiencing such a time. Bled of our sensitivity by the negative and stressful situations around us, we find certain persons who stand apart, like an oasis to those who encounter them. These persons seem to radiate a shining light which cuts a path for themselves through the fog, and as we witness their *serenity*, we find hope within our chest once again. Let us call these persons "mystics."

Jacob Needleman in his book, *Lost Christianity,* tells us that the soul gives us numerous times a day to wake up, but instead we struggle to satisfy ourselves with material pleasures or things. We stuff down all kinds of "fillers" to avoid the emptiness we feel. I call this misery "divine discontent"; others call it by different names, but anyone who has felt it will recognize it. Lord Buddha taught that the human nature *"desires the wrong things."* It takes a while before "the awakening one" in us is ready to shed these attractions, whatever they may be in an individual's life.

The Soul persists, even as dissatisfaction with our lives builds. Needleman says, thousands of opportunities come to us daily, but we look the other way because we are focused on creating this life.

It is the goal. We believe in our dream, or that whatever we are engaged in is right for us. Even when we know that we cannot change things, this discontent is signaling us that the time has come for a new design, a new plan.

Needleman uses the term "transformational impulse" rather than "divine discontent," and it is a more accurate descriptive term, but the latter is what persons can identify with more easily. The transformational impulse keeps calling until, at some point, some impulse turns us to a new direction, or provides the awareness needed for our quest. This shift ignites new awareness, new insights, and, if we are fortunate, may lead in many meaningful directions.

Rarely do we understand that the misery we are going through is the prompting of an impulse providing direction for us; or perhaps we feel that "godliness" is not even a part of our life. It is not a religious impulse, but rather a "seed," "germ," or "natural impulse," as are other natural biological impulses. The kitten becomes a cat; the puppy becomes a dog; and a godling becomes a god. "Made in the image and likeness of the divine," our natural goal is to come to spiritual maturity. The flower in the garden puts out buds, and in due time the buds bloom.

Just as we grow biologically according to the care of the body, the quality of food, the nurturing and exercise provided, so our divine nature has natural growth tendencies as well. Rarely do people think of this, but when we come in contact with a student of spiritual science, we become more aware of these natural growth patterns. As we advance in the care of our divine nature, we become aware that we are related to the well-being of all humanity.

Divine discontent journeys with us for the majority of our life, and we will struggle to escape its grasp many times. When we are less mature, we use pleasure and play to distract us. As we become older, we generally choose less stimulation, and as an oldster we generally find more peace and calmness through religion, or through alcohol, trips, or some form of ego satisfaction/gratification. Often people think it is sweet to see all the oldsters in church, but it depends on the consciousness of each whether it is "sweet" or "pitiful," especially if we consider that an entire life could be lived without gaining an awakened consciousness. Just being "good" or doing as "told" is no reward in itself. It may make us feel "good or safe," but we incarnated to become more than we were. To do so, we are to break free from the "group mind" to become an awakened mind, and deal with all the challenges of the quest within our own being.

Our earliest impulses as a human being are reactions to various sensations. This is a built-in challenge, for we either continue to pursue sensations, or we tend to become colder and harder, or withdrawn, which is in itself another form of sensation. Eventually, we tire of this emotionalism and we begin to seek more meaningful pursuits either intellectually or ethically. If, in our restlessness, we have been exposed to an impulse of the spiritual nature, a quest for meaning may begin. This may ignite the divine within so that we begin an investigation of a new sort, ignited via creative endeavors, inventive thinking, or by witnessing the spirituality of another.

There are enticing opportunities along the way to lose oneself in any number of new interests. In due time—this life or another—we will choose opportunities to advance. Our transformational impulse is still there, waiting to stir once again. It will return with its discontent, suffering, and daily problems. If we are fortunate, these difficulties continue long enough and are painful enough to wake us up. Part of the process is to strip us of our ego, the worldly part that defends us when in battle, or develops into a façade to help us through personality challenges.

I remember one day years ago when I fell walking to my studio. A worker seeing me immediately called out to me, *"Are you hurt?"* He began walking toward me to help me get up. I called back saying 'I was fine,' and with all my strength and pride gathered myself up, stood upright, and struggled to walk to the door of the studio and as quick as I could, entered. With knees bleeding, scratched and battered, I did not say, *"Yes sir, please help get me inside."* I was proud, and my pride carried me inside.

All pride is not a bad thing, but it is something we must learn to use wisely. Dignity and pride are part of our self-respect. False pride is that part of ourselves that cannot ask for help when we need it or admit we are wrong. We do not want to be on the defensive when another aspect, humility or vulnerability, can serve us better. Protecting the façade of our personality can inhibit our growth, but by releasing our defensiveness we can be open to seeing our error. By refusing help, we deny the other a chance to be of service, and we miss an experience of closeness. The personality dreads vulnerability, but it is necessary, as it allows others to approach us when they, too, have tender moments of growth.

If we do not wake up or "go back to sleep," as it is called, we have to awaken again. Experiences come into our life calling for deep thought and accompanied by pain repeatedly. This persists until we learn that the trick is not to go back to sleep, but to strive while awakened. The goal of inspiration is to assist the whole of our collectives, our family or group, to work together to keep one another striving toward meaningful goals. The transformational impulse is prompting us to evolve. Nature's natural way to advance in consciousness is "evolution." It is not as disputed as we think. If we choose to speed up this process, we consciously refine ourselves in ways we learn about by working with various spiritual techniques or a teacher. We apply all the ideas of awareness to assist us.

Each of us has had times when we have had to pick up our broken dreams, dust them off, and glue them back together. Such is life. However, the expertise needed to do this "gluing together" requires a source of hope! The hope springs eternal from within our own soul. If you are familiar with Margaret Starbird's work, you may remember her concept of the divine feminine holding "*the alabaster jar.*"

We each, in the more hidden part of our nature, "hold an alabaster jar" filled with awakening moments. This can be glimpses of awareness, moments of prayer, tender love and service to others, repentance, and a willingness to allow *God or the Divine or what-*

ever there is to guide us. We enter this confident state of mind and another day we lose it; the personality recovers its grip and we slide back into our old ways once again.

As we progress, we find ourselves looking for intimate answers about our own nature. Most often the human side of ourselves comes under analysis first, but later we extend this outreach to more subtle areas and search for even greater aid. We begin to ask simple questions such as: "*Why? Who am I? Why do not others see me as I see myself?*" This eternal search for answers leads us to the God-Spark through the closest contact one has: *within ourselves.*

As each meaningful step in our life is taken, we realize that we begin by being selfish, that is, thinking of ourselves only, and not realizing the *oneness* of Life. Each of us seeks to find inner peace for ourselves. As a greater awareness dawns upon us, so does the idea that all of us have the same need. Psychology shares this understanding and promotes ideas for bettering oneself, but until we realize we can go no further until we want for others what we want for ourselves, we are stopped. This process begins with a "love thy neighbor" impulse, but eventually becomes a Universal concept. We then become aware of the *one humanity theory,* or even embrace the idea of a collective transformation. Now we see that we are approaching a quest for the "nature of the divine"—called by any name—to become *our* nature.

Often, one feels overwhelmed or discouraged at the work they sense ahead. The newness of ideas wears thin. The curiosity is satisfied; the soul is weary of effort to battle ego. And the ego is much involved in its own importance. Add to this the weariness we have discussed of the earth-plane life, its depressions and its setbacks, and we see the once-enthusiastic person dropping by the wayside.

It is important to realize we do not lose the value of the experiences and strides we have made; we may, however, have to take "time out" in the struggle. Maybe we have done all we can for the balance of this lifetime … to begin again in another life, or maybe not; but the ground gained is not lost. At some point again, the soul comes to the crossroads of **actions** and here is where, with discipline and the wisdom in one's own soul, we can invoke the courage to begin again.

Not all follow a religious code; some follow "the book of nature," as some are more inclined to study nature and see its many interlocking relationships. This can be realized to the point that one develops a reverence for all of life—one that reaches above to other realities, below to younger kingdoms, and beyond humans to life in the cosmos. Our modern concern with ecology, with animals and insects, with solving problems of poverty, of ignorance and with violence, are really in this nature school of thought. We realize that the effort to become more at peace with one's self requires an expanding consciousness, not necessarily in following the ways of others. We find ourself learning to see things differently and contributing help to whatever issues we see. These first steps are precious, and signal a significant change from the sorrow and unhappiness of the uncomfortable, earlier periods. Some will find this understanding to be enough ... as far as they are ready to go. Some realize it is only a stage on the journey to a more profound inner life.

By recognizing the emotional and spiritual nature of oneself, one can become the person he or she is meant to be. We then cultivate the growth of the inner senses and sensitivity in such a way that we can allow the God-part of us to expand. To become a wise one, the effort must be done on a conscious level. Our society has more or less rejected the idea that we have mystics among us, or even have a need for them. Yet here they exist, unnoticed, quietly doing their thing: praying, meditating, serving, and loving. There is a "well-worn" pathway. Is it happening within you or around you? Is it growing in the hidden part of yourself without a name?

There is much need today for persons to label themselves "a mystic" in their own eyes. Let us think of the goals we set for ourselves when we consciously create an image for ourselves that allows for growth and change. As we do, we may choose to picture ourselves being serene, happy, and able to deal with whatever life dishes out. We make a conscious effort to find beauty in the world around us. If we can see ourselves with this creativity springing forth from within our own being, we recognize we are empowered to become whatever is our dream.

The mystic perceives beauty in the world in which they live ... not because the world is beautiful or not, but because all Creation is clothed in beauty, and as seekers we desire to see the beauty as recognition of the work of the Divine. Beauty is seen first with the physical eyes by admiring and appreciating objects and color; secondly it is seen in nature. Early on, a mystic sees that there is a natural beauty, a more subtle beauty. Next and in proper time, we begin to see the beauty in others, not surface beauty, but the inner glow, the kindness, the compassion begins to show, and at last, we can see the beauty of ourselves. We catch glimpses of the inner self with its soft glory.

Pythagoras taught that certain forms of illness could be treated by presenting to the attention of patients the figures of symmetrical geometric solids. He is said to have received this doctrine from the priests of Egypt. As the body of man is nourished by food, the internal psychic self is sustained by the contemplation of beauty. From this spiritual teaching evolved *"beauty is food for the soul,"* and so we recognize the need for human beings to behold beauty and order. Thus we understand how the Soul rushes to embrace that which substantiates its own inner disposition.

This is why it is so damaging when persons preach that "one is a sinner." We know, now, that if a person is repeatedly told, *"he or she is ugly, bad or dumb"* as they are growing up, they believe it. This damaged flower has difficulty ever recovering; thus to be told by an authority figure that *"we are sinners"* as often persons are, we now realize how damaging this can be. The path of the disciple is to grow into the strength and power of a brave soul on its journey to know God. If we feel inferior, we may never dare to go on the path that can take us to a loving God.

Mystics of today will not be the same as the desert mystics of long ago. A book of simple mystic teachings that spoke to me is *The Oasis of Wisdom* by David G. R. Keller, which makes the point of "choosing simplicity." This is the work of the mystic, true; however, you and I are to experience and respond to our time, culture, and the age of which we are a part. Too often we look with nostalgia at times past.

People of the future will wonder how mystics of our time survived in this materialist society. Some mystics will survive and grow, as we and others attempt to respond to current challenges. We benefit from the wisdom of the past by applying it as best we can in the midst of the environment our time offers. The "power of personal experiences" reminds me of the survivors of the holocaust, pondering how some were good to others, kept their truth, and did not sour or become unkind with all that violence around them.

We have to acknowledge that nature, art, music, love, and inner promptings have meaning. In daily life we actualize those values and reveal the nature of the inner self. We evaluate our surroundings and find what supports our inner nature. Learning to honor this part of ourselves is difficult for all, but for those of a mystical bent, to struggle to go further and to free ourselves from the "group-think" of our society is even more significant. It becomes important to give beginners, as we work together, the image of a "freed self" to work in faith. We believe that which I desire to be, I am becoming.

We imagine that, if society were different, it would be easier … but think like a mystic and grasp the reality that *it is our karma to be born where we are and to grow where we are planted.* Do not try to escape. Our task is to grow and become, and for whatever reason, here we are. Perhaps we are to influence the very society we are in, and that is why we are *stationed here.* Yes, it is quieter in the desert than in a city. Yes, many mystics did withdraw to find what they needed. You may as well. You may turn off television, spend money differently, adjust your diet, and simplify all your basic ways. We can adjust to our current times and value systems, to grow and to change the reality of our surroundings.

Finding what matters to you, and what is artificial, is the true transforming task. A lot of distractions are of no true value; toys fill the needs of the infant. We amuse ourselves with "toys" of false value until we mature: we come to perceive the world in a new way. We must come to see beauty where there was none before, to hear music within, or see gentleness in a new way. Mystics look for and see the God-side of both self and others in ways which we failed to in the past. We see with new eyes.

Hugh of St. Victor (1098–1141), a Christian mystic, taught we have three eyes with which to see. First, the physical eyes with which to see the material world, a mental eye with which to perceive ideas and concepts, and a spiritual eye with which to see the will of God.

From Ken Wilber in *Eye to Eye*:

> … Hugh of St. Victor … distinguished between *cogitatio, meditatio,* and *contemplatio. Cogitatio,* or simple empirical cognition, is a seeking for facts of the material world using the eye of flesh. *Meditatio* is a seeking for the truths within the psyche itself (the *imago* of God) using the mind's eye. *Contemplatio* is the knowledge whereby the psyche or soul is united instantly with Godhead in transcendent insight (revealed by the eye of contemplation).
>
> Now that particular wording—eye of flesh, mind, and contemplation—is Christian; but similar ideas can be found in every major school of traditional psychology, philosophy, and religion. The "three eyes" of a human being correspond, in fact, to the three major realms of being described by the perennial philosophy, which are the gross (flesh and material), the subtle (mental and animic), and the causal (transcendent and contemplative).

We sometimes see the word "anchorite" (Greek) used along with mystic, and this was an extreme way of life spoken of in the Middle Ages. Generally an anchorite was enclosed in a small space or shed attached to a church and stayed there until their death. Usually, this space had a small window through which people in the community fed them and in return the anchorite provided spiritual inspiration as best they could.

I am not proposing such a radical approach. I am envisioning modern individuals constructing a way of life that attaches themselves to "ethics, prayer and spiritual practices, service and caring" in such a manner that the group mind benefits by the grace gained from those living these more caring lives. There are two benefits: our soul grows and our society has spiritual leadership. Truly, the mystic builds a personal relationship with God first; the benefits to society are all by-products.

Sacred words may appeal to us; serving others may be our way; reading and studying, comforting others, or providing relief in emergencies—all make us reach outside ourselves to assist others. As mystics, we are to become aware of our relationship with others and with all creation. We see all of this well described in scripture from all faiths of the world, but we need look no further than the New Testament to see an introduction to the "seed within."

There is much significance to stories of the "seed" ... seeds contain the basic formula for the godling that is to mature into the divine being. Now we gain new respect for the seed of the divine sowed in the midst of our human experience. (We explored more about that in my book, *Esoteric Secrets of Sex, Passion, and Love*.) We begin to know the significance of the seed as we read in Matthew 13: the story of the sower.

The idea of the seed and teaching around it are exceedingly important. Within each human there is a divine seed waiting to emerge. It is buried in matter waiting for water and light. Our tears water this precious seed and it matters not, whether they be of sadness or joy. Likewise, as the light of the mind expands, it supplies the light needed until in due time the Light of the Soul beams upon it. The Real Self then blooms.

The seed or the spark divine arrives on the physical plane with a personality in which to mature. Scripture tells us "some seeds fall on rocky soil, some good soil, some begin to grow and dry up, and some have thorns." All of these examples have mystical meanings, as this is humanity's story. We ponder what is happening to the seed within us, and whether or not we have chosen to use well this precious opportunity to grow our seed to its fullest potential.

We can link holidays (holy days) to the same idea of stimulating the inner seed. Christmas with the water mysteries and Easter with the fire mysteries are to feed and provide us with certain energies to enrich our lives. Advent gives us a call, "to come" up higher. We are offered the focus and guidance to grow the inner nature. Likewise, Easter has Lent preceding it with seven weeks of focus. If desired, we can use these concepts in a dedicated way as opportunities to learn of Christ Jesus. We will come to know that certain veiled teachings exist; the hidden stories both hide veiled meanings and protect them from distortion at the same time. These are "clues" to what is happening within yourself as you advance into inner comprehension. The path to greatness is one of discovering the self within and learning to participate in the collective inner life.

Our inner life is the doorway to awakening spiritually. We have to resist the pull of the outer to make time for the inner. Said another way, we *embrace the process of growth rather than the products of the outer world* to nourish our "divine seed." Mysticism is process. Mysticism provides ways to stimulate the transformational process; some ideas will work for one, and others will best fit another. The eclectic mind and loving heart find nuggets among the thoughts that enhance our daily life and fill it with divine inspiration.

One of my favorite sayings, original I believe to me, is, "It is the work of the world to pull us off our path; it is our work to keep ourselves on it."

A summary of the three major transformation pathways are as follows:

The first is an intentional and regular exposure to the Light while we prompt a Light experience—every effort to be one with the Light. Disciplines: meditation, study, practice, commitment. The secret of this transformation journey, once awakened, is to do simplified steps consistently. Add chanting or singing: glorifying higher principles with song has long been a transformational tool.

The second is a sudden and profound experience of the Light. In today's world, it is the Near-Death-Experience or some other kind of unexpected phenomena, perhaps an out-of-body experience, or even seeing a discarnate. For some, a conversion experience breaks through the old consciousness and delivers a new perspective.

The third is the Bardo experience. The Bardo is a term most often associated with Eastern traditions, specifically the *Tibetan Book of the Dead*. This term represents the journey through the underworld. Torkom Saraydarian writes about the death experience (in English) in *Cosmos in Man*—(the easiest place I know to find it). Usually we think of "*bardo*" as scary, but we soon learn it is a real life experience as well as a part of the afterlife. Bardo is comparable to experiencing purgatory or hell on earth.

Often the afterlife in Western approaches is depicted as the astral world or lower planes. The Bardo experience is considered a particular part of a human physical life more difficult than usual life. This is a hard image to create and that is why it is usually thought of in an after-death sense. It is sometimes also known as the path through the Underworld. Here there are a series of painful, suffering and challenging experiences to be lived through by a Soul in an attempt to clear heavy karma, a heavy consciousness of serious addiction, sexual abuse, violence or cruelty … or whatever. A Soul is struggling to get the attention of the personality and offering it opportunities to wake up. To change, *one has to change the consciousness* and, when "hypnotized by negativity," a strenuous effort is required. It takes a tremendous force of will to make corrections, and that is what is needed. This effort may be required again and again before the one suffering wins his or her freedom to go another way.

In a Bardo experience the effort to make change comes slowly with many false starts. It is these many smaller efforts that add up in time to dynamic shifts in consciousness, thus allowing the Soul

to manifest a larger shift and a new beginning. It is these numerous shifts in consciousness that are so important. One has to make
profound effort, time and time again. Each effort is recorded by the
Soul and ultimately freedom is finally won.

When one experiences lots of losses, endures massive physical pain, but more often emotional pain with nothing working
out—this is the Bardo ... disappointment after disappointment,
one dream after another going up in smoke, continuous patterns
of pain-filled experiences. We cannot actually say "forced," but
stresses and pain offer small steps, through personal torment, to
pay off karmic debts or shift consciousness to, in time, break free.
The Bardo experience or the Underworld is a valid way to turn
toward the Light, but it is a most difficult path. It is hell on earth.
Tremendous effort makes small shifts, and even false starts are
vitally important to the long-range change one is attempting. It
is the effort and endurance put into these shifts in consciousness
that is so vital.

What this world needs are thousands of hard-at-work happy
mystics. Some of the ideas and suggestions available I would not
expect to work. I do not think a perfect course can be prescribed.
As we are individuals, the path itself is built by the conscious effort
of each individual and contributed to by several individuals coming together for this holy purpose. Building a mystical consciousness is achieved as one's heart and mind blend together. As one
builds right action, right thoughts, right feelings, right views, right
mindfulness, right intentions—all gleaned from one's own inner
source—these efforts flow from the personal Soul of each being.
Just as the Buddha expressed his teachings in this manner, the
truth is still there.

Later Master Jesus stressed, "love one another as yourself." This
great truth can provide the balance needed to confront the negativity of the world. The positive vibration of love is the most needed
force in our world—this includes love of self and each other. This
provides the force to overcome the problems of stress and tragedy
around us. If there is a salvation available for our earth plane, and

I believe there is, it will be through the brotherhood and sisterhood that we, as mystics, can generate from within. This radiance, one of serenity and peace, can flow outward to those around us. If mystical thought is the right action, we best be about our Maker's business.

Image a balance bar in your hands as you walk your path with its own challenges. See yourself balancing **love and dedication** with **study and will** ... each held steady. This idea of balance is ever changing, from the balancing required as an infant soul to a more stringent expression as we advance on our path. We often forget the balance of effort required between life in the material world and the energy demanded to blend with our efforts to grow in the inner reality; that is, what is acceptable to us as a healthy balance of behavior, study, research, and attention to inner life? What is an appropriate balance at one stage may not be appropriate at another. *To whom much is given, much is expected.*

When we are ready, we can find spiritual meaning behind most events whether we have tried to understand them or not: Halloween, Saints Days, Equinoxes, Solstices, etc. Having an annual saint's day book and reading it day by day can be of great value, helping us to recall ways others found to serve. I particularly enjoy *All Saints, Daily Reflections on Saints, Prophets, and Witnesses for Our Time* by Robert Ellsberg. This one is a favorite because it includes all faiths, and many not ordinarily considered "saints" by churches.

Philosophy versus Mysticism

The philosopher speaks of the Godhead impersonally, without qualities, activity, or being. The mystic tells of ecstatic union, actual contact with a perception of the Godly and a home of Souls; here we find the richness—the sum of the wise. This ecstatic union with the Oneness is that of which mystics hope, dream and speak. Yet there appears to be disharmony between the outer life and inner: to dissolve this disharmony is the point of each individual's work. Compare these discrepancies to the differences between a map and a landscape: both are true representations. A map charts a way to a destination; the landscape paints the picture to show what is there. Rules of the road are like the map; experiences are more like the landscape.

Philosophy is study on an intellectual basis—learning the theory of bodies and souls. Mysticism is an *actual experience* that then becomes a part of us. It affirms our magical moment of transformation with feelings, visions, perhaps beauty, even sound—the creative expression—the burst of comprehension of oneself as a soul. Thus, words become difficult; communication stumbles; we resort to symbols, poetry, parables, vibrations etc.

We must in some way learn to use the inner senses as we do the outer. The windows of our soul, presently being held in *limitation*, must open to experience additional realities. This is the beginning stage of the mystical life.

We first become aware of our inner senses by dreaming. While the physical body itself is at rest in sleep, the inner self produces dramatic experiences with the senses. In time, we learn there is a relationship between the inner and outer senses. To look at these with new eyes aids us to realize that the stirrings of the inner self— or basic self—have a distinct value.

We look at each developing chakra or consciousness center with its inner and outer expression or perception of the world. We learn to allow the "unnamed within" to activate. By understanding the journey to higher consciousness, we become aware of different vibrations, frequencies, and modulations, and the perspective they each have to offer. We realize that we all see the world through differing points of view. We come to grasp how several of us can see the same event and yet derive different perspectives of it.

This takes some time to grasp and for the beginner it is challenging. Abraham Maslow led the way to understanding these levels of consciousness with his Hierarchy of Needs. As basic survival needs are met, higher needs emerge. Inner pressure guides one ever toward a fuller expression of *Being*. These emerging needs push a human toward Self-actualization just as an acorn is pressured to become an oak tree.

Maslow's hierarchy suggests each level builds upon the latter. We need to grasp that we are evolving from level upon level (unless one is faced with some great challenge or trauma; then one usually regresses until rebalanced). Our basic physiological (bodily) needs consist of air, water, food, elimination, and rest. Another level of need has to do with safety and a sense of security. Here we need freedom from fear, order, and to reassure our security (as in "someone has your back!") and protection. This higher level comes into play as the need to be nurtured and loved.

We all want acceptance and caring; we want to give love and receive love; we have a basic need to belong—a kind of mutual bond that assures us of our value to others. As we continue to become, we find respect, and a sense of confidence. We desire something called self-love and positive self-regard. Self-actualization tops the list of needs, as this is the goal. We reach for our greatest potential, a sense of "peak experience."

The occult vocabulary utilizes the term "*chakras*" (or energy centers within the body). These centers serve similar roles as does a seven-level ladder. Each step both serves to offer another viewpoint and yet provides a place to stop, rest or rebalance. Chakras are located in the etheric body and felt in the physical. Each plexus center is, in non-professional's language, a cluster of nerves and delicate sensory systems built into the human anatomy to be activated as one moves from denser reality to a more refined one. Each human being evolves upon this ladder of awareness to become more sensitive to the influences coming from the higher world. These plexuses form the ladder to higher, more subtle awareness.

Each of us has an inner sense, that may or may not, be activated as we focus on these centers. The familiar term of *chakra* or the plural, *chakras*, comes from Sanskrit, meaning "wheel." We find much teaching about these energies in Eastern study. Energy centers are actual vortices of force latent within the etheric body. Generally we advance from a lower vibration to higher as centers develop and reveal themselves, most easily in an order: root, abdomen, solar plexus, heart, throat, brow, and crown.

The lower or basic center is the sacral center (root), which means "basic to life" in the physical body and is the contact that links the spirit vehicle and the physical body together. While a second center or plexus is located in the lower abdomen, it is usually referred to as the sensation or sexual center as this area is readily felt when aroused sexually. (An infant shows they feel sensation by rubbing a satin binding on a blanket to soothe his or her self.) The common location for this center is just below but near the area of the spleen and indeed, we gain a sensation of peace and serenity when comforted by a body massage or a compassionate touch.

This sensation center is also active when we are asleep and we begin to experience out-of-body experiences of astral travel. In this experience our physical body and spiritual vehicle separate and the non-physical follows its own desires to be active on more subtle levels. Commonly, we recognize this as an out-of-body experience. Frequently this serves as one of the surprises that aid spiritual awakening.

We begin to recognize these centers as we awaken to non-physical reality and become increasingly aware of higher vibrations and extended awareness. Eastern and Western concepts vary slightly, but not overly so. The most common plexus of our society is the solar plexus (dual in nature, includes the adrenals and pancreas); this is where we sense the strong feelings we get from fear, dread, or preparation for attack. We speak of this as a sick or sinking feeling in our stomach, or a defense mechanism that acts and feels like a shield when going into battle.

Moving from preparing to battle or competing with others, we advance to softening and experiencing love. *Our first work is to learn to love our self*: it is also the hardest. True love is not emotionalism. There is a warm fuzzy love for puppies and children and an attachment to others that exists in a personal way, while there is a cool, objective clarity for those whom we do not know personally. It is an impersonal caring, as for people suffering a tragedy or accident; this is a more distant response to caring for those who suffer but without a personal connection.

These two are sometimes portrayed as a "pink" warm love or a cool "blue" love of an impersonal nature. *Love-caring* contains all these three kinds of love: sexual, personal, and impersonal. The first step that allows us to care about others is to learn how to hold a healthy regard or love for ourselves. The second step is to recognize the feeling, or lack of feeling, when we experience other reactions. I suggest, when we learn to love ourselves, we are truly learning to love our "inner child." How can we love another until we love our inner child? This understanding opens the door to caring about others in a real way.

As the heart center, the thymus, opens, true love begins to flow; we experience moving more quickly from lower centers/chakras to higher. The heart (thus love) is the bridge; and from here we can move into higher consciousness. The three higher centers each have a specific and real purpose, although harder to explain and to grasp. It is important to think of the heart as a bridge and that we can make an effort to bridge the higher and lower. As the energy of the higher washes over the lower from time to time, it changes the function of a center. It changes the degree not the purpose. Now the drive of the lower centers will heighten in frequency, becoming softer and more sensitive as love softens them.

We are going to use a "climbing the ladder" approach, as the centers have a tendency to be felt in that order. Each one of us has an inner sense that will be activated as we advance spiritually. The throat center contains a rich body of creativity, often called "the horn of cornucopia center." It contains all kinds of creative ability and no one knows just how much until it is revealed.

"Gifts of the Spirit" are associated with these higher centers: the throat with clairaudience and/or inner guidance. The brow is associated with clairvoyance and higher will. It is not unusual for one to speak of "seeing the plan." The top of the head center, called the crown, contains both the pituitary and the pineal gland. It is associated with contacting the higher realms, and is the great goal for us all. A majority of humankind learn to think of this as "direct knowing" or "just knowing," the highest form of intuition there is.

Psychism, a response of the basic self, is a natural condition of the animal senses, and humanity is, after all, but a refined animal. Each of our senses can be quite active in the dream state. We know how powerful we can feel, see, and hear in the "behind-the-sleep" state. We can learn about dreams, brain wave frequencies, and the importance of this seemingly unaware state as we evolve. Humanity's animal senses have sunk below the level of consciousness in most; it takes but little effort to awaken them. Psychic development classes help do this.

Practices designed to assist one to awaken the senses teach us to value the development of the inner senses and to know that they have other purposes as well. An important realization is *not all psychics are spiritual, but all mystics are psychic.* Prayer, meditation, pondering, sharing and service are basic efforts to grow spiritually and to develop higher consciousness.

In due time, we are to learn to use the Inner Senses as well as we do our five outer senses. We must learn to allow the "*unnamed within*" to shine clearly through our personality and to be of value to those around us. As the shamans-of-old tell us, we must move from self-serving awareness and from sympathy to empathy. This comes slowly as we refine the personality and its ego identity. So why do we feel we should hide our "*extended sense awareness*"? We are here to learn how to appreciate and develop all our talents and creativity.

Important thoughts to ponder: Do you believe mystics are called or made? Discuss.

Answers naturally will vary with several common responses:

1. "I tried to be normal and just could not be. I was meant to be alone a lot and happiest when I could draw; I saw things, visions, that wanted me to draw them."

2. "I did not fit with most people. Friends I could really enjoy were rare and I was hungry for them."

3. "I did not enjoy what others did and I found I was happier with a book than with most people."

4. "I wanted to be alone and to use my imagination. Even as a child, I was accused of having 'too' much imagination."

5. "I am happiest living in my own world and few others really liked the things I did."

6. "We are living in a radical period of time and it is necessary to have a radical spirituality to be happy. Church is boring."

7. "We can get the nudge, but to respond consciously we have to get away from outside distractions and influences."

8. "I do not think most mystics can live in the house with others as they distract too much."

9. "If you are too mental, you do not fit any place. The soft people do not like you; the smart people want to argue and discuss but I do not want to argue. It is not easy to get acceptance. I do not want to be judged; others think this kind of talk is nonsense."

All of this tells us to stop looking outside ourselves and just try to have self-acceptance and *do not blame, shame or play the game.*

We must free ourselves from "game playing." That is so much a part of the "social personality life." Much of the outer world invests itself in social skills, distortion, out-smarting one another, or the breaking of morality codes, all of which are a violation to basic spiritual training programs such as the Commandments, the Beatitudes, and Buddha's Four Noble Truths and the Eight-Fold Path. These practices are guidelines to help us advance in expansion of consciousness or inner knowing.

If we hold such importance to truth, responsibility, and accountability, is it of less importance to allow the truth of our basic nature to show?

- *Did a psychic experience change the way you looked at life or change the boundaries of your consciousness? Was it frightening?*

- *Did a psychic experience, or an experience of extended awareness, seem "strange" or "weird" to you?*

- *Was psychism or mysticism taught to you as "wrong or evil"?*

- *Have you thought of it "as a gift of the spirit"?*

- *As a younger person, did you ever discuss psychism with anyone?*

- *Have you had a friend or one you knew experience anything labeled "psychic"?*

As we piece together the real goal of mysticism, we recognize what we really want is to "know" God. How are we going to do this? We may hope for an experience of immediate interaction with God. What we really want is an experience that we can grasp.

When we have a "true mystical moment," as it is called, it might be dramatic, such as an out-of-body experience. Or it may be *"just knowing that plant over there needs a drink of water."* Somehow, that plant has conveyed its need for water. Those are mystical experiences. It is neither philosophy nor religion; it is *"knowingness."*

Remember:
"Behind emotion is feeling; behind intellect is knowing."
—Carol E. Parrish-Harra

So, as we begin to approach mysticism, we move into a deeper and perhaps new awareness. From *An Outlook on Our Inner Western Way* by William Gray, we find a guiding concept. Imagine the spinal column as the center line with a line on either side. On one side we have what is called "occultism" and on the other we have what is called "orphic." Both are natural tendencies found within individuals. We begin by discovering which is *our* nature.

The orphic has a feeling, sensitive nature, and has a dedication to devotion; this can be devotion to family, work, not necessarily

God or religion. This one gets devotional toward causes, as it is one's nature to do so. On the other side of center, the occult (intellectual) nature awaits. Eliphas Levi,* the great Occultist said:

> Too deep a study of the mysteries may estrange from God the careless investigator, in whom mental fatigue paralyses the ardors of the heart. The occultist stands at the door to mysticism but often can go no further (because) for the desire for secret knowledge blocks the heart. Straight in the middle is a path to higher consciousness.

Put this picture in your mind and begin to weave both the feeling and knowing streams around the center column. This is what happens in our inner anatomy without our knowing it. The streams of energy on either side of the spine, create a caduceus, as they gradually ascend. As they weave higher around the spine, we rise higher in our integration of consciousness. Higher energy blends with our lower forces to create a situation for the moment of awakening. We cannot make it occur; we can only do the steady practice and prepare for it.

As we do certain beneficial practices and purify the lower centers, inner shifts and changes take place. Mystics dedicate themselves to the visualizing of a world with high ideals; this then tells us they aspire (positive emotion) to a better humanity and hold a thought for a wiser and gentler reality (visualizing or sensing divine possibilities). As progress is made in bringing hearts and minds together, the penetration (adventure) into the higher reality is made.

Orphic, derived from Orpheus, the poet and musician of Greek mythology, is symbolic of the most important mystery-religion

---

*Eliphas Levi (1810–1875}, a well known Occultist, was born Alphonse Louis Constant, of French descent. After studying for the Roman Catholic priesthood, he fell in love and was never ordained. Afterwards he involved himself with magic, ancient mysteries, and spiritualism. His version of transcendental magic is still popular today as is his view of spiritualism. His publication on *Occultism Unveiled* was published posthumously. He was the first to declare that the pentagram, the five-pointed star, when positioned with one point down and two upwards, represented evil. He is remembered as a key founder of the twentieth century revival of magic.

The Blend of Two Extremes Creates the Mystic

Orphic – – – – – – – – – – + – – – – – – – – – – Occultist
(Feeling, Sensitive)   Mystic   (Intellectual Nature)

---

training. The orphic-type person seeks experiences of God through the senses, as in nature, music, art, drama, and feeling. Pantheism is an orphic approach to spirituality.

Occultist, defined as one who studies the mysteries of the concealed or esoteric side of life, seeks greater knowledge of the hidden and ageless wisdom or gnosis.

Mystic is defined as a person with an awareness of a multidimensional reality who in seeking to have a personal relationship with God, bears witness to an expanded life, and uses their insight or understanding as best they can for the benefit of others. The mystic is a blend of the orphic and the occultist. (See *The New Dictionary of Spiritual Thought* by Carol E. Parrish-Harra.)

The "knowing" energy and the "feeling" energy of the chakras begin to blend and move, rising up the spinal column. We may remember swaying as we learned to enter deeply into meditation. Here we consider what is happening in the human anatomy as the sleeping energy within awakens, stirs, and then rises. This energy rises and falls as it moves through the various centers of consciousness. We experience grace in this way, and it is constantly at work, shifting and changing frequencies, helping each of us to better relate to the more refined, and more subtle realities we are beginning to experience.

What is the goal of this alive and active energy? Where does it hope to take us?

The goal has many names: Enlightenment, Salvation, Christ Consciousness ... and other traditions use their own terminology. We in Christianity are more familiar with the term "Saint." When we see certain individuals fervently seeking a personal relationship with the Divine, they are usually called a mystic. Certain others of this type, after evaluations by someone with ecclesiastical author-ity, could be labelled a "saint."

What then are the guidelines for becoming a mystic or saintly being? A very presumptuous question is: who knows how to become a saint? On the other hand, would we know one if we saw one? This may be the better question. Perhaps we can wonder about these thoughts together.

Sages, Wise Ones and Saints

A sage, a wise one, a spiritual teacher, master or saint, a holy one—as such one might be called in the Christian tradition—is a formal recognition given to someone after some stringent criteria is met by the Roman Catholic Church. Remember, there are many Catholic Churches, the Roman being the best known and with the largest membership in the West. As of yet, Mother Teresa of Calcutta is not a formal saint; although, I would venture to say, most of the world thinks of her in that way.

Look at Mother Teresa for a moment. What words would best describe this woman? If she had not been a nun, she would have been a powerful corporate head. She was direct, pushy, demanding, well-disciplined, dedicated, saw her vision and served it. Because she was a nun, to some this made it okay; but almost all saw her as "a tough cookie, hard to cross."

The grace in this situation was that Mother Teresa had a great cause and served it well. She engaged others in supporting her dedication, and her cause was so readily apparent that help came from every level of society.

Let us look at another of our beloved saints, St. Francis of As-sisi. He was a foolish well-to-do young man, who chased women and loved the rich life. In due time he went off to war to fight; he was found too sickly for the military and was sent home. In his ill-ness, he had an experience where he saw Jesus on the cross turn his head and speak with him. He "knew" he was called to build up Jesus' churches.

He denounced wealth, took off his clothes and walked down the street naked in front of his father and the village. Gradually, he attracted other young men to his cause. Together they lived in the outdoors, embracing a life of utter simplicity, and repaired churches that had been reduced to rubble. They had compassion for the uneducated and poor, working and singing songs most of the time. Francis felt akin to nature, praised the sun and moon and denounced what most of the people of his society worked hard for every day of their lives. He called himself "a fool for God's sake."

Francis of Assisi's vivid love of creation, nature, animals, the poor and helpless won him songs of praise, some remaining favorites to this modern day. One often sung in churches everywhere is "All Creatures of our God and King," with few recognizing he is the author. His terms, "Brother Sun and Sister Moon," became movie material, while he is noted as having said he was married to Lady Poverty—that is, not attached to worldly desires—and, as his young life drew toward the end, he spoke openly of "welcoming Sister Death." His identification with the Christ was so intense that Francis was one of the first recorded saints to receive and display the stigmata, the physical marks of the crucified Christ Jesus. Francis is one of the most favorite of saints among mystics.

There are stories of numerous holy ones who experienced God's presence in some unique way, such as Hildegard of Bingen (1098–1179).* In her time, although she was a nun, she would not be silenced; when she had an opinion, she let most everyone know. She experienced "something" that caused her to write, to sing, and to study. She rebelled against the usual life of a young maiden of her day. Fortunately, we have bits and pieces of her inspirational writings left behind to touch our lives today. We can see that there were liberated women … long before our era. Hildegard did not want a

---

* Hilegard of Bingen was a German nun and mystic who demonstrated a variety of gifts and talents. She wrote theological, botanical, and medicinal material as well as letters, songs, and poems. Feminists of modern times admire her visionary skills, admired by authorities, and a capable leader who founded two monasteries. She called herself "unlearned" and demonstrated simple strength and integrity in all her undertakings which made her music and visions more believable to others.

husband, children and the life she witnessed as that of most women around her. She had a greater vision of what our world could be.

Each society constructs its own kind or type of wisdom. This is the way life works in this mainstream. The society in which we grew up provided daily messages of how-to-be, and what would be our rewards. We learned to work hard, be good, follow the rules and become something. The message, always, is to be socially correct, yet few sages, saints, or inspired ones ever are. They frequently were considered "creative or bohemian," but to "march to your own drummer" has never been particularly acceptable, then or now. It certainly has not been openly encouraged.

We usually define saint as "one who hungers and thirsts after God." One who loves God with all one's heart, mind and Soul … one who places a higher value on another standard than that of the society of which one is a part. Jesus fulfilled the acceptable laws of his society, and passed the tests of the temple priests at age twelve. After being acknowledged by them, he set out to discover Wisdom's Ways as noted by other societies. In his early years, now labeled his "lost years," he journeyed beyond what was acceptable to that which was more "renegade wisdom." He sought the wisdom of the prophets as well as teachers outside his tradition in order to discover a relationship to what he called his "Father Within," which revealed more to him.

Wisdom, hope and peace do not dwell in a certain set of circumstances but instead in a person with a certain set of attitudes. Those who hunger for something beyond what his or her society provides seek characteristics such as these. They are graceful creations of individual choice, patience, and a willingness to stay open, in spite of ignorance and pain. As we seek a higher way, we discover a history of mystics and saints we can follow at a certain distance, but then we learn we must combine and develop our own attributes and journey in our own unique way.

The holy or the wise have an experiential relationship with God, called by whatever name, that we would choose to call "the Whole of Life." Here exists an experience of ever-expanding boundaries or rearranging of consciousness that provides a new and different perception of reality to replace the "old wineskins." It is well known that this new consciousness will continue to grow and rupture the container in which it develops. Therefore, we learn that our concepts have to have room to expand in order to contain their growth.

Reason and Passion

> Your soul is oftentimes a battlefield, upon which your reason and your judgment wage war against your passion and your appetite.
>
> Would that I could be the peacemaker in your soul, that I might turn the discord and the rivalry of your elements into oneness and melody.
>
> But how shall I, unless you yourselves be also the peacemakers, nay, the lovers of all your elements?
>
> Your reason and your passion are the rudder and the sails of your seafaring soul. If either your sails or your rudder be broken, you can but toss and drift, or else be held at a standstill in mid-seas.
>
> For reason, ruling alone is a force confining: and passion, unattended, is a flame that burns to its own destruction.
>
> Therefore, let your soul exalt your reason to the height of passion, that it may sing; and let it direct your passion with reason, that your passion may live through its own daily resurrection, and like the phoenix rise above its own ashes.
>
> —Kahlil Gibran

TWO

Building a New Awareness

PICTURE THE CHAKRA SYSTEM as a six-story building with a door at ground level, a winding staircase within, and open floor on the rooftop. At each floor there is a window from which we can look at the world. This gives us a particular perspective.

Currently within our body we are building levels of consciousness. The truth is, we are building these in our non-physical or more subtle vehicles. These various levels are clearly visible to many around us as we begin to explore (and *animate*) an inner life. Mysticism is an indication of a new awareness of life within a variety of dimensions that escapes our notice most of the time. Each level holds a particular view of life itself. When centered at any particular floor with its window on the world, we gain a different perspective or point of view.

Beginning with the highest perspective, we identify all seven points of view or levels of consciousness that humanity will, in time, develop. As enlightenment becomes ours, we will be as one standing on the roof top. From here we can turn in any direction and see with clarity. Here there is a sense of "everything" being clear. Called the "crown center," at this highest perspective we can experience and allow the Divine in us to receive the incoming energy of the Soul without effort. In this expanded awareness, we perceive direction and purpose, divine love, experience vision, or "just knowing," and learn to go with the flow. This is why many meditation practices begin by bringing down the higher energy of the soul through the crown of the head.

From the level just below the "roof top" one seeks to contact Higher Will. Insights as to the plan of life—from either an impersonal or more Divine perspective—will become available here. This center seems to function like a projector booth—open and light-filled. We use this center as we align our will with the higher will (the vision we may have glimpsed).

This third center from the rooftop (the throat, often called "cornucopia," for from here we speak "the word" to make it manifest) flows and overflows, filled with beauty ... words, music, and the impersonal emotions of caring, love, and tenderness. Often here we get messages, hear voices, receive impressions and/or the feeling to share them with others. Sometimes we feel so acutely open that it hurts, especially when first beginning to function from this charismatic center. Inner hearing is located here, as well as a personal unique flair in fashion or in social manners, which we see as asserting one's "individuality." Some may rebel or at least not subscribe to the social culture in which they live. The third center is the center of manifestation, due to the promptings "to give and to speak" which rule this center.

Below the throat, we reach the heart center that wells up to share the love of one's nature. As it flows through us, we may ache to help others, to work with healing energies; our words tend to be tender and of a healing, peacemaking type. We may find energy flowing down the arms to the hands, or the palms may feel swollen and full. We feel generous and can over-commit in this expanded state. The heart center is the bridge between the higher reality and more personal self-concerns.

Next, located at the solar plexus we find our self-centeredness. Here are located our personal ethics, confidence, strength, and a groundedness where duality is known as right and wrong. The rules or dogmas of our faith, social ethics, and culture are strong here. They have prepared us for outer life and the roles we play every day. The conscience is active and strong.

At the sixth or sensation center, we find we must discover for ourselves what it takes to have a good feeling. Emotions can run strong, up and down. All senses operate from here. The astral life (out-of-body) is based here and feelings easily amplified. We may either be frozen and not express our emotions due to pain we have felt, or we may be a "drama queen" that flies either high or low. Guided meditations can explore our personal symbology and insights to reveal what each means to us in a personal way. Acting out our feeling and emotions freely leads to "drama" with its own highs and lows. Drama always complicates our lives, as upsets can lead to behavior which is hard to chart and uncomfortable at best, especially if we are confident and experienced at listening to our feelings.

Next, at the base of the spine is the spirit-matter connection that holds us to the physical world. We have little understanding of our self as a soul, but there is much information stored in this connection should we find ourselves ready to explore. Herein lies the survival instinct. It keeps making us quest for security—food, shelter, mates—seeking whatever seems to fulfill us in our experience of life. We find we survive when it seems we can go on no longer, and yet this powerful effort to live comes forth from within, supplying stamina, insights and ruggedness we did not know we had.

We learn to see the relationship between matter and the vibrations of Spirit as related. We will learn All is divine life. Vibrations dense or subtle are both spiritual and we are building the discernment to understand the variation.

"Heart without mind is foolish; mind without heart is cruel."
—Carol E. Parrish-Harra

The Great Master Jesus introduced the concept of *"thinking with the heart."* All great mystics teach some version of this in their own tradition, and is an understanding that comes when we are ready. As we advance in awareness, we find that answers and insights come as "just knowing" to our most intimate questions.

Each different, cultural spiritual tradition builds a particular center of consciousness for the collective of humanity. For example, indigenous or native people of the world, by the power of their consciousness, are holding together the spirit and matter of this mother earth. Called "anchoring the planetary consciousness" each mind builds a container for itself (a material body through which to learn and express). The teachings about Father Sun and Mother Earth and respect for nature reflect this awareness to all of us. The native traditions of the world respectfully maintain this important connection in their prayer and ritual life that benefits all.

Most of the work done by the early goddess and shamanic religions was in the astral plane, as humanity developed its appreciation of the "spirit reality"—contact with the spirit world, deceased entities, and even "the little people." Thus began our contact with the inner world, although more strongly with some individuals than with others. These became the medicine men and women, spirit leaders and the mid-wives etc. Through time we have gleaned some limited respect from them (that still lingers) for their awareness of the human relationship with nature (which includes other close life streams), and the environmental issues this awareness continued to espouse. We regard our ancestry as significant, having descended from indigenous people, natives or pagans.

All our understanding of our personal chakras is mirrored in the experience of collective humanity, as we each are building our personal segment of our present-life wave. The solar plexus is the next to develop ... with its dualism. This process of discrimination has been going on for centuries and includes the work of age-old teachers who helped to define right and wrong for their people. It continues today with Moses and the *Ten Commandments* in the West and with Buddha and his teachings of *The Four Noble Truths* and the *Eight-Fold Noble Path* in the East. These introduced the sense of "right and wrong," "good and bad" to both "hemispheres of the world." Teachings suggest that most of humanity is ever building the rational mind. It is this work of the mental body to evaluate, judge, debate and make decisions; rational understanding is necessary for law and order to prevail in our own life as well as for society. This is the real work of the lower mental body, as the intuitive nature has not yet begun its interaction with higher awareness.

From the Godhead or Fountain of Life pours forth streams of life-giving energy that humanity has long struggled to understand. These powerful streams of energy have been identified by some as "Rays of Influence," similar to spiritual laws and/or invisible light, similar to a rainbow. Calling them by name and number helps us to have a common understanding of these streams; they are usually simply called "the Rays." These streams of power from the Godhead are known as follows and broken into two groups. The "Rays of Aspect" include: Ray One is Will, or Power; Ray Two is Love-Wisdom; Ray Three is Active Intelligence, Adaptability. The "Rays of Attribute" include: Ray Four is Harmony Through Conflict; Ray Five is Concrete Knowledge, Exactness; Ray Six is Devotion; and Ray Seven is Ceremonial Magic (Economy, Orderliness, Ceremony).

As we move more and more into the humanitarian age, the Aquarian Age, we will absorb more of these qualities of energies in which we swim. Aquarius is highly emotional and yet considered mental: a combination of Ray Five and Ray Seven with a dash of Ray Two to boot. This gives the heavily laden mind an intuitive charge that bonds with others. Ray Two reveals its efforts to take us all to the Oneness, consciously or unconsciously, while the mind easily expands and focuses on chosen arenas; Ray Five provides a strong mental mechanism, not easily penetrated, but loving to work; and Ray Seven organizes this mind mechanism into patterns. Uranus, the ruler, allows one to move rapidly from one subject to another. *The secret to utilizing this kind of intelligence is to find the patterns* and follow them with lots of willfulness/persistence.

Universal Energies carry each evolving consciousness toward the state of "perfected human." We are all related, and this is what the Oneness is about. In magnetizing something, anything to ourselves, we are pulling together the qualities we need to become consciously aware of the individuals, ideas, and events we need to enrich our life, even our lessons, to help us grow.

In my concept of *love bonds*, I promote the idea that we need a "*worthy opponent*," and I believe this is true in all meaningful relationships as well. We need someone who can contribute the quality or attributes we do not possess to our relationships and endeavors, whether marriage, friendship or business partnerships. These bring about the arrangements we find in families. Intentionally but unconsciously, we are put together because each one has something to add to the mix, and a unique combination often arranges itself in each of our physical families as well as in the spiritual groups we form.

We need "other than our own qualities" against which to push to help us grow strong. We may not like their physical personalities, or we may try to change or escape them; as we mature, we may learn to select personalities with qualities more compatible with ours. We enjoy the harmony we experience with these. With our "chosen families," we can feel more free from them, for example, when they rub us the wrong way; we feel we can escape and know we have choice. We rarely feel this with siblings or parents.

There is a terrible joke: A husband and wife are sitting comfortably in front of the fireplace one dark and damp evening enjoying the warmth. The man speaks, "*Mother, look at how peacefully that dog and cat are lying there enjoying the fire with us. Why can't we always be like that?*" To which she replies, "*Tie them together and see how long they are peaceful.*"

Progression of Consciousness

Progress in each life causes much exploration as the search for wholeness continues. If tests, or what seem to be tests, were understood in a more aware light, there would be less suffering and better understanding of why there must be these challenges along the way. By looking at the difficult spots in our lives today, not so much for a moral understanding as from a "peace of mind acceptance," we will find ways we can change or balance these upsets or land mines that lie along our spiritual pathways.

Master Jesus taught to "love thy neighbor" and that this mighty, but simple concept covers a multitude of sins. The Gospel of Thomas teaches that Jesus said, (verse 25) "*Love your brother like your Soul; guard him like the pupil of your eye.*" As we shift from our society's way of seeing things, to a higher one, we see there are many techniques we can apply. However, the Soul allows us free will to learn in our own ways and time. I have come to believe that to be a mentor to another, we must truly love him or her. If we cannot open our heart and soul to nourish a certain one, he or she is not ours to teach. Otherwise ego rules the relationship and not the Soul.

Although we understand there are levels of consciousness that do exist and that we are developing our abilities on many levels of being at the same time, most often we do not do this with a conscious awareness. We come to recognize the different levels to ourselves: emotional, mental, intuitive, as well as the physical. In time, we come to know that these levels mature at a "natural progression." This is the unconscious path, called evolution, by which most humanity advances.

Let us explore what it means to become more God-Like. Each religion posits different "rights" and "wrongs." This does not necessarily mean that we grow only by conscious spiritual intent, but unconsciously as well. In time we learn that each happening or event in our life teaches us something, and that we must remember that "God is ALL" … "Giver of All" … "Creator of all planes" … which challenges us to learn to use the creative force within our being for the good of all. As we become increasingly aware, we realize that our attitude, our kindnesses, and our humanity will guide us into actions that transform our understanding and our environment, at home, work, and play.

This implies that our personality—the material part of our being, the feeling and intellectual parts—has value in helping us connect to Divine guidance. The surprise of "*just knowing*" can be suspect when it comes upon us as a sudden *aha!* Yet, it happens. In a glance, you may see something that has always been there … but it never dawned on you before. You hear a lecture or comment and it pulls together two thoughts or truths you know but have never related previously. In a flash, there is a new meaning or realization. Now *you know.* These *"ah ha's"* are gifts of gold; they are truth for us from our inner realities dropping down into our conscious mind's territory. Now, we understand **now**!

One theory, spoken of more and more today relating to reincarnation, is that it is quite possible that many who have previously matured in the Oriental world are now incarnating in the Western world. Likewise, ones that have previously been Westerners are now incarnating in the Orient. Consider this: the cultural patterns of the East encourage humility, respect, and great sensitivity toward being a part of the Oneness, with less regard for the material plane. A modern idea is that these sensitives will bring their gentle attributes into our materialistic society. In return, people who advanced the causes of industries, inventions, and technologies, as well as the mechanization that marks our society are incarnating and contributing to the East at this time.

Souls who have had much experience in Western cultures suffer the *"poverty of abundance."* Modern Western societies often have so much material stuff that things lose their charm and no longer fulfill the individual. The quest for prosperity is a popular topic, but to be truly prosperous we need abundant health, happiness, opportunities, and so forth for our inner lives as well. We are learning that a more simple outer life leads to a richer inner life. The Westerner, now Easterner, is contributing to that economy and material world as they learn likewise about the values of "less being more." When we grasp a teaching known as *"voluntary simplicity,"* we find the foundation for a new value system as we mature. The concept is that *God will provide what we need if we first determine our real values and then trust.* We can now rest in the awareness that our needs are being met.

One student told me, *"There is a battle cry of the moment ... it is people before profit."* People who have found values that work for them have developed this idea. This is revealed in the comments of those who say "we can afford everything, *so what is most impor-*

tant for us?" Everyone who uses this way of thinking adds to the thought form of the collective which helps to correct the values of a distorted dollar-bill society.

All humanity is growing. Some consciously, some unconsciously, guided by natural evolution and suffering. Most often, our hidden past dwells just below our level of consciousness, and we must make an effort to bring it to consciousness. We can certainly search for insights from the past, but frequently this kind of new awareness breaks through unexpectedly—*ah ha's* that give meaning, to deepen relationships, memories, and familiar settings in ways that give value and help us *to know* hidden pieces of our soul's journey.

In due time we come to know there is more to life than judging ourselves and others. Most of us begin to realize that there is a bit-of-good in the worst of us and a bit of not-so-good in the best of us. We began in a most natural way to become aware of an extended capability to *"just know"* through the heart-mind connection. This is where the major level of development is taking place today. We are confronting the spiritual level of awareness called *"the opening of the heart"* and *"the building of the light (intuitive) body."*

Thus, we have come to the goal of Christianity, as given in the true Christian tradition by Jesus as he espoused, *"love one another"* … your enemies as well as friends. Christians always teach love, but how can others who have not known love know what it is? How can others learn to express it if they have not had it? We hear daily to "open the heart," and for the most part, I believe most serious students are in stages of doing so. We are to create a new humanity and a new world in the process. The results of an open heart are love, caring, generosity, giving the other the benefit of the doubt, wanting for the other what we want for ourselves—all are stepping-stones to real love … a pouring out of higher energies.

A lesson learned only intellectually does not have the same effect as a lesson learned on several levels, so let us contemplate these lessons as deeply as possible to gain all benefit possible. We can sharpen our awareness to derive all we can from all we observe. Some persons are naturally influenced by their feeling nature and emotional sensitivity, while others are more mental and want to know … *everything*. The mind questions everything. The paths are quite different and therefore the results are different. Yet we have to resist the desire to step down the "holy truths" to the mere rational level. Mystical awareness goes upward in consciousness and cannot be reduced to worldly understanding. It lifts us beyond the rational into the space where all Truths abide.

There are many paths leading to a *close* relationship, an "at-one-ness with the Divine." We can approach this Creator through art, science, theology, the intellect, or the emotions, all of which reveal the *Infinite Knowledge* displayed by the Divine, as we are made in the likeness of the Holy Image. The Creator needs us and we need the Creator to complete the design. There seems to be a certain point where the intellect fails. As we function more in keeping with the spirit of creation, we begin to be in touch with the intuitive part of our self, which again suggests the value of feeling to perceive that which is more subtle, beyond words and thoughts.

This process takes place automatically as we recognize the bounty of the higher world. We learn to love generously. We share, and we want for the other what they want for themselves; we celebrate the achievements of each, and we are grateful to be a part of humankind. When we unconsciously pour out *good, good* flows. When love is present, others may not know what they are feeling, but they sense it. They sense there is something different about us.

The Old Testament, the Torah, teaches tithing. This practice of sharing was considered a rule for those following the Hebrew tradition, whether through love and generosity, service, or other forms of caring—not just offering money. There are all kinds of ways to be generous with one's self and time, as we recall with gratitude all the belongings and talents we have received. Later this concept of tithing, of giving from our bounty, however small, became an important aspect of the Christian path.

The teachings of the Jewish philosopher, Maimonides (twelfth century), a famous Wise One, define the many ways individuals can grow spiritually. He defined "growth" through service and giving. It is my pleasure to offer these concepts that we may begin to practice them with a new depth of understanding.

There are eight degrees or steps in the duty of charity, not our modern use of the term as "donations," but the earlier meaning of *giving the other the benefit of the doubt.*

- The first and lowest degree is to give, but with reluctance or regret. This is the gift of the hand, but not of the heart.

- The second is to give cheerfully, but not proportionately to the distress of the sufferer.

- The third is to give cheerfully and proportionately, but not until solicited.

- The fourth is to give cheerfully, proportionately, and even un-solicited, but to put it in the poor man's hand, thereby exciting in him the painful emotion of shame.

- The fifth is to give charity in such a way that the distressed may receive the bounty, and know their benefactor, without their being known to him. Such was the conduct of some of our ancestors, who used to tie up money in the corners of their cloaks so that the poor might take it unperceived.

- The sixth, which demonstrates a higher understanding, is to know the objects of our bounty, but remain unknown to them. Such was the conduct of those of our ancestors, who used to convey their charitable gifts into poor people's dwellings, taking care that their own persons and names should remain unknown.

- The seventh is still more meritorious, namely to bestow charity in such a way that the benefactor may not know the relieved persons, nor they the name of their benefactors, as was done by our charitable ancestors during the existence of the Temple. For there was in that holy building a place called the *Chamber of the Silent*, wherein the good deposited secretly whatever their generous hearts suggested, and from which the poor could take, and where each identity was maintained with equal secrecy.

- Lastly, the eighth, and the most meritorious of all, is to anticipate charity by preventing poverty. Namely, to assist the reduced fellowman, either by a considerable gift, a loan of money, by teaching him a trade, or by putting him in business so that he may earn an honest livelihood, and not be forced to the dreadful alternative of holding out his hand for charity. To this scripture alludes when it says, "*And if thy brother be waxen poor, and fallen in decay with thee: then thou shalt revive him; [yea, though he be] a stranger, or a sojourner; that he may live with thee.*" This is the highest step and the summit of charity's "golden ladder" (*Leviticus* 25:35).

What about you and me? When we make an offering, whether in church or in any setting, do we think to *bless it*? Do we know what the *"intent"* adds to the gift? Consider this:

First, come to that special place within yourself where generosity can be aroused. Then feel the energy of the *Divine* within your being, and move to connect with the Sea of Consciousness who is the Great Creator of All.

Secondly, think or speak: *Energy Divine, do a mighty goodness within me and through me. I give thanks for this opportunity to acknowledge our Oneness. Amen.*

"The Truth is …You Cannot Out-Give God."

The mark of the opened heart is generosity and some have always demonstrated this understanding. The heart is the center or fourth chakra of the chakra system and the place where higher consciousness flows from self-centeredness to loving concern for all. *The heart is the bridge between the self-centered personality and the desired state of Higher Consciousness.* Here spirituality and materiality meet in the living of an ordinary human life.

Mysteries Are Hidden in Public

We learn to walk by walking, speak by speaking, work by working, and we learn to love God and humanity by loving. This entire
manuscript is intended to encourage our efforts in that awareness.
We must learn to love by building our love capacity; a two-ounce
cup is completely full at two ounces, a four-ounce cup is not full
without four ounces. In a human being we have the capacity of
expansion from a two-ounce cup, when personal love is the *most we
can do,* into the larger capacity as we embrace impersonal and then
unconditional love. We transform repeatedly like the dragonfly.

> *There is a remarkably unattractive insect whose gills force it to
> live in water for one to five years. Twelve or more times it sheds its
> skin; each time it remains water bound. Eventually it crawls from
> the muddy water to the top of a reed or up on rock. At last, after
> the final shedding, what it is to be has come to be. It emerges with
> a slender body and gauze-like iridescent wings; it is the beautiful
> dragonfly. An entirely new life-style is now possible. It breathes air,
> feels the sun's warmth, and it flies.*
>
> *This graceful flyer comes from the ugliest of bugs; repeatedly it
> has sloughed off the outer armor that is no longer appropriate. It then
> needs to pull itself out of the mud and water to a new life. Unless
> it does, it cannot use the power within. Had the dragonfly tried to
> cling to the old limitations, if it had refused to grow and change, if it
> had waited for someone else to free it, it would never have emerged
> to fulfill the promises of its birth.*

Until we move beyond that which keeps us mud-bound and
waterlogged—until we lay claim to the creative life force within,
and until we honor our life experiences and patterns—we are re-
stricted to the bonds of our programming; we are not free beings.

There is another story to recall. The lion story is our story, as
the lion is often the symbol of the untamed personality. He seeks
his way; he is powerful and strong, a beautiful animal. In Africa an
initiate celebrates having a dream of a lion. Each wants to dream

of a peaceful lion, which shows his beauty in a gentle manner. This is a sign that the personality is transforming into the refined being we are meant to be.

> *The story goes, a mountain lion preparing to give birth needs food for her ordeal. She goes down the mountain and kills a goat in a herd. In the process, she dies, but her baby is born anyway. Looking around at the herd, the baby identifies with it and believes he is a goat. He runs around grazing with the herd until one day Grandfather Lion comes out of the forest and sees him.*
>
> *Grandfather Lion approaches the cub, sniffs him, and finds he even smells like a goat. He grabs the cub by the scruff of the neck, carries him to a river and forces him to see his reflection. The baby mountain lion realizes he is not a goat and goes off with the grandfather to learn about his true nature.*

Aware of the high consciousness we carry, we work in order to use well the creativity of our Divine Lineage: no starving, no homeless, no unnecessary suffering or deprivation—what a dream! It is possible only with the collective genius awakening. Remember: *To those to whom much is given, much is required.* Too often, the privileged few have sealed themselves off selfishly from the world of pain, and from this, only hostility can result. To share a dream and invite participation gives others a good example.

Our society has now begun to appreciate these giving "creators" who impact those around them by recognizing what are called "CNN Heroes." Each year ten individuals, whose actiions resulted in service to others, receive gifts of money for their work, and one is chosen as the hero for the year and receives a larger dollar award. One such hero last year was an American builder whose son came home from battle as a multiple amputee. The son has a family and no hope of employment or gaining his own home. So the father built his son a home, but more than that … he started building homes for amputees with a mighty goal of "a home for each multiple amputee," and last year alone built forty-two homes.

In the ancient world, once the sincerity of a neophyte was recognized, those who *knew* nurtured them. They assisted others on the path of development within a given framework of training techniques and places which were kept secret from those with little or no interest. Rigorous disciplines changed the etheric nature of the individual. "Cleanliness is next to Godliness" speaks to us on all levels of Self. Think of this as the beginning of alchemy, a process of purification, self-discipline, intellectual development, and spiritual breakthroughs.

Most writing regarding the Egyptian Coptics or Essenes tell us how concerned they were with cleanliness. Historical stories record that bathing originated in the temples out of this concern. We know the Jews considered ritual baths to be very important. Master Morya introduced bathing pools as he taught cleanliness to be next to godliness and stressed that outer physical purity was the beginning step before advancing to the inner levels.

A great effort of character building was the foundation of all training. Tests were given—differing in nature from what occurs today because humanity was different then—but the first step was always physical training, such as proper hygiene, body building, yoga and a pure—almost Spartan—approach to daily life. Today we seem to receive our tests in the development of the non-physical, psychological levels of our personality. We know this as the psychological or psycho-spiritual self—the integration of body, mind and spirit.

The Divine design is for each one to assist another. As we find our own way, we can encourage, lift, or serve others as a tutor or guide. Each one helps each other. The next individual then embraces another, and so it goes; healing the world of *separatism* is the desired result. A way to think of this is that we are first a "seeker," then a "finder" as we discover particular ways that work for us and we share. Our own path may not be the same forever, but each stage deepens our consciousness as we progress and change.

Then we become the "doer," who is sincere and genuine in each practice he or she undertakes; the next step is the goal of "just being." Here one is just in perfect peace, knowing and living in communion with higher world, in both heart and mind. We each reach for this goal and the mystic leads the way by seeking out environments wherein serenity dwells. Thus, withdrawing from the busy world and seeking the forests or woods, the desert or hills, lends itself to inner peace.

PAUSE NOW: Think of this for yourself: How have you sought peace and quiet? Have you pondered this before? Have you actually left jobs or locations, friends or habits to bring purity and peace into your life? Can you see the quiet life drawing you nearer to it?

The Process at Work

The Christ Drama, or the Initiatory Path, unfolds within the Soul of each one. Each goes through a process of transformation, having his or her own conversion from darkness into light, no matter what the terminology. We each have our sorrows, temptations, movements of uplifts, as well as dark nights of the soul and death of high hopes. These are common experiences of the journey to become the wise one, the sage. Each human soul gains its birthright by facing the challenges of the darkness and doubt that holds it in bondage. The invoking of the Holy One, the Christ as Wayshower, is a cry for help, a seeking of spiritual power to assist the traveler on one's own way.

Within each of us there is a "redeeming power." In esoteric language we often use the term "Solar Angel" for the "Soul." While a bit different, they represent the same inner authority. Here within is awaiting the power for our journey, but we do not always know we can invoke this assistance ... or even know it is there. The long neglected but central message of the Christian (and Gnostic) tradition is: "the Christ in you, the hope of glory." This message gets lost in the formal orthodox structures that have become the Churches of today.

Religion, once the protector of the Soul, itself became lost. True religion is to be concerned about the discovery of each individual and his/her own divine selfhood. "Religion is the invocative cry of humanity and the evocative response of the Greater Life to that cry," so says the Tibetan Master (of the Alice A. Bailey material). At the same time, it has been said that there are no hatreds so great or as deep as those fostered by religion. This is the misinterpretation. The profound depth of emotional feeling and idealism that lie at the core of the religious impulse is overpowering. It is an impulse designed to bring forth the finest within each. It has been said that "fear" of the Holy, the sublime, is one of the greatest blocks humanity has to overcome.

We must have three ingredients to make our nature ready for living a holy life. These are first, having a self-organizing nature (the ability to learn from our mistakes and to reorganize our priorities). Secondly, we must have self-discipline; otherwise, we are like a person in a boat without oars. Third, we must aim for self-realization (we must dare to be more than we have ever been).

The choices or decisions we make establish Karmic Patterns. Actions merely follow suit. We live our entire lives with symbols, parables, dreams, and archetypes around us; we may or may not see them. We fill our buildings with statues of Liberty, drawings of Uncle Sam, movies filled with imaginative stories of good guys and not so good ones. We champion heroes and regret our learning experiences, thinking of them as "mis-takes" or accidental pregnancies—not understanding that each event/action is to stir us from our slumbering.

We gradually gain an overview of Life, making it large enough to hold our hopes, dreams, and wishes, and then we keep adjusting this view to the new and profound that we discover along the journey of experiences. This is the purpose of study.

The same "joy of sharing" that is encouraged for youngsters will live with us all the days of our life. To live is more than mere giving and receiving; it is a source of gladness to share, for the spirit within us knows the spirit within the other, and as they embrace, joy ignites. The basic rule is "give to live, share to enjoy."

All of us attune to something. Discover what you would like to be like and attune to it; likewise, if we fill our heart and mind with that which we hate, we become that. For whatever you hold in thought and mind, you become. We shape our lives guided by the intent we dwell upon and become whatever it is that is our guiding image. We must ask, to what are we attuned?

We acquire the ability to temper our will. It is our tool for choosing direction by letting it take each of us on our chosen path wherever we have so willed. Patience is a by-product of understanding the right use of will. All things flow along the way of appropriate timing. We eventually learn to "wait on the Lord"—we might call it "divine timing."

Cultivating "trust" involves our sense of knowing that *we are love*. It begins by receiving love from parents and caregivers, but it becomes divine when we *know* that the Universe loves us. Life loves us; we are each a child of the Universe. Trust makes us secure.

Humility allows us to give ourselves to that which is beyond us, more than we can do, more than we are now. We bow our head and plow forward toward the Highest that calls to us. We bring the lesser to serve the greater.

Our Creativity is the glue that mends the broken pieces back together. We all have nicks, cracks and scars. Until we love great, healing cannot happen. Creativity arises to allow us to rearrange our pieces in such a way that we can become new. We cease to be judgmental of self and others. Our sense of values change; we want for others what we want for ourselves. We allow our personality to soften; we quit living by the rigid standards of others and choose to be true to our evolving self.

Our new "discernment" glows in the dark ... we can now find our own way. In the past, the wisdom ways were passed down by the bard, the musician, the poet, the storyteller. There is a whole history of drama, pageants, Christ stories, and teachings, all shared without any church doing it. Wisdom has always had its ways!

Understanding gradually emerges that we are all one family. In fact, we are all One, and being able to find a practical application for our understanding assists us in finding the part we are to play, our role in the Greater Work. Wise ones come to realize that a "conscious realization of unity with God" is necessary, before we can be a blessing to others. A saint, wise one, an elder or meaningful mentor is one through whom the blessings flow, and this outpouring affects others on multiple levels.

As we open to the Heart Christ Center or the Center of Love-Wisdom, Lots of Vital Energy pours forth from the Soul. This floods the lower worlds with streams of energy transforming the self, then in turn, touching others. In group life, we are to come to live our lives in such a way that we each assist one another to realize a holy consciousness. We can hear the master's voice saying, "You will know them by their love."…

> We recall the Cherokee story about a wise old grandfather explaining humanity's power of choice to his young grandson. He says, "A fight is going on inside me."
>
> "It is a terrible fight and it is between two wolves. One is evil—he is anger, envy, sorrow, regret, greed, arrogance, self-pity, inferiority, lies, false pride, and ego. The other is good—he is joy, peace, love, hope, serenity, humility, kindness, benevolence, empathy, generosity, truth, compassion, and faith. They are locked in battle and neither will stop until the other is destroyed. The same fight is going on inside you and inside every other person, too."
>
> The grandson thought about it for a minute and then asked his grandfather, "Which wolf will win?"
>
> The old Cherokee simply replied, "The one you choose to feed."

All traditions pass on their "*wisdom*" stories in symbols and parables. In such a way, the listener can gain as much as they are capable of gaining. They can gain an understanding of the parables to the degree their inner or outer teacher has prepared them. It is wise to understand the power that parables contain. Truth comes in the language for which one is prepared. In the oral tradition there were no written scriptures; people spoke the stories or the symbolic truth in such a manner that others would grasp as much as they could.

As Our Path Emerges

1. Life has its ups and downs

2. Awakening and new understanding begins to change my path

3. One begins to question is this mine to do? not mine to do?

4. Clarity begins to stabilize direction

5. Focus comes

Here we see the path of the student as he or she awakens, turning toward the light and learning needed discernment.

Our faith celebrations also hold hidden meanings. "*Is there a Santa Claus*" is the perfect question. What about the hidden meaning of Advent and its real meaning? We have become a rational people wanting concrete responses; yet there are truths that lurk in other levels of understanding awaiting discovery. The rational reality denies subtle implications. Its truth exists in right-wrong limitations. Even crude illustrations have hidden meanings behind them, whether others agree or not. This denial happens to many as they are exposed to the subtleness of wisdom, whether it comes from within themselves or through another source.

A "mystical" experience informs a person of another way of *knowing*. It may be a sudden contact with another level of reality, a new way of knowing, or a powerful contact of a truth we cannot deny. Whether we understand this is possible in advance is not necessary; on the spot *we know*.

A symbol reveals one mystery and veils an even deeper one. While it seems to be *revealing* one thing, a deeper meaning awaits discovery. It is said that a symbol tells us one thing and protects another until we are ready. By placing a truth in the obvious, it is seen by one who is ready and is passed over by the unaware. It is accepted as "of no value" by the unaware because it is neither guarded nor hidden. The symbol for the mystical path is known by drawing a vertical line with a horizontal line crossing the vertical one.

The cross is an ancient symbol, not originally associated with Christianity. When we research its original meaning, we find the two lines had valuable meanings. The vertical represented Spirit coming down through the planes to density (at Earth). The horizontal is the earth plane on which we are manifesting physically. Below we see the vertical line flowing earthward; the horizontal can be crossed at whichever chakra represents where one is presently centered, but the goal for the collective is to be centered at the heart.

Make a circle enclosing the center point where the two lines cross. This is a symbol of the mystical journey, on which humanity has embarked. The vertical line represents bringing spirit and matter into relationship; the horizontal line represents bringing our will and higher will together. The cross in the center of the circle at the heart center brings this together. Incidentally, this is the astrological symbol for planet Earth and reveals the importance of "*thinking in the heart*" and the reason for which one incarnates in this particular place.

Astrological
symbol of Earth

Every icon witnesses to a truth; we may or may not perceive it. As with holy pictures of Jesus and Mary, saints or a known healer, each represents something about the quality and style of the one pictured. Another symbol commonly seen by all of us is the steeple on top of many churches. Do you know its meaning?

The steeple becomes narrower as it points into the heavenly direction because the path to the Higher World gets narrower as we progress.

Here is a photo of a headstone from a Turkish cemetery. Since Muslim people do not personalize them in the same way as Westerners, we look at this headstone and, if knowledgeable, we can see this is a friendly, loving woman. She always wanted to be fashionable, gracious, and loved earrings and jewelry. Just by the seeing the headstone we perceive her nature.

THREE

Overcoming Fear
of the Unknown

There is no death ... but do not take this life too seriously ...
no one gets out alive.

HERE WE PONDER A CUTE REMARK, but also a great truth. As we enter into metaphysical thinking, we learn "meta" means beyond or above the physical. We accept that there really is life in other dimensions to be experienced. The negative side of metaphysics is to accept whatever comes without thought. When people surrender the idea of "God" as a personal source of origination, they often lose their relationship with, and give up on, Spirit and the higher world. They no longer care to participate in the collective. They fail to realize that their contribution has value, and fail to take an active role in the progressive life of humanity. They feel powerless and fall into allowing others to create the worldview for the group mind. They then bemoan the outcome and say, *"I guess it was not meant to be,"* while their contribution may have made the difference.

At the present stage of "becoming," humanity realizes we cannot get out of this life without letting go of the physical form we wear. The personality we now wear is going to fade just like a blossom on a bush, but the bush still lives. *"I am the vine; you are the branches"* (John 15:5). The personality is the flower, but the soul is the bush. The sacred center (God-Creator) is the root. The part of us that blooms and gives its fragrance will come and go, but the soul still provides opportunities which our inner self needs to evolve. We call it "life," but as we broaden our picture, we change our long-range identity with the bush. "*I am the Soul*" becomes a reality as our consciousness expands and we realize that the Soul is the real energizer.

Our bush blooms and grows, but let us change this now to think about how the dense carbon-based body becomes the crystalline body that does not die. This cannot really be "known" without experience. What I am espousing is the difference between just learning about various philosophies of life and actually experiencing the mystical consciousness directly. We believe in a philosophy; we *know* in an expanded reality. To *know* is to experience an intimacy. When we know that we can trust our self, others, and the Source of Life, we change. In this awareness, we can be like the biblical flowers of the field. This is the awareness which the "*changing of the age*" is trying to help us reach. This is the goal of the Aquarian Age, the Mayan Prophecies, and many others as well—to reveal to us that there is more to our great reality than we realize.

As the earth is changing vibration, if we can move with it—and many can—all frequencies move upward, into a thinner and rarer altitude. At each lift we adjust, and in doing so we change into a more sensitive and more etheric individual ... or said another way, less materialistic. Materialism is not about money but about the beliefs we hold. Materialists do not accept anything beyond the physical reality. We each have to test the truth of our beliefs in the privacy of our own lives.

We are much more than the matter of our body. We move from the dense form to the etheric form, and this is what will happen to our world. The earth is lessening in its density, and the less dense astral world is growing greater. We are still aware of the dense reality where the "fight or flight" of survival exists, but we spend more and more of our time in thought and emotion where we see the astral or mental worlds grow in importance.

In 1974, the psychologist Dr. Lawrence LaShan wrote *The Medium, the Mystic, and the Physicist.* When it came out, it seemed near miraculous to see a Ph.D. in Human Development go out on the limb to address the "paranormal." He wrote a number of books such as *How to Meditate,* and compared mysticism and quantum mechanics. His research lead to *The Next Frontier* suggesting that the paranormal is explainable when compared to quantum theory.

LaShan sought to explain the paranormal reality to which our culture was waking up. His words comforted many, mostly college kids, ministers, and New Age thinkers. Psychologists examined the book and shared their comments; the "acceptance of unrecognized realities" had begun. A sudden explosion of Einstein, Kabir, Spiritualism and Buddhism swept the United States. All inquiring thinkers looked less suspicious when examining such long-hidden areas.

LaShan states:

> The mystical approach is known in every country and time for which we have records. It appears to be a search and training for an extraordinary way of being at home in the world, of perceiving and relating to reality. No matter when and where the inspiration arises, whatever the techniques developed and the disciplines followed, a marked similarity emerges. "All Mystics"... one of them, Louis Claude de St. Martin, wrote ..."speak the same language and come from the same country."
>
> They agree that the most important goal for man is to see more deeply into "what is," to go beyond his ordinary perceptions, to comprehend rather than merely understand the world. They agree further on the kinds of training and development techniques needed to move toward this goal. Further, they agree on what reality begins to look like when they have moved along the path. The overwhelming similarity in their conclusions as to the nature of the cosmos and the behavioral standards this implies for man has been remarked on by every serious student of mysticism.
>
> With the flower children and their fight for freedom, metaphysical thinking emerged only to change, grow and adapt rapidly within

the next thirty years until each minister and congregation, each art teacher and business motivator found the words—creative, intuitive, perception and talent—creeping into greater use. Psychic classes began to be taught and mysticism was whispered about in more ways than previously when reserved mainly for known saints."

In 1987 a scientific survey by Father Andrew Greeley, at the height of the breakthrough of New Thought regarding mysticism and/or psychism, he reported, "*Nearly half of American adults (42% at that time) believed they have been in contact with someone who has died, usually a dead spouse or sibling. That is up from more than 27% eleven years earlier.*" Other experiences, though, are profound. In 1973, a full 35% of Americans reported they had had a mystical experience, feeling "very close to a powerful, spiritual force that seemed to lift you out of yourself."

And one-seventh of those who have had such experiences—5% of the whole population—have literally been 'bathed in light' like the Apostle Paul. These experiences go way beyond intellect, and even beyond emotion. For a fifth of those who have them, they involve 'a sense of tremendous personal expansion, either psychological or physical'—a form of body mysticism.

Such paranormal experiences—by definition, lying outside the normal—are generally viewed as hallucinations or symptoms of mental disorder. But if these experiences were signs of mental illness, our numbers would show the country is going nuts. What was paranormal is now normal. It's even happening to elite scientist and physicians who insist that such things cannot possibly happen." (Greeley, 1987)

The Value of Suffering

Dr. Asher Barnwell writes of suffering in ways that shed much light on this harsh experience. In his insights, he says:

There are many aspects of suffering that have nothing to do with Karma as normally understood. Some suffering is necessary to create a widening of the consciousness. Therefore, suffering can be developmental. Other forms of suffering may occur due to what I will call 'functional' karma. By this, I mean preparation for future work, rather than being the consequence of past indiscretion. Another aspect of suffering has to do with our understanding of the level of reality we call Soul. (Barnwell, 1984)

We must remember that our planet is going through the *Near-Death-Experience* or the *Bardo* experience right now. Moreover, as all of us are offered the chance, we need to become mystics. We can choose to be "consciousness transformation assistants" or "midwives for the planet" as it births a new consciousness for all humanity. Facing violence and the addiction experience—especially sexual, alcoholic, and the drug experience—are Bardo experiences. We must recognize these are the energies of *hell-on-earth,* and we are required to form responses to these destructive energies and lend our efforts to help recovery to occur individually and collectively. We must find ways to be supportive of the advancement of improvement by money, political efforts, and personal one-to-one contributions.

So humanity lives through fear, darkness, pain, guilt, suffering, loss, and abuse. Each one of us faces these trying issues and we attempt to find a way to deal with them while living. When we think of certain holy ones whose lives are recorded as hard and testy—I think of the historical mystic, St. John of the Cross (1542–1591), or the modern mystic and priest healer, Padre Pio (1887–1968)—we will see pain-filled life-walks that are experienced as "going through the Bardo." Some fight the demons of humanity, and those who do, have some awful experiences in the tests they undergo to transform themselves … and planetary life.

Living through the destruction of one's family, falling into addiction, rape or violence, or experiencing Nazi Germany's dark hours—these all can lead to an awakening of our mystical nature. Remember how Viktor Frankl,* neurologist and psychiatrist (see Wikipedia.com), suffered under the Nazis, and his story.

Such severe situations combine to grant the human collective a new awareness. Darkness is the "unconsciousness prior to becoming conscious," even though this is not well understood. "Severe darkness" is the Bardo-in-action breaking down stubborn thought-forms.

We all begin in darkness as a seed in the ground. As mentioned here several times, the idea of the seed and the teachings around it are exceedingly important. Within each of us there is a Divine seed waiting to emerge. It is buried in matter, waiting for water and light. Our tears water this precious seed and it matters not whether they be of sadness or joy. Likewise, as the light of the mind expands, it supplies the light needed until in due time the Light of the Soul beams upon it. The Real Self then blooms.

Once I was asked to explore my own feelings of grief and pain. We each know this is a very hard thing to really do, but having had a lot of loss (and I believe all mystics have to look into a deep pool of grief to understand Life), I discovered my truest feelings: these always disappear in the light of day, and I find that I hide them from myself through my so-called busyness. So I share this pensive writing, tenderly:

> *Grief is a pain that stands in the shadows of my being. I dare not look at it or it will swallow me. Death has been so much a part of my life; it has been both my blessing and my enemy. Three times a child of mine has died; I have watched two other children suffer*

---

* Viktor Frankl [1905–1997], Austrian Jewish psychologist and significant to the Human Potential movement, had studied medicine and had an interest in psychology prior to internment at Auschwitz where for five months he was a slave laborer. He was liberated by Americans in April 1945. Frankl's concepts of engaging one's human potential was tested in the worst of suffering during these Holocaust experiences, but these shaped his therapeutic approaches as well as personal outlook. A most interesting teaching of his was found within the narrow boundaries of the camps; he shared that he found that only two races of men exist: decent and unprincipled ones; and these were to be found in all classes, ethnicities, and groups.

by living. I have grief for them, even more, I do believe, than the loss of those taken in death.

Grief touches me when my husband has low blood sugar attacks; I see him mindless and fumbling. He is not the partner of my forty years but a shadow of the man I loved. I see Grief as I watch my son unable to find his way and angry at me because I cannot help him. I have no more answers; I tell him he must do it for himself and he has it in himself to do it. He does not believe me; he bounces between love and anger of me, thinking I am cruel.

One dear daughter is truly selfish, yet she is finding herself. She is stronger, more capable than she knows, and I have to let her be tough so she can face life. It is grief when I cannot call her without her being rude. I pretend it does not matter, but inside I cry and turn to another task, so I do not have to think about her. I want her to express something more pleasant to me. I know I disappointed her; she disappointed me. I had to protect us—my husband and I, our home, and our hearts.

Grief has a hard heart and sharp edges. It pushes into the quiet hours and prevents rest; grief cares not if there are tasks waiting or a need for quiet. It masquerades as anger, fear, or busyness. It pretends to be gone until a thought or a hope brings it back. It is not one act or hurt; it is made up of pains glued together, forming a conglomeration of balls of pain. My nature is affected physically and emotionally. Stress builds up until I find a physical outlet: tears, sleep, or being outdoors for rest.

I walk around pain daily. Charles knows I cannot stand any more and, when it becomes too much, he has always tried to help me, not always in ways I would want him to, as he tries to resolve things in his own way. Now as he slips away in dementia, not even he can help me.

I reach to free myself and sometimes I think I do for a little while and then, if I look at the dark pile of shadows, I am in too much pain to pretend. I cannot cry; my tears have long ago dried up. I can only busy myself so the aches will go back into the shadows.

When I think of grief, I have to think of it at a distance; I cannot go close. I allow myself to feel apart, the shadow; I quickly then move away. I handle it intellectually. My heart no longer screams or throws up as it once did. Now I know it is Life that is neither "joy *nor pain." I do not allow either the great "ups" or great "downs" any more. I level out the highs and lows because I know one can only endure so much. This is how I can be steady or dependable. I allow love to flow even when I do not "like" things. Knowing this I find a different kind of peace.*

Philosopher and spiritual thinker, Nicholas Roerich in the Agni Yoga teachings, or Ethical Living as it is sometimes known, ponders and responds to Mable Collins' sensitive material in *Through the Gates of Gold:*

> Look into the deep heart of life, whence pain comes to darken men's lives. She is always on the threshold, and behind her stands despair.
>
> What are these two giant figures, and why are they permitted to be our constant followers?
>
> It is we who permit them; we who order them, as we permit and order the action of our bodies; and we do so as unconsciously. But by experiment and investigation we learn much about physical life, and we obtain at least as much in regard to our inner life.
>
> Pain arouses, softens, breaks, and destroys. Regarded from a sufficient removed standpoint, if we can be objective, it appears as medicine, as a knife, as a weapon, as a poison. It is an implement, which is to be used. What we desire is to discover, who the user is; what part of our self is it that demands the presence of this thing so hateful to the rest? ... for the benefit of our Soul, that we wage warfare inside of ourselves...
>
> ... if man's will becomes so relaxed with regard to it, he would no longer retain life in that state in which pain exists. Why does he desire his own hurt?

Nicholas Roerich answers:

> Because we use it to break through the shell of the seed of the Divine, within our self.
>
> Remember that the sin and shame of the world are your sin and shame for you are a part of it. The soiled garment that you shrink

from touching may have been yours yesterday, it may be yours tomorrow. Therefore, be wary lest too soon you fancy yourself apart from the masses."

Many sensitives are among us; you may be one. At some past point, you began the journey and at this time, you find yourself sensitized to the pain of others and of humankind. Maybe as a child you looked into a flower and it talked to you, or maybe you had an experience of seeing God in a tree or in a mountain, or likewise an experience in Nature, as many have had. Many children are sensitive, especially in our time. This is a sign of our "human refinement" (evolution) showing itself.

You may feel some of the pain of the human group mind; as such, you are helping humanity to become the Great Being it is to be. When this Great Being remembers who it really is ... the Child of the Most High ... there is much to understand and bear ... as we take upon ourselves a share in the responsibilities and burdens of the Holy Ones.

One woman spoke to me about the birth of her second child. As he lay in her arms, she knew that she had known this soul before. From deep within herself she knew that he and she had tried to get back together for lifetimes. Now it had happened. The woman, who had never believed in reincarnation or studied anything of this sort, found in that *knowingness* a "new reality." She was now ready for a more conscious path.

When we fall in love with someone, we generally see only the highest qualities in him or her, as we are blind to all else by our love. We do not see what we do not want to see; whenever we think of the loved one, we feel sensations of love and a charge of feelings in our astral heart center. This feeling is stimulated in much the same manner when we contemplate beauty, nature, children, or the Divine, the Higher World, or in whatever way we perceive through higher consciousness. No matter the language, when we love, our heart opens and continues to open ... we discover love in all its shades and frequencies. This is the same process as mysticism.

Become the Real Self

We have four heart centers, one in each of the physical, the etheric, the astral, and the mental bodies, not just one. The etheric body is the scaffolding or framework on which the physical body builds and conforms. The astral body is less dense, consisting of emotional matter or the desire nature. Likewise, layers of thought build a mental vehicle providing it an established record or "history" of the evolving ego. All the bodies interpenetrate the physical body and continue to evolve as we begin to recognize and awaken to our true nature as a Soul, or "Our Real Self."

These centers work within us, and together they make up the multi-leveled etheric-physical form. We use all of them as we evolve. We are well acquainted with this, our physical vehicle, and we become aware also of our non-physical vehicle (or etheric), which interfaces with it … and then perhaps we even discover the astral. As the etheric stirs, we feel emotion of some kind, mostly unconscious. When the astral and etheric work together, we feel expansion or contraction; at various times like these, our emotional nature begins to make itself known.

The astral heart loves or dislikes very personally and can be quite intense. Its role is to feel deeply in a personal way, and later to interface between itself and the mental body (mental heart). The mental body is home for the impersonal heart—more understanding and less emotional. This heart in turn "knows" and yet it is not yet the highest state of love. For as it opens, it begins to pull or draw down into itself energy from the next higher level, the Soul. The Soul energy, in turn, begins to flow into the mental body. We have a new kind of love, "unconditional love" (with the nature of Soul leaking into the personality).

To recount this, we have the physical heart working for the physical mechanical vehicle; the etheric organ interacts with the physical and opens to the astral (we now have personal love); the astral heart stimulates the mental heart, which loves impersonally. As the heart center of the mental body becomes active, it receives the impulses of the intuitive body; now the soul influence can make its "self" known as "unconditional love." Few humans have achieved so much; many evolved humans are loving humanitarians (working from the mental heart, still caring deeply in an impersonal way, and from time to time receiving droplets of intuitive wisdom).

The **first** step is letting the physical heart pump to benefit the physical organs. Awakening the feeling nature, it calls the astral nature to feel. This is a movement from animal instinctual drive—fight or flight—to awaken the "mind being" (the human) to kinds of new emotion and lets us feel the dualism of the animal-human drive.

The **second** step is when the instinctual/dualist emotions become focused in a personal manner, such as love, like, or dislike. We have feelings and we have focus, and when we see them or think of the one about whom we have personal emotion, this is where the astral heart makes its contribution with personal feelings.

The **third** step in expanding from the astral heart is to learn to love impersonally. We may know that we love this one best or more personally in our own astral feeling nature, but now we are able to bring enough "mind" into the situation to know that although this is my child or my friend, I can realize that he or she is not perfect. I can still see their good and not so good traits. I can still love yet be impersonal enough to see the human weaknesses.

This is impersonal love, which our pets, our children, and our mates need and want. They need not be perfect for us to love them, or for them to know that we see their potential. To love all others impersonally is our goal, and we must realize that each is on their own journey, just as we are. This journey to wholeness and holiness contains many rough spots, yet heightens the ability to learn through mindfulness; this is the development of the mental heart.

Impersonal love or empathy can be for the tree, the bird, a pet, and the love for another when they tell their story. We feel our heart expand "for them," even though they have a very different background and mannerisms. We feel compassion for the other although we have nothing personal with which to link their story to us. This mental heart and its impersonal love stimulates the intuitive body and the tender spiritual heart. It begins to "weep," and intuition begins to change the mental qualities into higher gifts. From scriptures we now read,

> To another the working of miracle; to another prophecy; to another discerning of spirits; to another divers kinds of tongues; to another the interpretation of tongues. (Corinthians 12:10)

Intuitive work includes discernment, discrimination, and a sense of invoking higher guidance. This awareness comes from a higher level of consciousness than rational thinking.

The **fourth** step is living in love unconditionally; here we come closest to the great heart of the divine. Loving unconditionally is "love-caring" from our spiritual heart as it is attuned to the Great Heart. We move from stage to stage, gaining the ability to care as much as possible at each step. Each time, we live closer to the open *cloud of knowable things*. Here we find ourselves at the very edge of knowing *with* the Divine. In this expanded state, we actually touch the love of God in all nature, a sense of Creator presence. When we experience this manner of sensing the presence of God in all nature, it is known as "pantheism," the worship of God through nature and its beauty. Remember, humanity is a part of nature as well.

In our quest for spiritual progress, we want this same openness to all humanity. The next step is astonishing, for it is really an expansion beyond the limitations of the mental dimension into the intuitive. It allows us another expansion … the unconditional takes us into the interface with the Divine. Here we enter the mystical (*maturing transformational impulse*) where we slip beyond the usual boundaries of discernment. This opening takes us into a *state of knowingness* that goes beyond the mental (either personal or impersonal) into the land of the *Divine knowing.*

Now we must grasp the similar expansion of mind as we did in grasping the expansion of the heart. To begin, we must acknowledge the brain and mind are different. **The brain is the physical mechanism, and the mind is the tool of consciousness.**

The brain itself has evolved from reptilian to mammalian, from mammalian to neo-cortex; now it is in process of changing from neo-cortex to pre-nodal or Divine. Similar to the heart, as one level after another of brain-mind development develops and becomes stable, the next level begins formation. The collective of humanity is advancing in its mental ability to use the earlier formations of the brain. Today as we begin the new era, humanity's overall "mental average" is capable of using well the three lower levels of consciousness (chakras).

Here we have traced the evolutionary advancement of the brain to create a better and more capable tool for the developing mind in order to handle the more subtle energies (frequencies) with which it is beginning to interact....

There are three kinds of reasoning to understand. The first is **logic,** an orderly sequence of thought toward a result. The second is **insight,** always dependent on logic. Here we take the logical capacity and combine it with ideas that have no relationship to logic and see that which is not obvious. This is "creative thinking." Third, we have **intuition** that is simple, direct "inner knowing."

As we begin our practice to develop higher consciousness, we often do ourselves harm by harboring lots of regrets about choices we have made or paths we have taken. Teachings tell us, "have no regrets." Often we do burden ourselves with such thinking, remembering the pain that resulted, thinking that, if we had made other choices, our life would be different. Studying an old manuscript that has much to say, I share:

> Many there are who secretly regret some lack of mental training and intellectual attainment: yet these same have within them aspiration —intuition. To them we say, **Regret nothing,** brethren: if the Powers-that-be, the great Lords of Karma, had seen fit to place you in conditions of life which would necessitate intellectual attainments and a comprehensive education, you would have been so placed. Many there are on earth at present who, in past lives, have stored within them all that education and intellect could bestow. During this incarnation their development lies along the love-wisdom, or intuitional path, thus leaving the physical brain unclouded in order that wisdom previously stored within the soul can register, or be reflected, upon a less clouded and crowded outer consciousness. **Regret nothing.** Accept the conditions of your life as they present themselves with a thankful heart, knowing them as necessary at the present time. (*Illumination Vol. III, The Christian Mysteries* by The White Eagle Lodge of London)

Paramahansa Yogananda said,
"Change no circumstance of my life, change me."

Our goal, often called *Christ Consciousness,* is also known as *"mystical awareness,"* for it reveals the Oneness or Wholeness of Life. The mystical approach is one of simplicity; such a path works to bring the inner and outer natures together in an "honest set of values." By this, I mean a set of values that we personally can honor, not because a church or temple taught them to us.

We might say we acknowledge "*the web of life and its interlocking relationships.*" We buy into the concepts that speak to us and we practice them, knowing there are other concepts that work for others but you are not "with them" as of yet. One leaves room to build on to one's own value system or ethics as they awaken to them or find they have value for one's own self. The idea is ancient, and we are once again re-discovering it. Operating at the edge of our group mind, we begin to know it as a true reality.

Pir Zia Inayat-Khan offers a valid way to think in his salutation:

Fellow Travelers on the Endless Path,
   May the remembrance of the … births and lives of all of the holy Prophets, fill our hearts with peace and hope…. As the Earth orbits the Sun, the soul circles the Divine Essence. As the Earth has its home in the Sun's photosphere, the soul lives, moves, and has its being in the Divine Light. As the Earth is made of stardust, the soul is a ray of God.

Expansion of Consciousness

Our human nature has developed well and "divine discontent" advances. We pursue various goals and desires; nothing satisfies … time passes. We seek inner peace … begin to ask questions and hear of an acceptable approach to spirituality.

When you are trying to grow yourself out, you are pressing against your own limitation. That is the importance of *seed thought* meditations. Just like when you want to make your body stronger, you use exercise techniques; here you are assisting your mind to advance from limited mind to contact Divine mind.

We begin to meditate, follow our path, or read, or study. We expand the mind repeatedly. It is like blowing up the awareness to make it larger, larger and larger. There is more room, more sensitivity to the new, more subtle energies we contact. We allow higher dimensions to give us impressions, intuition and insights. The subtle intuitive energy that can come into our mind is the so-called "Christ or Buddhic Consciousness"; "the cloud of knowable things" is another name for this divine world of thought.

Picture in your visualization a black and white page where individual black dots are shown against white paper. Now imagine magnifying this on a copier. Each time the picture is enlarged, the white area becomes larger; it expands along with the dots. It is the same with expansion of consciousness. Each enlargement means more capacity, allowing greater consciousness to be realized. The attunement we are making is to this enlightened area and the effect is *expanded consciousness*.

Some realized this high consciousness prior to Jesus, most notably the Buddha. Other master beings had experiences of entering into the interface between abstract mind and the intuitional plane. Master Jesus was able to anchor this *holy consciousness* in his physical and to carry it into his ministry. As the subtle influence vibrates into the abstract mind providing us with additional ways of knowing, we advance toward the goal long held before humankind as the holy state of awareness or enlightenment. Humanity is realizing that it is the Divine Child of God.

When we began to do conscious work on our spiritual path, we may have begun by just being interested. Perhaps we studied and became inclined to join a spiritual class; it may have been meditation or the charm of cards, or an art class that grabbed us. It can be anything that helps us to begin magnifying our "image-making ability." Some of us have a fear of imagination; it should not be so. "*Image-making ability*" is creativity and a gift of our higher self.

A title often used as a foundation for these kinds of teachings is Spiritual Science. Here we find the science of becoming more who we are or who we are meant to be "spiritually." When one enters into these classes, one begins to prepare the mind to recognize what it experiences. After study, we might recognize a personal experience from the variety to which we have been exposed. A near-death-experience is the most common one today, one that thousands of Americans have had and are having. In having one, a sudden profound experience of expanded reality hits us. Suddenly we know something more; *we know with our knower.*

It is not taught, it is caught!

We become aware that in the deepest part of our self we can say, "I felt a presence, or I felt a different kind of love." This blends *knowing* and *feeling*; this blending is not just "knowing" like the intellect produces, but a more complete sense of *feeling and knowing with a surety*. One might say, *"When it feels like this, I just know."* When we have this feeling, we are bringing the energy of the transcendental part of our feeling nature to register on the heart. At the same time, we bring perception down from the higher centers. We are beginning to "love with the mind," and that is a major part of knowing God. When we begin to comprehend this true meaning of mysticism, we realize that mysticism is not philosophy nor is it religion.

FOUR

What is Truth?

VICTOR HUGO SAYS, "*There are no esoteric or hidden truths; everything is luminous within mind.*" He taught that the developing mind is capable of penetrating all levels of thought. What is mysterious to one may be clear to another. Therefore, there are only truths that we have not recognized yet. Eventually everything is luminous (is filled with the light of mind). The teaching of the things of spirit are said to be mystical. That introduces a term we of the Christian tradition call "the gifts of spirit." All gifts of the spirit are mystical experiences. We cannot make them happen; they occur or they come upon us in their own way. When we have an experience that takes us out of our usual consciousness, we must give value to that experience.

As children, we were encouraged not to talk so much about our own experiences so as not to build ego. Experiences can be labeled "imagination" or "not true." Now as an adult we do realize we have precious moments of inspiration and we must learn to value these as a touch of spirit; we do not let others downplay them. If you are a private person, you may not be ready to share them with anyone else. This is really a guidepost for your own progress as you are maturing. The bush is blooming.

From Corinthians 12:4-11, we learn:

4) Now, there are diversities of gifts, but the same Spirit.

5) There are differences of ministries, but the same Lord.

6) And there are diversities of activities, but it is the same God who works in all.

7) But the manifestation of the Spirit is given to each one for the profit of all.

8) For to one is given the word of wisdom through the Spirit, to another the word of knowledge through the same Spirit,

9) To another faith by the same Spirit, to another, gifts of healing by the same Spirit,

10) To another the working of miracles, to another prophecy, to another discerning of spirits, to another different kinds of tongues, to another the interpretation of tongues.

11) And the same Spirit works all these things, distributing to each one individually as He wills.

Modern Understanding of the Gifts of the Spirit

When we look deeply at the Gifts of the Spirit from biblical writings, we have to consider how our modern understanding assists us to understand them. We see how humanity looks at these happenings today, and we see them differently than how they were understood in the past. We shall take a modern look at these terms as we ponder just what we would call this gift in our present terminology.

Starting with the term **wisdom**, we would translate this experience into expanded awareness, higher consciousness or even an enlightened state. A wise one often shares their perspective with awesome impact on others who find the newer perspective to be an insight quite beyond their own.

Likewise, **knowledge** becomes divine inspiration, channeling, or a new, previously unknown or little understood concept. Many examples exist of modern-day channelers revealing information, that has been previously unknown to them, by inspiration from an unknown source. A "source" may be seen as a spirit being, a guide, a teacher or collective that works from the spirit realm. Somehow, a contact with spirit is established and it now provides prompting as well as guidance to an individual who dwells in human form.

Faith as a term is often applied to the branch of religion to which we belong; this is actually incorrect. Faith is a belief to which we are dedicated; and it sustains us. It has strength to empower or fortify us through its connection. Best described by the acronym "*Finding Answers In Thy Heart,*" we recognize that what dwells as truth in our own heart signals us when ideas or behaviors either support us or fail to. This way of *knowing in the heart* is called "intuitive knowing." We feel and know the rightness of something by this inner awareness.

Healing, of course, means to make whole. We experience healing on every level and through many means. Natural healing occurs by harmonious living, clean air, exercise and healthy food. We know healing also happens by the transfer of a powerful energy charge. This can be delivered by *laying-on-of-hands*, massage, by Reiki, and other popular energy transferring techniques. Healing can occur by prayer and/or the sending of positive thoughts, or one person sending energy to another.

The technique of sending positive energy over a distance to another is *absentee healing*. So, for clarity, healing techniques are named *touch, absentee, treatments, or self-healing*. A general rule, attributed to the many healing examples in the Bible stories about Master Jesus, is that spiritual healing requests should have the permission of the one to whom the healing energy is sent, to be in keeping with spiritual ethics. This does not apply to remembrance and prayers for the deceased.

Probably the most difficult to define are spiritual happenings called **miracles**; we interpret the term to mean "unexplainable." Down through the ages churches have studied miracles and the science of the day was called upon to prove the validity of the happening. However my understanding of such events is that since we do not grasp all spiritual laws or possibilities, such events as these are representative of "the operation of unknown or little known spiritual laws" of another level. Likewise, telepathy, telekinesis and dematerialization appear miraculous, but my belief is that these are in harmony with higher laws conforming to a yet-to-be-revealed higher understanding.

Prophecy is little understood; it is far too often confused with prediction. A prediction is the reading of a pattern that, if maintained, will manifest; if change is desired, change is required. Prophecy is a revelation of the unknown coming into manifestation according to the higher will of the force or power. There is a difference, subtle but important, to be understood. Our own ruling powers point in a given direction and are preparing our future: this is prediction. Prophecy is even more unknown, things yet to be determined by the Higher Will of the Divine or the will of the collective, and often quite futuristic. For example, as the Piscean age closes and as humanity is more empowered by Aquarius, humanity will become more mental in nature and less devotional. Here the greater authority is the influence of an incoming influence, Aquarius, which is not yet strongly empowered.

Now we face **the gift of the spirits** that we will meet in the world of deceased, known as the discarnates. As we open ourselves to those dwelling on subtle planes, i.e., not dwelling in physical bodies, we find we meet many influences. This is not unlike going into a crowd at a football game. Here we find all types of former human beings, angelic beings, extra-terrestrials, meta-terrestrials, good guys and not so good. We could contact saintly ones or liars, our previous relatives who would like to give us advice (whether they know what they are talking about or not), and beings just out to experiment as we find in our own hometown.

The hardest *gift* to understand is **speaking in tongues.** This descriptive title reveals its work; here the practitioner is being emotionally stimulated in the heart and throat areas by a moving, quivering energy in the emotional body to an intense degree. The description of the activity is joy, soul expressiveness, and is known as the Singing of the Soul to its Maker. The English formal name for this experience is *glossolalia,* and for some more literal Christian denominations it signifies an adoption by the Holy Spirit and an indication of one being taken into Her care.

The last referenced gift of the spirit, **the interpretation of tongues,** is likewise a working of Spirit in such a way that it is taught that, should a legitimate experience of speaking in tongues occur, there will always be a giver (the speaker) and a translator (the receiver) present. Practitioners of these experiences recognize that for the *interpretation of tongues* to occur there must always be one present who can understand the message.

There will always be at least one present capable of perceiving the meaning of the glossolalia; there is according to teachings always one or more present that are capable of grasping the message(s) even if it is multilevel in its meaning. This experience of understanding the message is also considered a divine gift and, until one has had such an experience, he or she may have no understanding of such. Likewise, one may have never undergone such an experience previously. This is not a cultivated experience and may never occur in the life again.

In the Western mind, gifts of the spirit are just that—gifts. However, in the Eastern understanding they are natural results of spiritual practices. They are natural results of stimulating the inner spiritual energy, and its arousal has certain unspecified results. The energy that awakens and begins to move within the body is Kundalini, in the East, and as the Holy Spirit in the West. Both are speaking of various manifestations of Spiritual Ecstasy. Some experiences are more emotionally based, stirred by devotion and love. Others are mental in expression, with dedicated focus arousing the energy. Either occurs because an energy focus has developed either in the feeling nature, or in the mind. Activity of the kundalini can become a topic to explore and study in depth. However, the guidance of the teachings is not to focus on the lifting of the stream of energy, but to let it find its natural way of manifesting. It seems less troublesome and confusing if allowed to follow its natural pathway and in its own timing.

Therefore, we find in the search for truth that which is *mysterious* and *occult* is for the most part simply a range of facts that few have yet explored. When one expands the mind and takes in a larger horizon, the interrelation of a multitude of hitherto unknown laws, which, from the former viewpoint, seemed mysterious, are now grasped.

Some hidden truths are identified as "Hermetic Principles" or "Spiritual Laws." Seven in number, they are: 1) Mentalism, 2) Correspondence, 3) Vibration, 4) Polarity, 5) Rhythm, 6) Cause and Effect, and 7) Gender (from *The Kybalion* by a disciple). Within the framework of these laws, numerous variations are defined by religions and cultures. These influences maintain and support life through the processes of chaos, creation, orderliness, and destruction. The idea exists everywhere that the old is, in time, destroyed and a new creation built through many stages of growth and change.

These various "gifts" or phenomena may be experiences that we have already had and did not realize their significance. Déjà vu, insight, intuition, discernment, discrimination, and dreams, can be very significant, but we need to know also that depression, despair, loss, grief, and painful experiences are of importance in our nature. They also often bring us to our awakening. Near-death experiences, as well as loss and grief, are ways of awakening us to quest also, and to begin our path.

As developing mystics, we try to live in the here and now, to live in the eternal now, and we have to learn how to do this. However, the human being cannot; he is a mind being (one who lives in mental compartments and is largely learning to think); yet, he/she has to learn to find peace and to live in harmony to calm the restless scanning ego. Until then, each living person exists in a trap. Humanity has learned to call what has passed, "the past," and the yet-to-be, "the future," with only a small space in between. All of our spiritual endeavors focus upon our need to perceive God's Presence in the immediacy of the present moment.

Past – – – – – **NOW**– – – – – Future

To be a mystic is to make "now" larger and more significant, with past and future having less and less power of influence. What do "the lilies of the field" that are cared for and "the sparrows of the air" mean? We also have the teaching of Christ Jesus about "*the kingdom of Heaven is like unto…*" (*Matthew 13*). These six examples are: 1) a process of working with Tares, 2) like a mustard seed, 3) like leaven bread, 4) like hidden treasures accidentally found, 5) like a pearl in a field, and 6) like a dragnet of fish. These lessons are all instructions to the sower to cultivate a certain something in their being. When one catches a glimpse of what could be meant, one has a moment of insight, a breakthrough of understanding the true nature of reality. It represents the ability of Consciousness to expand.

All these instructions are for us to cultivate a certain kind of *knowing* within them. The plant and animal kingdoms do not have to struggle with the past or future: they live in the here and now. We can learn to as well; we will expand beyond the rational mind and live in expanded awareness … mystical awareness. Another important key is in *John 18:36* where we read, "*My kingdom is not of this world.*" All of this reminds us that the people of high consciousness are to be "*in this world, but not of it.*"

We program animals as we draw them into closer human behavior; in puppy training we teach them or program them to do a certain behavior—tricks, or to obey our wishes—but they have no rational mind to pull them to past or future, or equip them for decision making or priorities. They are gradually learning more and more obedience to the master. To dispute this, science is now telling us the animal kingdom is developing more and more of a capacity for being trained, and I would say this is to be expected as they evolve; they are also building more solar plexus capacity.

There is a lot to be said about spontaneity or staying in the here and now. The teacher, Ram Dass, taught a lot about the richness of staying in the *Be Here Now* approach to life. The Bible calls this "eternity." This eternal *now* ... getting into the place between past and future. This is where peace exists.

Past – – – – – **Eternal NOW** – – – – – Future

In the Christian faith, we accept that, when we die, we are going to eternal life somewhere. A major reason for learning in church is "to earn a good eternal life." This is the basis for *heaven vs. hell* teaching. The mystical perspective is that no moment in eternity is any closer than any other moment; it all exists now ... not at some distant point in the future.

In esoteric teachings, we learn to realize that at least some sense of eternal life is to be realized while still in this material world. It is a doorway to the realm of Higher Consciousness. We want to find a completely centered *"peace of mind"* place of being that is eternally *"in the presence."* At the end of an earthly life, we continue to live in our spirit form at the level of vibration to which we are comfortable by a formula we all try to understand. This can be higher or, unfortunately, lower, calculated out of the life we have lived.

A perspective I appreciate is *"Heaven is a high state of consciousness: purgatory is being on the spiritual path as we purify ourselves, while some are stuck in hell right here and now."* If we look around and attune to the Earth, we know this is so.

A deep effort in the art of character building is the work we begin on earth as an inner-directed person. We ready ourselves through the spiritual progress we make. We will take this with us at the end of each life. Soul growth registers each time we embrace spiritual training. Many are working off old karma; some are awakening; some are dedicated to growth. Tests of differing sorts have developed over the ages, beginning with physical training, such as hygiene, body-building, yoga and a pure, rather Spartan approach to daily life. Today our "inner development of the psychological personality" formulates the test; we know this as the psycho-spiritual self, or the relationship of body, mind and soul. *The building of the light body has its emphasis here.*

Many times people call mystical studies "the study of truth," but this is not correct. Truth is the reality of things as it registers with each one at a particular period. This is his or her current truth. But, truth changes, with our experience and with a change of perspective. A mystical experience is one without the exercise of our personal perspective or exercise of will. One has a direct and immediate confrontation with what one *knows* to be the Ultimate, called by whatever name.

Biblically we know of the Holy Spirit as God's Wisdom. In *John 14:26 & 27*, we read:

> 26) But the Comforter, the Holy Spirit, whom my Father will send in my name, will teach you everything... 27) Peace I leave with you; my own peace I give you; not as the world gives, I give to you. Let not your heart be troubled and do not be afraid.

Sophia, as the Inner Teacher or Guide, is the companion of the mystic as consciousness expands and dialogue with God comes forth from the hidden resources of the inner life. She, Sophia, often called Mother Wisdom, walks as a companion with those who pursue the mystical and spiritual transformation.

We have to gain an understanding of the divine feminine, in that we did not have it in our society as we matured. She is a part of the Creator, as expressed through both the Father and the Mother Nature of God. We come to know She is active in all creation. Understanding Sophia comes gradually and progressively:

1) The first and densest expression is as Mother Nature, the intelligence that is innate in all kingdoms and sees that each has an active process of Life.

2) The second expression of Sophia is as Psyche within our basic nature where she directs our body functions without our conscious thought, accepts programming, has feelings and emotions but without rational thought. We know her best here as our

inner child. In some traditions we call her lower Sophia (lower psychism) for this psychic effect that warns, gives feelings that influence, and directs us unconsciously.

3) Third, we next come to know Sophia as our intuitive guide, who prompts our behavior and is the wee small voice that guides us as we listen inward. We mature spiritually in the care of Sophia as she directs us as a prompter who walks beside us to keep us on track.

4) Then lastly, we come to know her as the Bride of Christ who overshadows and walks with us across the burning ground of the path of initiation, activating the divinity within our personal life. Known as Shekinah to the Jewish mystics, She was known throughout the Mid-East, as "She Who Dwells Within assisting to guide us back to the Creator."

All matter (mother forms) contains an inner spirit and this truth, though known to the ancients, got lost in the separation of "religion and science." We began to believe humanity was a living spirit. Now with the discovery of Sophia, we expand our consciousness to know once again that all is alive: the web is unbroken.

It is wise to reread Proverbs with the idea that here is the Wisdom of God. Translated into the early Christian writings by the Greeks, Sophia (meaning God's Wisdom) speaks "*her*" words to her people. By not capitalizing the word "*wisdom*," we do not read it as a name, let alone the name of Mother Wisdom, the Holy Mother of us all. *Agape, logos, koinoinia,* are all Greek words that long ago made their way into translations, however "*Sophia*" became omitted as the patriarchal structure was formed.

From *Prayers to Sophia* by Joyce Rupp:

Light-Bearer
Eternal Lamp of Love, remind me often of how much radiance comes from the glow of one small candle flame. When my spiritual

window is heavily clouded, and your abiding love seems far from me, restore my belief in your vibrant presence.

When I doubt my ability to be a bearer of your light, shine your truth and wisdom into my faltering spirit.

Radiant star in my heart, in every generation you pass into holy souls. Thank you for the illuminated beings who have touched my life with their goodness.

Your light shining through them has inspired me and filled me with spiritual energy.

Assure me that I can also be a Light-bearer for others, a clear window of your eternal starlight. Stir and whirl your dynamic presence in my being. Stream your loving kindness through me.

I will open my mind and heart to your presence as you greet me in the unexpected and the challenging. I, too, can make a difference in my world because of your radiant light shining through me. Amen.

When we step from the path of religion to the path of spirituality, it is into Sophia's care that we render ourselves. A reading from a Gnostic writing affirms this:

And now, therefore, as I have come, I have opened the gates of Light and I open the ways which lead into the Light. And now, therefore, the person who will do what is worthy of the mysteries, let that person receive the mysteries and enter into the Light. (Pistis Sophia, chapter 135, p. 356)

In the traditional church, we use *1 Cor. 4: 1:*

Let a man so account of us as to be the ministers of Christ and the dispensers of the Mysteries of God.

We have similar readings throughout the Bible in the books of *Proverbs, Job, Wisdom of Solomon, Song of Songs* and others. I suggest *The Divine Feminine in Biblical Wisdom Literature,* annotated and explained by Rabbi Rami Shapiro. Read about Wisdom with awareness and gain a deeper understanding of what Sophia has to offer us, as we perceive the mystical spiritual teachings available. I recommend *Proverbs 8* as the first chapter to read.

Mysticism is the next step beyond humanitarian love, whether we truly understand it or not. *Agape* is the name most commonly used for the outpouring of Divine Love. It is perceived most often as an outpouring from above, which it is, but it is also a human heart-mind connection ascending from below. Love arising from within the individual heart center in a grace-filled and freeing moment races upward toward the higher centers to meet the *down-pouring* energy of the Divine. Those capable of loving in this manner are individuals who truly love from their heart and mind. The *lots-of-vital-energy* pouring down from the higher planes blends with the ascending love to create a purely Divine love. The beloved and the lover embrace as one.

Disciples have a process to move through in their journey. Defined in different ways in different traditions, traditional Western paths use the terms: Awakening—Illumination—and then Enlightenment. Let us ponder the process together and see if, indeed, we can understand the principle of *"love with a new love"* to which we have been introduced.

Awakening is the secondary influence embedded within the human nature. This in time stirs and makes us become conscious of a path to higher consciousness (the primary influence being survival). A capacity for fresh insights and intellectual awareness grows, leading to a state of liberation from conventional thought and openness to a new perspective, which enters the consciousness.

An exciting period of the discovery—with a new and another perception of reality—dwells right alongside our limited one, of which we were very unaware. An example: when we discover a new word and are excited, then suddenly we hear the term all around us and realize it was there, but we were not "tuned in" to it. Now somehow we have reached or earned the privilege of knowing it is there for us, if we so choose.

Illumination, occurring as Light (perception, understanding, and realizations) ignites within the mind; concepts are comprehended, and the mysteries of life stand revealed. The light overcomes the darkness within us. Think of these as "we are unconscious and becoming conscious"; we use language like "in the dark" and "coming into the light," for example. All humanity is moving on a continuum of dark to light; some are ahead and some are behind, but we are all Souls moving on forward in this process.

The period between illumination and enlightenment is the longest period of growth. During this time, you are growing through experiences, "ah ha's" and realizations; you are making progress in the move toward illumination. Through the process of nurturing the word, perception and intuition, you are nurturing your soul. Amidst the learnings, intellectually, emotionally, and intuitionally, you grow out your own spiritual Self.

From the mystery tradition we hear we are to learn to "think in the heart and love within the mind." Our society well understands I.Q. as intellectual quotient; we understand more and more about E.Q., the emotional quotient. Now we are learning something about S. Q., a spiritual quotient that was left unknown as we discovered earlier equations. These perceptions from higher mind (S.Q.) are good for all and act negatively to no one. Here as we seek our higher good, we get in touch with a higher good that will act for the wellbeing of all. Here we find a concept that must have been known earlier and is still known by the mystics of old and, again, of now. It certainly is a hopeful one. I recommend you spend time becoming acquainted with the SQ assessment on the website www.iitransform.com; I suggest you will find this intriguing.

Here we learn that those who benefit most are those who have been successful in this world and are asking the familiar question, "*is there not more to life than this?*" Many individuals reach a natural state of wanting to make a positive difference in the world. Are you one? As we are going through transitions in our lives, we find the many questions that lead us forward with our goals bless others as well. Most of us are anxious to spread our new discoveries. As our ethics become ever clearer, we want to support the ideas and products that make the world a better place in which to live. As you find yourself feeling and saying such things, you recognize that your own spiritual self is becoming the leading component in your new state of awareness.

> **Enlightenment** is supreme discrimination; a state of mind filled with spiritual wisdom. Enlightenment is quite similar to salvation, as understood in Christianity, when the Christ-Within, called by any name, rules the life, having reclaimed one's intrinsic nature from the limitation and distortions of the instinctual self. There is no greater goal than to reach this holy state and to share yourself with your co-walkers on the path. (*The New Dictionary of Spiritual Thought* by Carol E. Parrish-Harra)

Enlightenment or Self-Realization comes at some point, not because you now know everything: it means that, if you ask a question of the higher nature, the answer will arrive in some way. Enlightenment, then, is:

> a natural process ruled by biological laws as strict in their operation as the laws governing the continuance of the race.... This, I believe, is the purpose for which you and I are here—to realize ourselves ... to bring the soul to a clear realization of its own divine nature. (Gopi Krishna)

The mystic experiences an awareness of a multi-dimensional reality and discovers his or her personal connection with the Higher World through a great "*love,*" and witnesses to that expanded life. This is done by stepping down his or her subjective understanding as best he or she can, or one may be also very quiet about his or her ideas. They do realize their "*truth*" is different from others, and generally "*know*" it is richer and larger than that of most average individuals.

They may know themselves to be either an orphic, or an occultist, and they make the effort to blend these as they continue to build their path. They do not proselytize because they know from experience these ideas will only work for those that are ready.

Mystics often do not have the words or the desire to explain themselves to others. (People not well understood are often ostracized or ridiculed.)

Every tradition has stories of persons that have actually transformed their flesh as well. There are saints with no deterioration of the physical form after death. Fascinating and profound, the method of transforming the body is labeled as **Union** in some traditions, meaning it is merged with the higher vehicles. There is no more incarnation. It has also been called Union with God, but it means the body, soul, and personality have been purified and "*cooked*" into one. The experience of the Earth initiations is complete.

"Creating the Celestial Body" is the term used by most wisdom traditions currently for the eventual change we will undergo. Our carbon-based body is to become a light vehicle or, as is said, the carbon-based body becomes the celestial one. The Bible tells us we have a physical body and a celestial body. We do not believe this; we think it means astral body; but, in fact, it implies more than we understand.

Some in the culture of ancient China saved their cut hair and fingernails all their life so upon their death the pieces will be buried in the grave or tomb in order for the person to be ready for their use in restoring the body back to life. In Orthodox Judaism, as in some more fundamental Christian denominations, there is a belief that the Messiah will resurrect dead bodies upon his coming; likewise, some Orthodox Jews even retain amputated body parts for burial with an individual. With these ideas floating around, you will see how great a difference there is in Esoteric or Mystical Thought regarding all of this.

Most of what we call "apparitions" manifest from the "building of the light body" level of achievement. This rare experience assists humanity to continue to be inspired. We aspire to the greatness of these holy ones. Theosophical literature teaches that there are at least sixty master beings caring for humanity at all times. I certainly think of Master Jesus and the Planetary Hierarchy in this way. Those holy ones, who have walked the path of humanity, can assist us much more than ones that have not. This is another way of understanding *"being in the world and not of it."* We are a part of humanity's group mind, but we can be in the higher vibrating part rather than in the mundane, even though we are still in material bodies.

To understand better this transformation process, we continue to use examples. Remember, we are talking about years or lives, not a short period. However, remember also, there is "recapitulation" which explains the re-tracing of steps each lifetime to get us back ready for fresh growth. Recapitulation means to recall, repeat, or re-experience. Generally, we spend at least five to ten years in reca-pitulation. Many today are currently experiencing this awakening period, although, of course, some are awakening in each period as newcomers to the path. Recapitulation advances one rapidly com-pared to new growth, which proceeds more deliberately.

Awakening can be quick or the process of awakening can be to wake up and go back to sleep, only to awaken again at another experience. Gradually one realizes they are on a spiritual path and invest themselves in it more as a seeker.

Mysticism does not usually interest us until we have advanced enough to begin preparing for illumination, so says Flower Newhouse, a noted modern mystic well versed in the subject. She enumerates steps along the way as:

- Longing to directly know Go ... deep hunger
- Definite acts of seeking God ... searching, study, lectures
- Self-Surrender ... giving up of the lesser will
- Consecration ... detaching from ego desires and habits comes more easily

It is not through our own cleverness that we are able to move on and to change. Rather, it is the spirit of the inner light investing itself through us as directions, instructions, and inspirations. Finally, we find we are transformed from one stage to another until what we did last year, or five years ago, seems heavy and earthy compared to what we feel in this living eternal moment of God. (*Christian Mysticism* by Flower Newhouse)

In the **Illumination** stage, one must be in the process of purging or purifying themselves of food, habits, and thoughts in such a way as to know that they are on a path to Higher Consciousness—and that this path may be long. "Insights," as Paul Brunton calls them, are these most common impressions prior to deep intuitive *knowings*. During this period, there is often something like a breakthrough of the Light. For example, if you are walking on a dark path at night and the lightning flashes, you see the pathway more clearly. The lightning flash ends, but now as you walk down the path, there is a picture of what lies ahead in your mind. We begin to speak to others about the "insights" we have; these are flashes of expanded awareness, but does not indicate we have reached *"enlightenment,"* although often this part is misunderstood.

This second stage, Illumination, usually lasts for a period of years/lives and develops a more or less *"wise being."* We admire these individuals for their efforts, ethics, and wisdom. They persist in finding their way without much outside guidance; they listen within and let the rest of the world have its rules, while they have their own value system and they live it.

Some years ago, a Jewish Rabbi, Abraham Joshua Herschel, dared to challenge *religion* by suggesting it should be *spiritual*. This man was a coworker with Dr. Martin Luther King and marched with him at Selma, Alabama. Rabbi Herschel taught that prayer, which he called *"the song the universe sings to itself,"* is useless unless it is subversive … *"shattering pyramids of callousness."* He went on to say, after marching for voting rights alongside Dr. King, *"I felt that my legs were praying."*

One of the very misleading questions of salvation/enlightenment centers upon the concept of *"salvation by works or faith."* I personally believe it is both, and that one cannot work without the other. Whereas some persons employ their own definitions of *"works"* and *"faith"* (Ephesians 2:89 and James 2:14) … neither of which allow for the uniqueness of the individual "son or daughter of the Most High." "Faith" is *"finding the answers in the heart,"* and "works," as in *"work, for the Lord is coming."*

Mysticism teaches neither; rather, it is following the voice within and obeying the Inner Presence. It is most likely to be both. Truly, for the mystic as it is for the disciple, they are one. This is natural as we consider that humanity is preparing for its first collective initiation. We must dare to ask: *is it enough to go to church on Sundays as a part of a faith tradition without struggling with issues of slavery, mistreatment and abuse, war, and other negative social issues with which our society suffers?*

To be a mystic one can be a member of any philosophy or religion, but their ideas go far beyond the essence of a determined path. Mystics are within all traditions because they have arrived at an understanding of *"many paths, one goal."* The goal is High Consciousness. Ethics and principles of high consciousness are the practices open to all; some also have a religious practice or have matured through a philosophic approach.

> In Eliphas Levi's case, as is well known, the discord between the occult and mystical ideals was resolved by his return to the Catholic Church. Characteristically, he "read into" Catholicism much that the orthodox would hardly allow; so that it became for him, as it were, a romantic gloss on the occult tradition. He held that the Christian Church, nursing mother of the mystics, was also the heir of the magi; and that popular piety and popular magic, veiled the same ineffable truths. (*Mysticism* by Evelyn Underhill, pp. 162-163)

We use the word **Enlightenment** a lot when speaking of subjects like *"expansion of consciousness."* Specifically what does it mean?: a state of mind filled with supreme discrimination, a mind filled with spiritual wisdom. Quite similar to "salvation" as understood in Christianity, enlightenment acknowledges that the Christ-Within rules one's life. We experience enlightenment after having reclaimed our human nature from the limitations and distortions of instinctual self and filled it with the wisdom that flows from the highest planes. Each faith has some word for this blessed state.

A mystical Christian would be one who seeks to grasp the Oneness of Life through the lens of the Christ. The concepts of Jesus, the Christ, in mystical teachings, are accepted as Jesus, the great teacher, having received Higher Consciousness (the Christ) and speaking from that level of Wisdom. Blessed by or filled with this high consciousness is what we all want, as we would be Christed (*Enlightened*).

The early church found itself struggling with a collapsing Roman Empire, a number of other old religions, and a need to become important, especially after it became a national religion under Constantine. Christianity was searching for a simple doctrine it could teach the people, versus the complicated wisdom of the Gnostics, which were many and within all traditions. We recall there were Greek, Roman, Celtic, Asian Gnostics, plus others, and their path was not an easy one. It required a new kind of lifestyle that witnessed to its validity and simplicity. As a solution for the guidance of the general public there developed what came to be called Christian Literalists (very similar to our fundamentalists of today).

The Christian Literalists transformed themselves ultimately into the Roman Catholic Church after the split in about 1000 AD. Gnostics of all traditions—Jewish, Greek or Pagan, as well as Christian—sought a certain kind of realization, not unlike Paul's Damascus experience. They sought to connect with an inner life from which they could experience the fount of knowing and inspiration. They "*knew*" God and they lived according to this, not a code impressed upon them by an outer authority.

In the ancient world, the truly knowledgeable ones assisted others whom they deemed worthy—within a given framework of rituals and practices in chosen places kept secret from those with little or no interest. Rigorous disciplines designed to change the etheric nature of the individual were practiced. Think of this as alchemy, a process of purification, self-discipline, intellectual development and inner life breakthroughs.

They used a simple formula to teach the *Way* to know this inner state of Oneness and called it **Life**. To them **Death** was the name of the unawakened, as in the Bible we have the line, "*Let the dead bury the dead.*" They taught, as Master Jesus had, that "*the Kingdom of Heaven is within* you," and whoever knows himself shall find it. "**Know your Self.**" The spiritual quest is continually one that confronts each one of us with, "**Who am I?**"

Normal men set dogma and church laws into form and made them subject to hierarchal judgment. Rituals, on the other hand, while it is true that unworthy persons can initiate them, are usually set into motion from a holy one to another whom they have deemed worthy. Alternatively, an enlightened one, to benefit ones worthy of special transferences of grace, can institute rituals for grace-filled deliverance.

Judgment is a solar plexus capability and subject to the right-wrong, good-bad perspective. This is not mysticism; it is rational mind at work. Mystics are seeking peace and insight within themselves; they seek reconciliation between the inner self and the outer. A major purpose of a sacred ritual is to strengthen the spiritual self for its role in seeking an enriched consciousness. The grace of the ritual helps us to grow into our authentic self.

What we know today as the Eucharist is actually ceremonial magic. As we enter the rule of the Seventh Ray (the Aquarius Age is ruled by Uranus, the ruler of Aquarius), we will see more and more the power of economy in all areas. New ways to acknowledge the right use of energy, conserve resources, talent, creativity, and expand our respect and understanding will emerge. Certainly, it is seen in spiritual ceremonies as healing prayers and laying on of hands; also in understanding human beings as creative resources, and labor as a resource rather than leftover or wasted talent. Alert individuals will see with more clear vision into the invisible world, whether it be true seeing, or a deeper awareness through the right use of senses, and they will be able to contribute to the general well-being of the groups with which they surround themselves.

Becoming a Conscious Soul

The journey and practices of the Gnostics, as condemned as they are occasionally, are the same or similar practices that are used today to awaken the inner mystic, and this is what we are striving toward. This is not to say that all ideas of the Gnostics will be once again accepted; some will be, but a great similarity in style and freedom will be the norm. To find one's own way, to have one's own experience, to honor and deal with others with high regard, is the goal.

We want to be conscious persons—alive and well—on as many planes as possible. This is the intent of this work, and all mystics practice all or most of these guidelines to bring about their own advancement. Those who seek to become conscious beings will once again find open doors and certain suggested keys. Meditation techniques are steps in this practice. "Soul-infusion meditation" provides the lower intellect with practice so it can learn to attune to the higher vibrations of the Soul itself ... to grasp the vibration of Senzar, a mysterious language of the Mind that transfers great quantities of insight from the "Cloud of Knowable Things" into the mind mechanism in a rapid, non-linear symbology. This knowledge must be transferred into words to be able to articulate the information that has been given. This experience is considered sacred teaching, which must be turned into recognizable thought.

This inner language operates somewhat like this. First, the subtle frequencies of hieroglyphs or sacred symbols will be *sensed*, and then this contact becomes changed into a more subtle vibration, which then turns into a vague thought, which becomes "wispy" impressions, which we try to put into words to describe what we contacted. This is the foundation of becoming conscious; we live with one ear turned to the outer, while the other listens inward.

Upon this foundation, we begin to unfold the soul, and all wisdom practices are to assist in this flowering. A wise man once said, "The process of initiation can be understood as the same process as reading. We begin by recognizing the alphabet and progress to spelling a word. In due time, we can read a sentence, and only after that can we begin to grasp the meaning behind the material we are reading." This is the process of becoming a conscious soul.

Synthesis is the activity of the soul to bring the pieces of the incarnated nature together to blend with our higher nature while we let go of some unnecessary aspects. We do some self-study and seek to spot some patterns or attributes to enhance and see some hindrances we do not choose to continue. At this point, we discover how our own inner senses assist us in our process of becoming.

Albert Einstein reminded us that "*the Intuitive Mind is a sacred gift, and the Rational Mind is a faithful servant. We have created a society that honors the servant and has forgotten the gift.*"

We must "*see/perceive*" in some manner a step or two at a time to be able to become more than we happen to be now. We integrate in this way. Most of us can perceive only a short distance at a time … we take the next step so the following one can then be seen. Esoteric divination tools can help, as well as the study of astrology, rays, and esoteric psychology.

We begin to watch for the design of our life, for a pattern that repeats or is delicately unfolding. We study the higher plan for humanity to try to catch a glimpse of pieces or places wherein we might fit, while paying particular attention to our inner voice.

To awaken our creativity, we stimulate the inner fires through aspiration, dedication, study and service. We seek to integrate our talents and gifts for the use of the higher plan for humanity as understood day by day.

As we see the harmony and the opposites, the sameness, and the differences, we learn what helps and what hinders. We seek to understand our style, our qualities, and embrace the new we need to cultivate without being untruthful or manipulative to others.

For our idealism to be effective we need devotion and caring to develop aspects of our feeling nature, as well as the active mind formulating its understanding. We add practices that enhance traits or attributes we are choosing to develop. We call down and bring spirit into everyday life, and seek to lift our outer expression upward day-by-day, knowing some days feel more successful than others, but realizing also that inner achievement is different from outer success.

My understanding is that there is a natural progression of growth moving from evolution to experiment, thus leading us to learn and express whatever we have experienced. Consider three levels that seem to follow this pattern.

(1) Each incarnation we begin life anew, recapitulating our knowledge and working on learning new lessons of some kind. The result is that additional facets of expression may be added to our human nature (such as changing from male previously to female presently, or being wealthy in one life, and limited means in another).

(2) In time, we gain entrance to discipleship where our experiments of life deepen and expand into other dimensions. We strive for love-wisdom to add value to our life, and through service our expression touches others. Service teaches generosity of spirit.

(3) As the Soul truly comes to live in our life, or we should say, as we live as a Soul-Infused being, we will dare to stand courageously for our beliefs. Thus, we gain new strengths, and we receive initiations from the higher world … *we earn stars in our crown* as the common world sees it!

Collective wisdom has given us some hints to improve our perception of the Higher World by offering simple steps that can make sacred the path we walk. The majority will find these helpful in building a sacred way. *We need to realize that something is sacred because we make it sacred.* As it takes on more and more significance, its value to us changes.

Blessed by our active heart, we are directing a kind of conscious intent (this is of great importance) as well as loving energy to the sacred object, perhaps a rosary or medal. We therefore treat such differently than we do "non-sacred" things. We need to note that what is therefore sacred to us is not automatically sacred to someone else. Our "something" is sacred to us because we have made it so by the love, blessing, and respect that we relegate to it. Anything can become sacred by our making it so.

The spark within you has infused you with divine life or divine energy, but maybe you lived many years without this understanding. As you gained an awareness of this "inner life," you began to live differently, did you not? What is sacred to you? Stop and think. Do not take someone else's list; think of your own. Be true to yourself.

We want to make our home a sacred place for ourselves but likewise for others we accept into it. Suggestions: To make your home sacred, the first step is to make an altar and dedicate your home to the Hierarchy or Christ Jesus, whoever truly matters to you. Then bless each room and extend your love energy into every room.

Next step, either walk your property line or sit and visualize yourself walking these lines. Surround the house and the property with protection of the higher beings and your love. Place this ring of protection all around the property and around all within it. Then work to maintain the good vibrations you have created. Repeat this from time to time and remember to say prayers for your home, your intentions etc. If we really believe "thoughts are things," we must exercise this awareness.

Now here is an interesting related thought: the traveling or wandering mystic has the goal of "making sacred" the environment wherever they walk, dedicating the territory to the divine or to God. This was particularly true if they were in "dark" areas, not yet converted to the God they knew, and they felt that this was their goal. Missionaries especially held this great goal in their hearts. In some ways, this is what we are doing when we visualize a "light-filled earth." We usually temper our prayers with "may the higher will be done," and not necessarily in the name of a particular religion or deity.

To become a Conscious Soul, we organize our spiritual practices … find some you can use in your own style. Adapt as needed, but gather the reasons for such practices.

- *Conclude each day with a simple review. Greet the day when you awaken.*

- *Study and add pieces to your lifestyle as they appeal to you; drop them when you tire of them.*

- *Knowing how we see Life shapes life, so we become more interested and involved in the destiny of the greater life of Humanity. Begin to know thyself to provide a sense of honesty about strengths and weaknesses, lessons and learnings. We become genuine now.*

- *Dare to love the Self within and see the inner child as worthy of loving. Personality is but the child of the Soul; it deserves love.*

- *Face life courageously, especially when fear threatens to take over. Seeing the significance of these challenging moments helps us to respond courageously.*

- *Grief and loss, sadness and trials are a part of the human condition. The Wise have taught us this is the place of sorrows. We come to bring Light, not by denial, but by taking necessary steps on the path or in darkness, understanding these are the testing moments of building character.*

- *Learn to see kindness, goodness in the smallest actions. Let these acts lighten the heavy heart … bringing joy to others whenever possible. Be like the sun and shine on the just and the unjust. Enrich others because you know the Divine within.*

- *Respond by expressing gratitude for your blessings; foster thanksgiving in your heart. Forgive and release what would hinder you. Much of life is on your side as you transform; the treasure is deep within.*

- *Follow what makes your heart sing. The part of the plan that calls you lives within, hidden from sight, but it sends forth positive energy to empower you to respond. When happy, we tend to be open and sharing from our center. Be 'available' in order to deliver a blessing to others. Love, serve and smile.*

- *Look at the world seeing the glass half-full and be delighted in your discovery. Support the good and see it expand, as does the capacity to see it. Attempt to see the inner essence of each one you meet, not to judge, but to help you develop the ability to see the Divine in the least as well as the greatest. Both are distortions, but if you can find the essence, you will find yourself.*

- *Celebrate Life. Cultivate humor. Respect all kingdoms. Be honest.*

—Written for her class by Carol E. Parrish-Harra, 2007

Direct Knowing Is the Goal

The mystic works to become One with God, whatever this might mean to the individual. To experience this *direct wisdom* is the goal of Christian Mysticism. As we make contact, we receive teachings, revelations, vision, and messages through the higher senses. The inner world or planes, or inner reality, contains "the many mansions" of the Bible or "the inner schools" of esoteric teachings.

We are a part of a new inner-directed society that is forming. It requires us to discern what we truly value prior to bringing it into our lives. We are in the middle of building an educated (spiritual) awareness of "what is worth what." We recognize the value of thoughts, actions, and simplicity, even though we have not always thought in such a way. Today, some already are more influenced by inner values more than money or other false values of our society; together we, the awakened, are transforming, and gradually, therefore, our society is changing.

Mystics continuously try to clarify their own values. Spiritual viewpoints and practices become "ways of life" and must be refined once again. A mystic looks at relationships for what goodness they encourage. What value does money have for this one? What gives it value, and what worth is it? What services have personal value? How are values recognized? Friends are of value for what we each can contribute to the lives we touch. There is much discernment in the mystical process. Inner-directedness does not usually have to explain all of its rationale. Inner-directedness brings new awareness, and that newer awareness takes precedent over old thought. We use inner direction to find our personal value process and continuously upgrade our comprehension.

A mystic is not necessarily one who will stand out in a crowd; they are not a marked person except to those who know them as their true self. Like attracts like in that situation. They are not necessarily an obvious contemplative individual; this is why the term "inner-directive" has developed. He or she can be overlooked, as they tend not to attract attention to their process except to persons who ask or are themselves students of wisdom. Whether recognized or not, mystics are always a force working to make change. They are always intent on raising the vibration of wherever they find themselves.

Here we discover a main importance of the mystical life. It is the use of *intent*. One intends to have a relationship with the Creator, called by any name. One intends to be honorable and virtuous; invisible values rule one's life. A code of ethics has emerged from within, not necessarily as anyone else's, but is so intentional and with such integrity that one holds his or her self to these standards in spite of the challenges that arise. This calls the word "inner-directed" naturally into being. It acknowledges that there is a source of insight, awareness, and direction for this one that comes from meditation and contemplation, study and right relationship. All kinds of confusion exist about contemplation. One of the most beautiful definitions I have seen is:

> Contemplation—A deep and dynamic state of conscience, in which the being is placed in a direct manner before an inner energy source, and from it gathers vibrations that then radiate to the world. True contemplation is not obtained by human effort; therefore, there

are no formulas to reach it. Prayers, thoughts or exercises, whichever, cannot induce it. However, the peaceful seeking of union with the essence creates a receptive inner environment for such a state to arise. When it is established, contemplation brings seeds from the future stages of evolution. Absorbed by immaterial conscience, the individual ceases looking for paths, techniques and methods of ascension; just a single course, unique and real, remains. In contemplation, sadness and joy/happiness are unknown, but one is fulfilled in silence. Yesterday and tomorrow are unknown. Today is one's whole existence. Nothing is expected, and one is not intended to arrive anywhere, for the journey is mapped for us at a higher level. (*Esoteric Lexicon* by Trigueirinho)

A friend and often a "challenger to complacent Christianity," author John White writes:

Sacred traditions and metaphysical schools of thought generally agree that reality is multileveled and that each level of reality is composed of differing energies or of matter with different degrees of vibration and density. At one end of the spectrum is purely physical matter; at the other end is pure spirit prior to its manifestation as matter and energy.

This spectrum of substance is one of the two primal forms of God constituting the cosmos. The other is the spectrum of consciousness. Together, they are the inner and outer aspects in a deathless body of light, the perfection of the human body-mind. (Excerpt from "Resurrection and the Body of Light," *Quest Magazine*, John White, Winter 2009)

The effort we make suggests that, as we live our lives with more attunement to our inner self, our intuitive self leads to a struggle with judgmental and opinionated thought. Hear the difference. We may say to another, "this is really important to me." Not, "You are wrong or a bad person because you don't share the same opinion as I do." One is *opinionated* because thought has been given the issue; the other is *judgmental* because of the labels "good or bad";

two perspectives have been attached. As we grow into our higher self, we have to learn to tell the difference within ourselves.

Gnosticism is "*direct knowing*" and comes down through history as a practice of those known for being in touch with Sophia, Divine Wisdom, or Daath in Kabalah. This ever-increasing awareness leads to direct knowing of the Supreme Triad. It is, indeed, the blending of the mind of the heart with the mind of the knower (intuition). Esoteric Christianity speaks of this as being in touch with the Holy Spirit, a person of the trinity. She guides all of us toward the Holy Consciousness of the Son, as we know the Christ. She blends with the Christ (Love) and Sophia (Wisdom) to form Love-Wisdom.

Think this way, please. We have to "*think something*" before we can say it. We have to open the heart before it can "*love.*" This is the work of the Christ to teach us love; then when we love with our mind, it helps us to have the "wisdom" that can flow to better bless the situation. Love opens the way, and then wisdom can come into our awareness as to how to better live and serve. The first step is to "really care" (to love) ... then the wiser part of our consciousness begins to lead our actions. This combination creates love-wisdom. It is no longer two separate streams of energy, but Christ-Sophia made new by the combination.

Sophia is "*wisdom*" in Greek, but there her name was capitalized and personified as personal and feminine. In time, it changed under the leadership of the church, still translated as *wisdom*, but without capitalization or personification. In the Biblical books of Proverbs, Wisdom of Solomon, Song of Songs, Job, Psalms, Ecclesiastes, and Wisdom of Jesus Ben Sirach, we find references to Sophia and her role at work with humanity. Sometimes known as the Holy Spirit of Wisdom, as in the Apocrypha and other Gnostic texts, Sophia is re-emerging.

By losing the teachings regarding Kundalini, or Shekinah and/or Sophia in the West, we lost the part the feminine played in Creation. Without an awareness of Her, this provided another downhill step for feminine values within organized religion. From the Hebrews we learn of *She Who Dwells Within*. Wisdom is *She* who opens the ever-ascending ladder to "direct knowing." This awareness grows within as we develop the knowledge and activation of the ascending chakras. The West has discovered most of its understanding of the energy centers through the Eastern approaches regarding chakras, or through Kabalah and its Sephiroths.

The respect for Sophia or *direct knowing* is affirmed for us in *The Gnostic Gospel* by Elaine Pagels, one of the direct translators of the Nag Hammadi Scrolls (codices dating back to the fourth century) named for the site of their discovery near the Egyptian village of Al Qasar in 1945. Here we find much understanding of the Gnostic approach to direct knowledge. The Gnostics themselves believed a variety of concepts as they emerged from all faiths, including but not limited to Pagan, Jewish, and Greek. As Christianity was spreading through the regions, it had similarities to the perennial wisdom teachings the people could recognize, and they accepted, or sensed, its value. The practitioners felt a natural affinity to the Truths they already held.

While Christians and Gnostics took opposite stands, each claiming to represent the church, and each denouncing the others as heretics, the Valentinians took a mediating position. Resisting the orthodox attempt to label them as outsiders, they identified themselves as fully members of the church. But, the Valentinians engaged in vehement debate among themselves over the opposite question—the status of Catholic Christians. So serious was their disagreement over this question that the crisis finally split the followers of Valentinus into two different factions.

Were Catholic Christians included in the church, the "body of Christ"? The Eastern branch of Valentinians said, no. They maintained that Christ's body, the church, was "purely spiritual," consisting only of those who were spiritual, who had received gnosis. Theodotus, the great teacher of the Eastern school, defined the church as "the chosen race," those "chosen before the foundation of the world." Their salvation was certain, predestined—and exclusive. Like Tertullian in his later years, Theodotus taught that only those who received direct spiritual inspiration belonged to the "spiritual church."

But, Ptolemy and Heracleon, the leading teachers of the Western school of Valentinians, disagreed. Against Theodotus, they claimed that "Christ's body," the church, consisted of two distinct elements, one spiritual, the other unspiritual. This meant, they explained, that both gnostic and non-gnostic Christians stood within the same church. Citing Jesus, saying that "many are called, but few are chosen," they explained that Christians who lacked gnosis—by far the majority—were the many who were "called." They themselves, as gnostic Christians, belonged to the few who were chosen. Heracleon taught that God had given them spiritual understanding for the sake of the rest—so that they would be able to teach "the many" and bring them to gnosis.

The gnostic teacher Ptolemy agreed: Christ combined within the church both spiritual and unspiritual Christians so that eventually all may become spiritual. Meanwhile, both belonged to one church; both were baptized; both shared in the celebration of the mass; both made the same confession. What differentiated them was the level of their understanding. Uninitiated Christians mistakenly worshiped the creator, as if he were God; they believed in Christ as the one who would save them from sin, and whom they believed had risen bodily from the dead: they accepted him by faith, but without understanding the mystery of his nature—or their own. But those who had gone on to receive gnosis had come to recognize Christ as the one sent from the Father of Truth, whose coming revealed to them that their own nature was identical with his—and with God's. (*The Gnostic Gospels* by Elaine Pagels, pp. 115-16)

The Gnostics taught that each one had to have their own experience of the Divine. This was the meaning of "enlightened." It became "salvation" with the Christian Orthodoxy, and salvation meant "healed of separation from the Source," called by any name. Most others from a non-Christian background considered Jesus as the Teacher who brought a reformation and rejuvenation to the Jewish faith.

Considered a Kabalistic mystic, Jesus was teaching his followers how to connect with The Father God. His major offerings were about his loving father and ways to comprehend a holy life. He took disciples and followers, seeking to give to them teachings about Creator, the Higher World, and how to live in peace. Various faiths used different terms for this Source of Life: Creator, Father, Mother, Quetzalcoatl, Father Sun-Mother Earth, Lord, The Divine, Thunder, Perfect Mind etc....

This was the long-awaited God Man, as the Celtics spoke of this Great One, who was promised to come. The Jewish people had prepared for their messiah for eight hundred years, before his birth. Many recognized Jesus as the One, and his disciples proclaimed him the long-awaited Savior. These ideas spread throughout the near East among communities with large Jewish populations, and then Paul became the voice speaking to the gentiles. If you are interested in the inner story of the seeds of Christianity, read about the major streams that developed as portrayed in *The Brother of Jesus* by Jeffrey J. Butz. This is quite factual, easy to read, and most informative (page 162):

> These observations on the nature of orthodoxy and heresy become clearer when one understands that the word "heresy" comes from the Greek "haeresis," which carries the root meaning of an "opinion" or a "party line." Therefore in the strict sense of the word, all of the early Christian Communities had their own heresy—their own opinion about who Jesus was. It was only many years later—at the Council of Nicaea in 325AD—that by a majority vote it was permanently decided what would forever be the acceptable heresy, which then, by definition, became orthodoxy. (Butz, 2005)

The Gospel of Mary Magdalene is also a Gnostic Gospel, recently discovered and translated, that offers a new view to most Christians and another look at Jesus and his disciples other than the traditional gospels. Here we find an interesting view of Jesus' relationship to Mary Magdalene and the relationships among the disciples.

A number of Gnostic-based writings will surprise many; some may be offended while others will understand the archetypal picture presented. The concepts are hard to take if you have been a loyal traditionalist and are only gradually changing. If you have studied for years, your reaction might be, "Oh, my goodness. Here it is in writing!" (Books of this sort are: *The Jesus Mysteries, Jesus and the Lost Goddess, The Laughing Jesus*: all by Timothy Freke & Peter Gandy.)

While I personally believe Jesus to be the "archetypal man" for the "possible human," I believe it is a good exercise to read these views and determine for ourselves what we believe and why. With Uranus bringing us much new information about a veiled past and offering it to the public, each one will have to decide for his or her self what they want to believe, or what it is that inspires each to be the disciple the world wants and needs. In the coming era people will be more independent and more tolerant as we learn to think for ourselves rather than accept "concepts" at face value.

FIVE

Consequences of New Vibrations

IN THE FIFTEENTH CENTURY, Joachim of Flora prophesied that there would be in the future a new age that would be the age of the Holy Ghost. This is the age of Sophia, in which she declares, "I unite all things." Sophia, the god-bearer, is the inner mother. We have all seen the pictures of the Divine with the Christ on her chest, most often called the Theotokos. The incarnating Self within each enables us to be born again to a new comprehension of our outer world. We are born of spirit now, as earlier we had been born of matter. This maturing inner self is being known as ChristoSophia.

Please turn your attention inward. After each Invocation, I ask you to respond with the OM.

> *O Lord Christ, fill our hearts with love, compassion and peace no matter the circumstances of our lives. Respond, "OM"*

> *O Sophia, grant to us ever widening eyes with which to see the true power and beauty of our world. Establish great harmony and wholeness in all the kingdoms. Respond, "OM"*

> *ChristoSophia, grant the love-wisdom we embody to bring forth the Divine that it might express well the gifts and talents with which we are blessed. Respond, "OM"*

Now take a breath and move your attention outward. Are you ready to embark on more thoughts for the new?

There is much speculation about the era we are entering. Will it be as good as promised or as bad as feared? The Mayan feel it will be wonderful in outcome as the new humanity comes about. Let us look at it in a number of ways, new yet old ways. I begin with a brief introduction of the changes in vibration we undergo, spoken in astrological language. Do not feel you have to know astrology to understand this; you do not. Astrology helps us grasp a bit more about the new influences which are affecting humanity and it helps to have a rudimentary understanding of "The Seven Rays."

Uranus, the mundane ruler of the so-called forthcoming age, influences Aquarius by delivering a strong Seventh Ray influence that strengthens and encourages particular areas: ceremonial magic, ritual, economy, organization, formulas, and technology. It regulates areas that it strengthens.

Uranus has both a strong mental influence and a powerful emotion as well. It can change directions readily, but always supports measured steps; for example, with computers you must have a certain predetermined password or program to enter or move from one action to another; this is an important aspect to understand about the Seventh Ray. It is respectful of the right use of resources, measuring devices, and formulas. Think of these as "recipes" … the blending of this and that to make life more harmonious.

Jupiter, the beneficent, is Aquarius' Esoteric Ruler and is a planet with a kind and beneficent-caring influence. This is a Second Ray influence, which provides much hope of love and transformation to a struggling humanity. We are moving from a group mind charged with devotion and emotion, but often lacking compassion and understanding for others. Too often, the Sixth Ray influence can become narrowly focused and fanatical in responding to anyone who dares to differ in opinion. Jupiter gives the benefit of the doubt to others and desires Humanity to recognize more of the sameness and less of the differences of others. Jupiter will help

RAYS, THE SEVEN

Seven streams of force, or emanations, from the Logos express individualized attributes of divine nature. Each bequeaths its quality, color, and sound as it impacts consciousness. The seven Rays are divided into three major Rays of aspect and four minor Rays of attribute. The Rulers, or CHOHANS, of the Rays are also known as Seven Spirits, ELDER BROTHERS BEFORE THE THRONE, MASTERS, or (in Eastern thought) Seven Great RISHIS.

RAYS OF ASPECT

RAY 1 WILL, OR POWER

Each Age is ushered in with a flood of Ray 1 energy, which relates to politicians, those learning to use will, the science of true statesmanship/government, and those mastering techniques of manifesting power. The strong influence of Ray 1 creates the initiator with leadership abilities. Its color is red; its chohan is Morya.

RAY 2 LOVE-WISDOM

Relates to the sciences of meditation, social evolution, psychology—all sciences of INITIATION, which produce the true psychic. The strong influence of Ray 2 creates an intuitive, maintainer with teaching and healing abilities. Its color is blue; its chohan is Kuthumi.

RAY 3 ACTIVE INTELLIGENCE, ADAPTABILITY

Relates to the history of EVOLUTION, laws governing humanity, OCCULT use of money, the science of communication with the CLOUD OF KNOWABLE THINGS. The strong influence of Ray 3 creates a mediator with a philosophical nature. Its color is yellow; its chohan is The Venetian.

RAYS OF ATTRIBUTE

RAY 4 HARMONY THROUGH CONFLICT

Relates to the science of color and sound, study of ETHERIC BODY, science of crisis, tension, and new emergence. The true artist surfaces. Its color is green; its chohan is Serapis. It is said, this is the personality Ray of most of humanity today.

RAY 5 CONCRETE KNOWLEDGE, EXACTNESS

Relates to the study of life and space, specific awareness of energies, laws of the cosmos, and hidden chemistry, the science of the soul, meditation, and right use of mind. Unlocking science of electricity and esoteric healing. Its color is orange; its chohan is Hilarion.

RAY 6 DEVOTION

Relates to the science of approaches to the Higher, the mysteries of INITIATION, the science of service, worship, and devotion to duty. New awareness of the unseen world emerges. Its color is indigo or rose; its chohan is Jesus.

RAY 7 ECONOMY, ORDERLINESS, CEREMONY

Relates to the science of cycles; soul and personality; orderliness; divine simplicity; ceremonial magic; and finance. Its color, purple; its chohan, St. Germaine.

---

to bring about a renewed understanding of the concept of *"walking in the moccasins"* of the other.

Uranus is the personality ruler of Aquarius, as said earlier. Aquarius is a constellation ruled by Ray Five; scientific, researcher, inventor and at the same time emotional, yet stubborn, fixed and determined, this influence will continue to search for answers to current issues as they arise. A Ray Five influence is clean, simple, effective and measured. By utilizing the mental and intuitive capabilities of the higher energies of these incoming new influences, humanity will begin building the new civilization. Uranus loves beauty; and will set into motion research that bodes well for both nature and culture. Aquarius, Uranus, and Jupiter work together well and "can do strategy well" when called for, as in planning and feeling the way forward with careful examination. So we see that Rays Seven, Five, and Two combine strong influences for our future.

Many of us, worldwide, watched the Royal Wedding of Prince William and Catherine Middleton, now the Duke and Duchess of Cambridge. It was of particular interest if you know wisdom teachings. It was a goddess festival with all the significant pieces. It was a commitment ceremony, yes, but balanced in importance of masculine and feminine qualities: the tenderness blended with the power displays; the freedom of her (Kate's) choices spoke of equality of male and female.

The many trees moved into the church spoke of the importance of Mother Nature, as they were to the Celtic people and therefore the historical bloodline of the English. The one bridesmaid spoke of simplicity with young ones around her, invoking "fertility" and the desire for and importance of family. The display of kisses showed respect for affection and values rather than just devotion to duty. Respect for the old tradition became readily apparent, but did not overpower the fresh and new. Beauty was simple, ordered, and intelligent. The word was "keep" not "obey," suggesting "care," protect and nurture. Yes, This is how the new era enters … so subtle, yet respectful of older traditions.

Aquarius works in intellectual spurts of creative thinking. Under this leadership we will see Science and Spirituality coming together; the transforming of humanity will advance toward its potential. This Ray Seven Uranus and Ray Five Aquarius will be able to make some needed breakthroughs, both in helpful technology and in a more humane approach to the global human condition, no matter how humanity drags its collective feet.

The virtue attributed to Aquarius is humility and the building of humility begins when we realize we may not be correct, right, or have every answer. **We each must confront the arrogance of our own personality**. The characteristics of our personality reflect our culture. We can think of the training of our society—our materiality, our education, our churches or religious teachings—all are to help us fit into this dying culture. Where we lack healing for our personal wounds, we lock into bad behavior. Thus, childhood experiences build the "box" that produces personalities and then the personality fuels the drive to sustain ego.

Now the Age of Aquarius introduces the energy that will help build humility within humanity. This trait is gained by learning how to resist the personality's misshaped ego and be true to the leadership of our higher self; we obey our guidance whether we like it or not. The challenge is to detach from personality and be subservient to the part of our self where there is harmony "with higher will." To do such, we begin when our various programs recognize that *"our lives have become unmanageable."* We already see how various desires, habits, or addictions *"controlling"* our lives have neither made us happy or fulfilled.

> Much more than our own growth and action is involved in the life of our planet Earth. We are part of an inter-related system of planets, stars and galaxies, and even astronomers tell us now, other galaxies. This means that we participate in a great circulating flow of energies far beyond our own, and belong to a gigantic pattern of relationship, which it is hard to conceive. But, in this recognition lies the meaning of "entering the zodiacal sign of Aquarius."
>
> … But the transit from one sign to another is not an immediate happening; it takes some 500 years for the influences of one sign to take over fully from another, and this period is always one of difficulty and confusion. Here lies the cause of a great many of our present problems. (*Entering Aquarius* by Michael J. Eastcott and Nancy Magor, p. 24)

According to the hermetic saying "as above, so below," the human and nature kingdoms' activities are just a reflection of the cosmic forces that act upon our planet. One of the major difficulties an eager humanity has with the future of our world is knowing that

Uranus—who is forcing the leap in vibrations and thus changing our consciousness—is telling us that it is time to take a next step, but this won't happen immediately. **We want it now, immediately … instant gratification.**

However the vibrational leap that will modify earth and humanity will not do so in a few days or years. Rather we must understand the truth of wisdom teachings and realize that it takes about 350-500 years to make this "leap." At the present time (2014) we have about one hundred twenty years yet before we are totally into the Aquarian Age. At the same time, we are changing every day. In cosmic time a day is *"as a thousand years,"* or we may realize *"a thousand years is but a day."* We will have all the time it takes; we are leaving the puberty of humanity to become the divine human.

This step creates an upsetting paranoia: mental illness, plus violence, and addictions, are all signs of the transition period we are passing through. A vast share of our people will suffer these ills. The human psyche has to adapt to the structure, which has to accommodate the new incoming vibrations arriving. Everyone has predicted humanity will suffer during this stage, but there is also hope that some will move smoothly ahead, combining the collective social wisdom with the wisdom of the inner nature.

No one really has said "just what all" humanity will suffer … fear, competition, anger, mental stresses and physical stresses are all caused by facing change and the unknown. The end of any cycle brings upheaval because of the new frequencies. Some tectonic and meteorological changes are to occur due to the adjustments that the Earth itself must make. As well, the mental and materialistic mindset will disappear, and instinctually we will know it to belong to the "old vibration," because this has been a part of the *rule of a few* to have financial control and dominance over the whole world.

Not all the present instability and discomfort is the end of the world, but it is the end of a worldview that simply must be leaving to make room for the new. Torkom Saraydarian said of this stage of development:

This planet is sick. It is stated in the Ageless Wisdom that people are now living on Earth exactly the same way as people did on the moon. The moon was eventually destroyed. The same thing can happen on Earth. A crazy person can start a war, or a person using drugs may push the wrong button. Either way, even if accidentally done, it would be the end of this planet.

A Great Teacher, M(aster) M(orya) states that, Cosmic cooperation is achieved only when you are drawn to Hierarchy. This is vertical cooperation. There is no other way. Hierarchy is the Captain. Hierarchy has great intuitive antahkaranas and communication systems, which keep it informed of what the Soul of the Planet is doing so that It can adjust humanity with the advancing Soul of the Planet.

Cosmic cooperation in this life begins when you have a vision and when you begin to perceive the Hierarchy and follow the steps of the Christ.... As you advance toward the vision, a fire is created within you that galvanizes all your movements and leads you into Oneness, into a life based on Oneness.... Our basic responsibility is to learn the science of cooperation. This is our future destiny.... We can never understand cooperation through education; we can only understand it through the heart.

The heart will reveal how everything in nature is one. Let us strive to be a part of Oneness, instead of living apart for ourselves. (*Cosmic Shocks* by Torkom Saraydarian, pp 146-48)

The earliest mystics in the Christian tradition were found among the priests, hermits, anchorites, and before them the Gnostics, both men and women. There have been mystics in every period. We can trace them in the East, West, holy men, and holy women. They have been religious, scientists, and artists. They have spoken to the world of the Higher World: the earth circling the sun, the beauty of the higher world, places and dimensions we still do not grasp. The ancients recorded the earth circling the sun before Galileo came to testify scientifically to the fact.

Mysticism is not people orientated; it is spirit orientated. It is a possibility for individuals as they reach a certain kind of consciousness. The time has come in the collective life for a "leap" forward to move upward. All will move, some ready for higher consciousness. Those on the cutting edge are ready for a new reality; others will come soon afterwards. As we work through these so-called *shifts*, we are establishing a chance for greater contact and interaction with the inner planes, which is really a term for relationships with other dimensions of creation. We could apply the six-story building theory to this shift, as it is a movement from one floor to the next higher (more subtle) one. The seventh floor is on the rooftop—no restrictions.

What does mysticism do for us? As we become the possibility that lives within, we find a "timelessness" that pulls us into the hidden crevices within ourselves where there is an unknown awareness. In time, it bursts us out of ourselves as a personality into the spirit being we truly are. As we quest, we expand our ring-pass-not repeatedly. We reach awareness and live there for some time, and then other awarenesses burst in and we see life differently and begin the process again. We live out each experience until the energy of it is gone, and in time, another may come, and we are invigorated once again.

Mother Theresa had an inner experience with Master Jesus while traveling on a train through the mountains in India. She went to her confessor and reported it. He told her to keep quiet and see what happened. She did and came to him again, I believe, two years later. It was still real, alive within her. He then suggested she consider it valid and go to the Pope. Years later in her memoirs, she says she never had such an experience again, but served her entire life from the power of that contact. This is the power of the mystical experience: whether it lasts long or short, we work from the energy of the contact.

It is important to realize that the great shift we are undergoing is that the consciousness of humanity is moving into our planet's more subtle form. A great many of our human population is expanding beyond the dense form of Earth and are reaching into the more subtle form of our world. Knowing spiritual teachings helps us image some of this more comfortably. It is much similar to an out-of-body experience; we do not miss a thing; in fact, our senses are sharper and we perceive more.

Therefore, I want us to keep in mind the concept "a thousand years is as a day and a day is as a thousand years." This says to some it will seem fast, and to others it will seem very slow. This understanding also addresses the "rapture" theory to some degree, although I cannot conceive of it as such a frightening event as is portrayed. Life moves steadily forward and seemingly in a natural manner, not attempting to ignite "terror" in the hearts and minds of the human family. We are to believe also, that the Universe loves us and is raising us to be cosmic creatures bringing love-wisdom throughout the universe.

The greatest work of the Mystic is to Live Love! Each chakra has a different expression of love energy. As progress is made, we are to cultivate such high frequencies within ourselves that we emanate a love from the solar plexus that affirms all humanity is becoming one family. The heart says, "No judgment." The throat center wants for all of humanity the very things we would want for ourselves and what will bring happiness to each.

This kind of love culminates in a vision of everyone having his or her needs met and recognized as worthy. Social values do not depend upon possessions, although we will continue to have possessions. There is a higher manifestation of caring that includes satisfying humanity's basic needs. The Mystical Path includes peace within our inner nature as well as the outer.

The Era Ahead

When we read about the new era, we think of a new world culture, a foundation on which an evolved humanity can build a new worldview or new civilization. We think of space travel, beauty, and opportunities undreamed of; we might say a New Vision to benefit all planetary life, but also we think of a more enlightened people. We envision all humanity coming to an awareness of "right relations"; I think of this as *"all humanity becoming one family."*

The new consciousness that humanity is building will: (1) care for the earth, (2) recognize the importance of heart-centered leadership, and (3) develop healthy egos, nurtured by good psychological and spiritual health. These qualities form the conscience that is forthcoming so that we express care for the Earth as embraced by ecologists and care for the indigenous people of all traditions, and thereby gain access to their wisdom so as to safeguard concepts like love for the "four- footed ones" and "all my relations."

A concern for the Earth is natural as soon as we understand that this planet is our lifeboat for the dense physical dimension. It is a school where actions move in slow motion to benefit our learning process. Earth is our schoolhouse. Some graduate and go out of the boat into a greater arena … these are called Masters, Teachers and Spirit Guides in different traditions, but they are still concerned about the "little ole school house."

Heart-centered leadership implies that the rulership by "solar plexus logic" will end. Those who truly have a greater concern for the health and well-being of the younger kingdoms, as well as concern for the common good of humanity, will earn the appreciation of their brothers and sisters. One of the commandments states: **"Honor thy father and mother"** as a guideline for healthy, happy living.

My spiritual training taught me *"all mothers and fathers are my mother and father"* and *"all children are my children."* With this idea, one is to treat all as if they were your parents and/or your children; thus, indeed, *"all are my relations."* We are all karmically bound in this web of life together. The open heart is our leader in dealing with all others! A rich paragraph I have treasured is below; I have long since lost the author's name. Enjoy!

> **Healthy purified egos** *will allow each unique personality its rightful opportunity to grow and express the rays of its make-up. Yes, from infancy we will strengthen the qualities of the soul, not just the psychological needs of each. Just as we now invest time and effort in proper diet and sports, we will recognize the positive and negative traits of each personality, and we spend time nurturing in ways few*

understand as of yet the spiritual self of each. Parents will begin the effort, teachers and mentors will continue the work, and as children become adults, this will continue as their personal work.

This inner world or higher reality is the spirit world, or heaven, or the dreaming reality of the aborigine, or by different names in other traditions. Humanity is moving forward and into new vibrations to a new consciousness and breaking out of old thoughtforms and powerful restrictions. Havoc is happening, as in remodeling a home. We make a mess before we can rebuild.

Nostradamus refers to a lost generation. First, think of the great losses we must undergo to make such a change. The violence, mental illness, and addiction are real, and so is the price humanity must pay in response to the *transformational impulse*. We must come to realize we are really one human soul and live like it.

Many of us know intellectually that, for us to evolve into what humanity is meant to be "as a God-Being" or the "Possible Human," separatist attitudes must change. This is a clear occult teaching, and knowing it is good, but to know it intellectually and not have the well-being of the plan in our heart becomes an obstacle to the power-seeking occultist. The mind can be brilliant, but the heart can still be stingy.

There has always been some who are ahead and some behind in the advancement of the collective. If we desire to work from the higher levels of our own nature, we have energy now to assist us. We can bring heart and mind together and build the mystical awareness we need to progress in our own journey. At the same time, we assist all of humanity to take the next step and open the collective heart and higher awareness.

Think of steps we might take to care for and nurture the higher qualities of this human animal to transformation and refinement. We watch *Animal Planet* and are amazed at how long it takes to rear a baby elephant or a panda bear; we are now learning it takes thousands of years to bring forth a fully developed divine human. We must remember that it is our reason for being.

We are holding a vision of a fragile possibility. It is old, yet ever new. The seed is in human consciousness; from the ancients we have known of the possibility, from message after message from the Wise Ones of each tradition. We are pioneers of this reality; it is fragile, and we can produce the thoughtforms and love that can manifest in this possibility if we have the courage—much like the founders of any new country or project which is led by Spirit. This new vision of a new kind of humanity is gradually being spoken about publically, especially to counteract the idea that each person is born a "sinner." We naturally outgrow the limitations of the old when we replace them with a more enlightened vision, hope, and thought-form.

The challenge and obstacle is to allow/encourage each personality to bow to its inner nature, soul, or spirit leadership and depart its materialistic traits of seeing only the benefits of selfish behavior. Our part is to hold the inner life as important and to be a "Johnny Appleseed" for the new possibility. We are to step out, step up, and step into our best self and show it is so.

Just as the dragonfly must pass through its many seasons to be able to be the iridescent beauty of the air, humanity is on a powerful journey to become a Divine being in body. I would say at the fourth or even higher level of awareness (thinking of the example of a multi-story building), it is a natural goal and a natural occurrence.

In some sense, this is like the newborn pup or kitten which is born with its eyes shut. To survive, learn to eat, run and play, it needs to have a mother to wash and care for it before it can do so for itself. Humanity is born needing the same care. It is not born with its inner eyes open or its inner awareness. It has to have spiritual care from within to become what it truly is.

Now the experience of Life often does trigger spiritual emergencies and an entirely new kind of growth begins. A wiser collective is now emerging as a progressive mind versus a frightened fundamentalist one. Again, this is the influence of the new era.

One must gain entry into the new mental room that humanity is building in some acceptable way. Some feel threatened by this expansion and wish to continue in the known rather than face the unknown. They would rather not have to discover that behind their truth, there is a more subtle truth. This is currently happening in technologies as we know, but it has always been so in many areas of life. We had to make a move from the horse and buggy to get the automobile. The major difference was that Life (time) moved more slowly in the past; that is not the reality of today.

As the age of change is upon us, we face new translations of old understandings and this affects time itself. It may be hard to grasp how time can speed up or slow down, but this is a realization of perception. The closer to the finish of the hourglass, the faster the sand seems to flows out. This is what we are experiencing as the old era ends and the new is upon us.

The world's mystical traditions have always recognized the role of this inner self to evolve, each individually as well as assisting the collective. It is important to realize the power of "lots of vital energies"as evolutionary in nature. This power is actively doing battle with the involutionary forces of selfishness and self-centeredness in our time and within and through us.

I have an understanding of Love that is not held by many, but I would like to offer it to you now. Each one of us is a facet of the whole; this whole is the One Humanity that is attempting to emerge, and eventually this healthy group mind will win out. Now, remember Jesus' saying, "Love one another," "Love fulfills the Law," and other references to love. Love is to be the identifying mark of Jesus' followers. Now, think about the "facets of the One" being attracted to one another. Natural attraction pulls them together. Love is the glue that makes them one.

Think: **Love is the glue** … as the facets love one another, they join together. It is not romantic love, or family love, but a kind of evolutionary love that has little meaning at the average human level. However, it is this evolutionary Love that will mold us together as we become one at the higher levels ... ponder this. I think L-o-v-e is glue!

Societies have a keynote just as a family does. This note or tone is a frequency on which they predominate. As each person has a unique note, when two individuals blend their life force, the tones blend, and then create a tone of a new frequency. As babies are born or adopted, they add their notes to both the family and the collective.

This causes the collective to sound on a slightly different note, or we might know it best as a thought form, or an identity with a reputation all its own. Relationships add to this collective tone, for example, groups such as a football team, a church, a political party, or a country. We see the importance of individual keynotes as well as that of collective relationships. Their importance is immeasurable, whether large in number or small, for the impact they make.

Advanced souls have a higher tone and seek to lead or create a higher or guiding keynote; advanced tones magnetize others together and the collective grows. Some souls lag behind and grow at a slower rate. Souls are assisted by the tone of the group, and they become a part of or are affected by the service of others. All souls have to deal with the tone they create, alone and with others, as they find themselves involved in group work ... *service*, as it is known. More advanced souls assist the younger; leaders have to exert more effort to make a stronger tone when working with younger souls, or less aware individuals.

Ways exist for elevating the group vibration, the thought form or spiritual tone of a collective relationship. For example, take any person who presents the challenge—it may be learning to work together, or something karmic in nature. It may be your blessing yet unseen, or something to provoke you and the other(s) to new growth. Use these wise ideas:

- I will hold that relationship or individual in *respect*.

- I will speak only *good* about this situation.

- I will intentionally create *constructive thought forms* about this situation.

- I will *forgive* the situation and myself our differences.

- I will realize *all are doing the best* they can to bring healing.

- *Before bed,* I will *ask heavenly help* to bring benefit to this relationship.

- I will keep *silence*—no comments, only inner work.

Karmic relationships are between individuals destined to connect to confront unlearned lessons from the past. This means there will be conflicts to see if each has learned to respond more wisely than they would have in the past. Generally, any of four situations can result:

- The individuals incarnate into the situation for lifetime, e.g. relatives.

- The situation is open-ended, so the outcome depends upon the growth of each. If they both grow, they can stay in relationship. If new growth is possible, they may remain together; without growth, they will part. This can apply to spouses, lovers, friends, business partners.

- Destined to part, these individuals will come together only to part; that is the goal. Have they learned to part without creating even more hostility? They locked into this situation from previously creating handicapping ties. Examples can be loving parents that tied the child to themselves by never allowing them to leave home and mature, i. e., "mama's boy," or "tied to the apron strings," or a child who would not mature into a self-supporting adult; they did not develop the courage and self-confidence needed to leave their security.

- A dependency that became so unhealthy the two souls needed to battle that weakness within each. They return to grow strong and to have the courage to leave situations when they find them so damaging.

"Dharmic Soul Mates" are those of us with a shared goal. The word "dharma" has many meanings, but here it is the sum total of all the teachings, and represents the duty one has to spread the dharma or highest knowledge both to oneself and to others. Our individual karma has prepared each of us for this situation, and we are to do our part to fulfill the objective of assisting others. Here we find that a relationship or group effort can bring collective growth, and become a karmic structure that locks players together in a shared goal. On the other hand, some relationships or groups can become open-ended, and grow apart. Then each can make a decision to go or stay. If the group is destined to end the relationship, the project will fade, and many of these souls may have to work together again in the future to resolve differences and see if they can work together more harmoniously.

Counterpart Soul Mates are individuals brought together for growth and support of each other and they tend to work together well. They have spiritual growth to achieve, but their lessons are not with each other. These individuals support and help each other meet their challenges, and reflect back good karma or "rewards" to each other.

All relationships, whether rough or pleasant, are for the purpose of new growth, as is the reason for incarnation. One of the hardest experiences a soul can have is that of betrayal. Here one seeks to apply the wisdom of his or her soul to the situation, and any one of the collective can grow or incur karma because of their actions. The group relationship will bear the results, and many people will grow and others will regress according to how the tests work out.

A worldwide community under the care of the higher world is in the formative stage. A conscious understanding of this does not end our personal struggle or growth. It is not just a nice thought-form, but also a "*wispy*" power blowing through the inner world impressing itself on the planetary blueprint. Each age has a work to do, and ours is the Oneness we are striving to discover.

The Mayans say our society teaches us three major "**lies**" and we have to come to realize this to move ahead with wisdom. Let us look at these:

- *Job loss is bad.*

- *Time is money.*

- *There is never enough.*

The indigenous way of looking at these ideas is very different from our customary Western way. Let us try to see their understanding as we look at each of them.

"*Job loss is bad*" can produce fear within us, but we can see job loss in another way. It is a way to have *freedom* from what you were doing and to give you a chance to gain new opportunity.

The teaching of "*Time is money*" can be understood as "*no, it is not just time, it is your life.*" Your physical life is passing with each hour and is much more valuable than money.

"*There is never enough*" may seem to be true at some points, but is not consistently so. There are plenty of situations where too much of most everything challenges us. This challenge is to confront materialism. We are entitled to what we need, but most of us have far too much and we must learn that it takes energy to maintain so much.

As we seek spirituality, we must learn to examine our lives and see what we are magnetizing to the life we are developing. Rarely do we understand *intent, karma,* or the many *spiritual axioms* that are affecting us, whether we know them or not. We have to wake up to the idea "*we are souls*" with roles to play.

We must become charitable to ourselves as well as to others … not critical or judgmental … for these energies destroy the awakening we have begun. Indeed, this is the intent of those who attack you for any new idea or new spiritual practice you may have begun. Others want you to stop changing, to stay the same. You scare them with your new ideas and ways of life. To intimidate you into stopping your changes is the goal. Watch!

Most of our actions are not great earth-stirring happenings. It is within our daily attitudes that we initiate the "cause" of the "cause-and-effect wheel." Knowing this is a major clue to our quest for higher consciousness. The truth is that God has given us *role-sharing* in the evolving Creation ... the ability of the God within and without to blend together in the creation of a world—inside our head, if not outside our being—that expresses our true spirit.

The mature mystic is in search of the flow of the God Consciousness, whether understood as Cosmic Consciousness, or Father, or Mother God, or Sophia, or Holy Consciousness. They long for the opportunity. Many long for the peaceful state we are calling *Love-Wisdom* to flow freely in and around them as well. They are that; this is the "Om Tat Sat" we hear in the East. We might use the word *saint* for mystic in this statement, but it is inaccurate.

There is no "mystic" label authorized by church authorities in average modern life. It is a state earned from within and realized privately, or granted by others observing the individual.

Some mystics, because of circumstances, training, periods in the life, or the society to which they belong, find themselves existing within the realms of religious expression. This is not necessarily because they accept the dogmas under which they live; here, they find the protection their society has to offer. Others find themselves totally at war with religion and its restrictions. Religious fanatics tend to be dogmatic, regimented people, not mystics, even though persons commonly confuse the two.

> *A favorite saying about the spiritual path is: seeking perfection and enlightenment is like looking for a flashlight when all you need the flashlight for is to find your flashlight!*

The word *mysticism* comes from the word, *mystos*, meaning "to keep silent," and because of this "keep silent," disciples were taught not to discuss, but to keep their experiences to themselves, so as not to dilute the subtle implications and fullness of their immediate experience. The term originally applied to those initiated into some mystery cults and a word taken from the Greek schools. It implies knowledge of divine things not accessible to others. Gradually, it took on a broader meaning: *"Don't talk about this to anyone but your teacher."*

About the time of the Inquisition, this secrecy became a life-saving protection: that is, *"something we don't talk about, because if the world finds out, it will try to tear us apart."* Often others will reference the *"influence of the devil"* in some way, and we tend to become quiet, especially when terms like *"demon"* or *"devil"* surface, because Biblical words carry a lot of punch. We face judgment even to dare to think a certain way, and this thinking is seen as either good or bad, depending on who you are with, and the depth of their understanding (or ignorance). All of this reminds us of the distorted group consciousness in which we dwell.

As a sensitive one, we can touch gently the beliefs of another, but just as we want the privilege of freedom of thought, we must grant freedom to the other. A gentle touch may do no damage, but if anger or fear is aroused, it may take a long time to heal. Be gentle in your quest, and extremely respectful of where others are on their path.

Holy Consciousness Changes Us

Some interesting Eastern concepts teach that each human has seven demons to confront as they realize higher consciousness. Some believe that a passage in the Gospel refers to Jesus' healing Mary Magdalene of seven demons. This is more important than most understand. Many think "the demons" were migraine head-aches, menstrual problems, depression, or other female ailments. But some Eastern ideas go further and suggest that, when Holy Consciousness comes to us, it brings about a natural healing of inner human frailties.

Sophianic teachings say that opening to the Holy Consciousness (or as more commonly said by many today, "the acceptance of Christ into our heart") dissolves the seven deadly sins common to the human condition. We know them as: pride, greed, anger, envy/covetousness, sloth, gluttony, lust.

When we gain the Christ Consciousness by the help of its grace, we are purified of these frailties. Certain antidotes help us understand and assist the process. These are:

- oneness heals pride

- creativity heals greed

- love heals anger

- knowing heals envy

- power heals sloth

- temperance heals gluttony

- respectful sexuality heals lust

> **"The impulse to sin is not sin, but to consent to sin ...
> is indeed sin,"** said Meister Eckhart.

Sin (or "ignorance') is a tool that our basic nature uses to lead us into pain, loss, or suffering in some way, and thus learn our lessons. Our failings aid in creating within us a desire to transform. Often I refer to these experiences as *Self-Inflicted Nonsense*, yet these struggles provoke the very testing experiences which culminate in lessons learned. We bring on the necessary pain to cause ourselves to get out of the box (society's *maya*) in which we have found ourselves.

In seeking Truth, we have to be mindful that other ideas of truth exist as well as our own. Each values his or her truth and, as we tend toward mysticism, we will become aligned with a greater view than average individuals. Especially when change comes to humanity as fast as it is today, Fundamentalism rises up in order to slow down the world culture from such a rapid shift. There is a certain relationship between the two: expansion and contraction. The law of duality teaches that a more liberal perspective will propel others to defend a narrower view to maintain a collective balance. In this duality, each sustains the other.

As we explore spirituality and its expansion of consciousness, one must recognize that religious fundamentalists have a role as well. Fundamentalists by definition have already made a choice to give allegiance to more constrictive points of view and choose not to embrace broader perspectives. The term "fundamentalism" has come to denote a literal translation of scripture, which is not comfortable with a deeper meaning of a concept, parable, or teaching. The term can apply to any field, not just religion. In addition, persons with a more narrow perspective do not appreciate the mystic's sense of conviction. Nor does the mystic accept the literalistic view of the fundamentalist.

In a time of rapid shifts, the explorer plots the new and the fundamentalist accepts what has served before. A dual attitude develops between the two perspectives that we see manifesting in politics, religion, economics, and all of life. One can only stretch so far until the other comes into play. If expansion runs wild, there would be no stability; if restriction rules too strongly, there will be no progress. There is always a pull involved between our inner selves and our outer reality. We find this conflict best represented by the comment, "Yes, but…," followed by an opposing statement to whatever is said.

The idea of study is to learn how to put all of this information into a spiritual perspective rather than a materialistic one. First, we must know the rules; and then secondly, we must get past the rules to a place where they do not limit us anymore. We must grant freedom to others to get freedom. We grasp the awareness behind the rules and then push back the limiting boundaries for greater expression. Gay marriage is a modern example.

So first we meet the new thought; second, we must understand or make peace with the new issue (e.g., deal with our own feelings);

third, not want another to have less benefits or less rights than ourselves; and four, with a new understanding, we can take a stand.

As we adapt our understanding, we can gradually facilitate contact with something of the invisible world with the awareness we need to know the higher will for our lives. Each of us discovers the path within ourselves as we systematically find our way. This is the symbolic meaning of "*dropping crumbs to be followed*" in fairy tales. We, indeed, pull our personal path together piece by piece as we go. We, in turn, leave crumbs for those who might follow.

We hear the charge to **stay the course**: we use prayer, meditation, love, and service—the same disciplines and practices each disciple has used from the beginning to fulfill their part of the plan. We receive the sacred "food"—inspiration—to fortify ourselves on the quest.

When one says, "*in my guidance I was told*" or "*this is how I know,*" we ponder just how does one just *know* with his or her inner knower. This flash or awareness comes as a vibration, a frequency sensed and understood; it brings both a feeling and a knowing that blend to provide a new awareness. We speak of a guardian angel, or solar angel (different systems use different terms) vibrating the message at the edge of our mind. **Remember, the brain and the mind are not the same.**

Brain is the physical equipment. Expansion of mind is quite different. It is the process of developing a larger and larger capability, with more space and more ability to translate or step down a vibration or impression to a rational reality (the understanding held in our intellectual mental body). When channeled material becomes too flattering in words or too glamourous, we say, "*It is of the astral reality.*" Since we want *higher will*, we seek a more impersonal and objective level. Persons often need instruction in the pyramid of techniques about all of this, and a mentor can provide much assistance.

The more subtle realities make up what we call higher consciousness and involve certain initiations on the path. Until such time we can walk the path alone, the human family has guardians to help. While names differ, occult studies introduce "solar angels." Not all planetary systems have solar angels, but Earthlings do. The key is that our own mind mechanism must resonate comfortably with whatever we perceive for these presences or energies to register in our awareness. Until then we *cannot know* with our *knower.*

As a "working" mother, something much criticized in the 1960s, the belief existed that a good mother did not go to work and leave her children. Even when forced to do so for economic reasons, the working mother was often considered a questionable mother. The mystical way, likewise, "forces or entices" us to follow our guidance and, when we begin to do so, we take hesitant steps not knowing where they will lead … to acceptance or to rejection.

Sometimes people get on a spiritual path thinking life will get easier … but no. While it is true that the shepherd may carry a young lamb, the sheep are expected to walk. This may be different as one follows a social or a dogmatic path, but not on a spiritual one. There is far too much to learn in the higher world, and Pandora's Box has merely been opened—we have just begun to learn the "how to's" of the newly discovered realities.

The most pain-filled, the most challenging, and thank goodness, the best years of one's life come as this journey unfolds enough to occasionally be able to recognize its many blessings and synchronicities. Someone may say, "*I followed my guidance and it led to the worst experience of my life.*" There is no promise that our guidance will always lead to happiness, but it is our commitment that will lead to wisdom.

There is an occult teaching that says a lesson seemingly out of context will give us the gift of learning that cannot otherwise come to us. Something within us attracted or magnetized it to us and we eventually have to face it. When we have mastered some growth, or learned or mastered something, this learning will change the balance of this life and those of the future. We have to *know this from within, not just because someone says so,* or we could not have found the courage or strength to meet the challenge.

At this time, humanity is particularly learning about addiction, sexual abuse, and violence because it is a part of the human journey not well understood. This painful journey through hell on earth is the very underbelly of humanity and has long been labeled "the bardo." Expressed as "a breakdown can be a breakthrough," we grow in unique ways. The blending of the changing ages and various mindsets have created a field of chaos that allows the dregs of our group mind to surface.

The collective has to deal with emerging attitudes. These acts of chaos are to awaken all of us to the negative prompting of the astral plane, such as collective hostility poured into the astral plane by riots, violence, etc. I particularly am concerned by the acceptance of violent movies and television, a tolerance of "lesser crimes" as we witness wanton acts of child molestation, pornography, and robbery. Frequently these are brushed aside saying, "We do not have sufficient staff to investigate all complaints." The damage done by tolerating or accepting such behavior leads to even more lack of self-restraint. Wisdom teachings of various traditions share a great deal of humanity's collective wisdom as all began from the same root and have merely branched out and adopted different cultural expressions. However, we note, life's lessons are quite similar as we progress through the learning experiences we all need to evolve on our path.

SIX

Exploring the Shadow

WE KNOW THE SHADOW GOES WITH US EVERYWHERE. Likewise, it goes with us on our spiritual journey. Who or what is it? The most common answer is, "the part of our self that we do not like."

Think of our "shadow" as the part of the personality that we attempt to keep out of sight and are not desirous of owning; we prefer not to be identified with these particular traits. It is like when we read an astrology description and there are negative as well as positive traits about each sign. We tend to claim the good and deny the negative. We are likely to do the same with our personality traits, claim those we are proud of and deny the ones of which we are not proud.

As we study our self, we identify characteristics that we think are strengths; we amplify the ones with which we are pleased and attempt to disguise the ones with which we are uncomfortable. Our greatest work remains to bring the highest potential of the invisible aspect of our nature to express these truths through the framework of the personality. In all probability this is not the work of one lifetime. This brings up the question of reincarnation, and the major quote remaining in the modern versions of the Gospel that offers us a reference.

1) And as Jesus passed by, he saw a man who was blind from his birth.

2) And his disciples asked him, saying, "Master, who did sin, this man, or his parents, that he was born blind?"

3) Jesus answered, "Neither hath this man sinned, or his parents; but that the works of God should be made manifest in him" (Matthew 9:1-3).

The above scripture tells us that Jesus as a teacher could have addressed the issue of reincarnation if he chose to … however, most around him already shared that belief at that time, so there was no reason for him to comment. This story was chosen to be in the Bible so it was not unduly offensive at the time the Bible was being constructed.

We need to ponder the reference. This little tidbit is enough to whet our appetite if we are alert. While the early church did not focus on reincarnation, it chose not to encourage the belief. The church wanted immediate obedience, and this thought allowed individuals to put off dealing with religious obedience rather than becoming the staunch persons the church wanted. This is where the "power play" of the new structure began.

Reincarnation is just one way of looking at the growth pattern of the Soul. I personally believe there is a Soul with many experiences of life for each of us. Each personality life (of the Soul) is like a day in the life of the divine being we truly are. If I live and learn a certain amount by the end of this personality life, the Soul has had one more life/day in which to learn and grow. I do not think it necessary to accept reincarnation, but this is a way to look at the issue. We rarely speak of reincarnation without karma, and I feel very strongly about it. The acceptance of the concept of karma ignites all kinds of social issues and causes us to move carefully in whatever we do.

One other thought about the daily life of an individual as *one day in the life of the Soul* can be remembered when we think, "A day for the divine is like a thousand years and a thousand years as a day." This really says God does things in his own time and we grow in our own time. I think we can have all the time it takes to grow our divinity. Some will move ahead faster and some more slowly. Just grow!

Let us find another way to examine the little-recognized companion, the Shadow, that so closely identifies with our ego. Particularly think of "niceness" as a part of the collective shadow of women; we are to be *"sugar and spice, and everything nice."* It is okay for boys to be *"frogs and snails and puppy dog tails."*

Because of our collective experience, the feminine group mind has cultivated a strong mistrust of other women who might be *nicer* than we might, so we pretend. We develop tools of seduction and dishonesty, hiding that we do not feel *nice enough* all the time. We say we are *"hurt,"* not *"angry"*—never *mad* or *sad* but always pretending *"glad."* We become victims, or at least the feminine part of one's self does. Strong feminine natures do this, and not just women, nice men also!

Males have a collective shadow as well. It is competitive and egotistic. Each believes he is to be *ever strong,* ever *in charge,* ever *virile,* ever *masterful* ... anything less is failure. Being feminine or sissy was condemnation in the master masculine era. Males ruled life, and the feminine walked three paces behind. Now we are entering a time when we need both natures to be whole. We are learning the male nature can choose to be tender, while the feminine aspect can be fierce as nails ... when need be.

Years ago Ann Manser, spiritual teacher, gave this example to help us understand the shadow:

> Imagine you are in a darkened library equipped with a flashlight to use to find your present life purpose. You look at your book of this life and can see only that book. A few faintly illumined books show around it, while all the rest are in the darkness.
>
> Walk to another spot in the room, and now, where you were originally standing, is in the darkness. A new part of your life is visible and in the Light; the other events are fading. The past only is visible when focused on it. The other perspectives we cannot see clearly now are in the shadow.

We all carry wounds, regrets, past happiness, loves, events, as well as hidden talents, abilities, traits not yet developed. Full awareness has not yet dawned on us. We have deep insights yet to perceive, and tests to take that have not come upon us yet. All this potential is waiting for us to discover, and it is a part of the shadow. We are developing new skills and capabilities all the time. We make errors that must be rectified as we continue to travel our path, and these embed themselves within our soul to be resolved.

We can only guess that Grandma Moses, the famous artist, did not know when she was a young woman that she had artistic talent. As well, we do not know our capacity as an inventor or a parent until the occasion arrives; yet, the capacity is there, waiting. We may not know our meanness or harshness, wickedness or kindnesses, as well as our nurturing capability, until they "hatch" within our self.

Events of our life birth new inner strengths, or blend inner forces together to create new potentials. This is the work of the shadow … to grow a more talented Self, and align our High Self toward Soul Infusion. Transformation takes place as this blending and shifting takes place. The mystic is not to deny his or her shadow, but to try to see it, to recognize and integrate it. Participate consciously in the discovery of the shadow; do not attempt to escape it, but learn to work with it and other processes that hasten the transformation process.

Death is our major transformation, a complete movement from physical reality back to spirit. How do we dare look at Death and the withdrawal process when we are in the physical? Death is a sober topic we want to avoid and usually we do. As a minister, we have an obligation to help others examine their purpose in life and what are appropriate actions. As such, each one in this role has probably dealt with death more than an average person. We visit the sick and dying in homes and in hospital; we share the tender and precious moments of fear and of hot grieving pain, as well as witnessing the struggle of unfinished business. We close eyes that have finished their views of this dimension and bless the bodies of those who have vacated them. There is the surreal work of what the mystic witnesses and learns. Up close and real, one's view of Life and Death changes.

Death of a loved one is a heart opening experience for most; it is where one leans on the strength of others for love and much needed courage. Death is feared; it makes us vulnerable so we hesitate to reach out. Our weakness scares us. Death touches the delicate part of our being while beckoning for the best in us to come forward. There is a role for the strong one, while those left behind are weak, both in knees and in hope. Facing the fear of being swallowed up by the dark empty hole made by the departure of the one we love leaves us with the painful experience and the grief. This thought reminds us that, some part of each day, we choose to look the other way.

Those suffering know, "there is a long drawn out pain, a slowly building wave of grief that begins at the bottom of the belly and climbs to the heart from which there is no escape." It cuts off the breath and wracks one's being. It is overwhelming and finally when over, it leaves us spent. Weakly we finish the sobs and rest, only to allow a fresh start and another pain. Death cuts into our joy, our pleasure with life, our love and our ability to be rational. We think it will never end … and it does not. It changes, but when after twenty years something reminds one of the child that never grew up, or the tenderness of grandmother's fragrance, we recall the love, not the pain. Death is a foundation for the living and loving of our lives; it is mulch for every additional experience. We give up the sharpness of original pain and "turn the event under" to wait for better control of our feelings and thoughts; and when that pain returns, it brings back the goodness gleaned by loving another so deeply. Memories become precious. Each death becomes as precious to relive as each birth, both unique in their own way. One blessed side of the coin is Life … and the admittance price is Death.

In the language of spirituality, we speak of the struggling inner parts of our nature as the *Dweller* and the *Angel*, neither perfect nor terrible. Consciousness is merely expanding. We gain consciousness as we walk our path. We do the blending throughout the experiences of each day. It is a process of gradual openness and caring that brings heart and mind together.

There can be a look in the eyes that says, *I am judging you,* just as there is a look that is compassionate. Long has it been known that the eyes are the *"windows of the Soul."* Remember, there is the *"evil* eye" technique or a way of using the energy from the eye as a tool to weaken as well as to energize. This is primarily making an attunement using a technique of focusing upon the acupuncture points with the *eye in a weakening manner.*

Christina Grof, well known for her Holotropic Breathwork, is a significant contributor to our understanding of the struggles we encounter as we seek to embrace our spirituality. Contributors also to the burgeoning field of Transpersonal Psychology, Christina authored with her husband, Stanislav Grof, *Spiritual Emergency: When Personal Transformation Becomes a Crisis* (1989), and her own book, *The Thirst for Wholeness: Attachment, Addiction, and the Spiritual Path (1994).* She writes clearly and is easily understood.

> Many of us are taught from earliest childhood to seek satisfaction or answers outside of our self…. At first these things appear to satisfy us; then, after a while, this desire for things turns against us, and it becomes an addiction.
>
> Then later on when I started working in the addiction field, I was surprised and delighted to find that therapists used many of the same ideas I worked with, but expressed them in somewhat different language. What I'm excited about now is being able to bring these two worlds together. I feel that the addiction world is already doing the kind of work that transpersonal psychology has been moving toward — bringing the spiritual dimension into psychology. I think that the transpersonal world could benefit a great deal from the grounded practical earthbound spirituality that's practiced in the recovering community.
>
> For instance, there are many who have been involved in spiritual practices that—as they say in AA—have their feet planted firmly in mid-air. They are interested in collecting experiences and moving out of this earthly realm into other realms. What I have most appreciated in the recovering community, is that it is a much-grounded daily practice, focused on bringing the spiritual experiences into everyday life. That is something that for me personally has meant a great deal.

There are many good approaches, and they all help us do a part of the work of building a higher consciousness. It is not just being "saintly"; it is an awareness of other dimensions and the experiences that can and often do occur in them. In this case we are examining a part of the Bardo path. We must in fact, get down and dirty as one struggles with the transformation practice. A mystic *knows* there is more because they have met the pain, and recognize it.

Prophets and priests, if they become a "mystic," often seem to depart from their worldly goals. It does not mean they become hermits, they do not, but they shift their views and warn us regarding the direction the collective is going. The priest follows the rules and tries to teach others to do the same; church officials want to enforce the church laws and dogma. Mystics want *to know* the will and ways of God for themselves; the purpose of their transformation is now directed toward that aim. *"To be in the world, but not of the world"* becomes the goal; to see *the error of the world, and love it anyway,* is the work of high consciousness.

We are to realize it serves the Divine to have it that way. We come to truly trust: The Creator created the plan and set it into action. To help the individuals who are ready for inner peace to find it, and to allow others to struggle ... the drama continues. In the quest for higher understanding, we even have to come to trust our own instincts regarding choices and events, impressions and knowings. We will not always have a mentor, so this inner sense of trust is ours to build (and it does grow as we do). As transforming moments happen to and for us, we can no longer hold the truth as it was; it becomes a larger Truth that is increasingly Cosmic in nature.

When someone goes too fast (youth in particular or immature souls), one tends either to become frightened or to retreat to a fundamental belief or guilt. The more adventurous one is, he or she may ask searching questions or seek out new ideas and other help. To do so, we must overcome the fear. Sometimes we must face offending the group consciousness with which one has identified. Greater importance is to be given to one's own boundaries. At times, this causes one to search for a new group. This may be spirit's way of moving one forward, but a sense of overwhelming doubt prevails. "*Spiritual emergencies or psychic emergencies*" are names we have given to these concerns. There are knowledgeable individuals who can wisely assist in these situations, and the mystic, familiar with such, is a good one to approach.

Something we must address here is the issue of drugs. They are a means of inducing mystical experiences. However, few, if any, healthy experiences are achieved as a result. Drugs, even acceptable medical drugs, can induce altered states of consciousness. Persons can be "drugged" out of their minds; this in no way brings about mystical experiences and can, in fact, be detrimental. There is an interesting and informative small book by H. (Torkom) Saraydarian entitled *The Fiery Carriage and Drugs*, which contains a powerful warning for us all:

> Drugs, at best, open a window to the astral plane. They break the astral world, a fantastic world full of glamorous, illusive colors and forms. No drug can elevate consciousness higher than the astral world. We know that the astral plane is the plane of delusions, and whoever is caught there cannot easily return into the light of reality. (p. 34)

There is a great deal of additional valuable information regarding the subject, as well as recovery from drug use to help the healing process. As maturity continues, the journey begins in earnest. All psychic workers, trainers, or healers need to be reasonably comfortable in their knowledge and experience when attempting to assist others. Few books properly cover all these topics, but it is a field to which more scrutiny is being directed. Someone who has made the journey becomes the best guide.

Many hesitate because the appearance is so similar to some touches of mental illness. Due to this similarity, unless someone has had experience of the psychical or mystical, it is very hard to understand and even harder to be comforting and supportive. All healers need to understand the psychic pain these little-understood situations cause.

As each one of us strives for the ever-developing sensitivity and love for humanity that we need, tender moments will arise. The perception of the Soul develops as we attune to life with all its experiences. In our self-defense, we begin our eternal quest for the God-Self to fortify and direct ourselves. As the God-Self comes forward in our individual life, it naturally flows outward into the world around us—ever loving, ever healing, and ever encouraging others to question, to search, and to attune to the Source Within themselves.

Let us look closely within our deeper nature and recognize every experience and every wise decision, every renunciation faced, every sacrifice made, every holy prayer sent, every book of spiritual thought studied, every soul-awakening action … has brought you and I to the experience of today. We realize we guide two selves at once: the physical and the spiritual. Moreover, it is necessary they parallel and support each other; these levels of us are intertwined in the journey. Each of us has an obligation, as we come to know our inner nature, to bring forward the highest and finest we can for the world around. We work not just for ourselves. It is not an obligation to the outside mundane world; it is an obligation to the God Within.

We must remember what we are attempting to do. Just as ice melts to be water, water heats to become steam, and steam evaporates to return to ether, we go through stages of change on our way to godliness. In embarking on this quest, we call down higher energies to be with us and to assist us to make the necessary changes so we can become that upon which we have set our heart.

In the respected work of Evelyn Underhill, she explains better than most the "dark night of the soul" that dedicated questers often experience:

> But the mystic, like other persons of genius, is (hu) man first and artist afterwards. We shall make a grave though common mistake if we forget and allow ourselves to be deflected from our study of his growth in personality by the wonder and interest of his art. Being,

not Doing, is the first aim of the mystic; and hence should be the first interest of the student of mysticism.

The most intense period of that great swing back into darkness which usually divides the 'first mystic life', or Illuminative Way, from the 'second mystic life', or Unitive Way, is generally a period of utter blankness and stagnation, so far as mystical activity is concerned. ... The self is tossed back from its hard-won point of vantage. Impotence, blankness, solitude are the epithets by which those immersed in this dark fire of purification describe their pains. It is this episode in the life-history of the mystic type to which we have now come. (*Mysticism* by Evelyn Underhill, pp 380-81)

An age-old formula is: we travel from orthonoia (mechanical behavior, or to keep straight,) to metanoia (to go beyond or higher than), through paranoia (a state in which the mind is deranged, taken apart and rearranged so that a more clear perceptive of reality might be experienced). Paranoia is a condition well understood by mystical and sacred traditions.

Spiritual disciplines are to ease the passage from a limited state of consciousness to a higher state of awareness. At beginning stages we use various practices to rid ourselves of old undesired habits and build a new framework for the new life we envision. Because many have not experienced metanoia, the role of paranoia is likewise not well understood in our culture. It is most often seen as an acerbated dead end, rather than a precondition to higher consciousness.

Evelyn Underhill suggests in *Mysticism*, that we look at the Dark Night (of the Soul), from two points of view:

> 1) we may see it as a psychologist, as a moment in the history of mental development, governed by the more or less mechanical laws which so conveniently explain to him the psychic life of man:
> 2) or with the mystic himself, we may see it in its spiritual aspect as contributing to the remaking of character, the growth of "the new man"; his transmutation in God" (p. 382).

The discomfort, confusion, and suffering in paranoia is due largely to the destruction of illusion or ego. Self-realized individuals understand the process and know that transformation (all three stages) becomes the pathway to enlightenment.

While such experiences are often confused with mental illness, as the appearances of psychotic incidences are quite similar, it is always wise to keep this in mind with an unknown situation and obey good mental health precautions. When an experienced individual shares with one in the midst of their own frightening experience, they have a depth of insight to offer. Working with others in spiritual emergencies allows one to learn by experience and provides some good and careful advice.

It seems that when the higher centers have been submitted to the continuous strain of a developed and illuminated life, then the accompanying periods of intense fervor, deep contemplation, visionary and auditory phenomena do their inner work. As we attempt to live in the midst of average modern-day life, the swings back into negative bouts seem almost unavoidable. Perhaps they are necessary wisdom points setting up our future transformation.

This psychological explanation must be adapted to fit most artistic and highly creative individuals. We can expect no less from spiritual persons, saints, or suffering servants of the Higher Way. In these moments of the shadow's "presence," one unfolds in the darkness; the once complete inner assurance is swept away and only blind stubbornness of the memory keeps the personality together. By holding on to gratitude for each "happening," especially the hard and not so pretty, we are progressing. To truly claim gratitude for each event, unkind and kind, losses and disappointments, as well as good and happy moments, we are becoming loyal, dependable, and worthy of trust of the higher ones—in spirit and in body. We are proving our dependability, a loyal member of the spiritual triad and trustworthy.

By releasing our pain over our unworthiness, over past hurts, over seeing our failures, we are lightening our burdens. We will have "reviews" of our past always; this is part of going forward into the light, if we want to call it thus. My musing about the pain of daily learning brought these thoughts. Ponder and write your own.

Pain is like a lingering fragrance, slight, ever present, breaking into flame from time to time. It lingers in the background like a dull sound until it bursts into full blast … taking many little bites, until we scream, leaving us no place to escape but to bare the anguish, until it hones us to a fine point. Eventually the heart can bleed no more.

We recall the not-so-great experiences and see how we could have responded more wisely, but failed to do so. Now we know, so now we do the correcting effort. Just as we build new habits, new attitudes, new awareness, we must expect to re-work errors, sorrows, when we see a higher way. We are only now achieving such through the image-making ability in the inner reality. Here, in the privacy of our own inner life, we do the healing work or enlist the aid of a trusted mentor. We release and let go, so we can go into higher reality without so much baggage.

In recent years, the American Psychiatric Association has approved Spiritual Emergency as a DSM-IV category in certain states, when this kind of help is needed. As a dedicated spiritual one, I would recommend that we be careful in choosing a counselor. Such a one does not have to be of the same tradition or viewpoint as your own, but they are not to damage your own soul either.

Choose carefully from the advice of others on your path, as to whom to expose yourself and your precious inner awareness. You want respect for your insights and regard for your journey. Remember, many see only a narrow path, not a broad one … thus, the very choosing of one with whom to "reflect" will take inner work, but do not give up. There are good counselors who work with an understanding of the Soul. Ask for referrals as you quest.

Spiritual Emergencies

As we journey into the mystical unknown, we are to be prepared for disappointing or confusing experiences. Of great importance for healers and teachers is to have an understanding of *Spiritual Emergencies*. While once called "psychic illnesses," the terms overlap as one scans the field. Warnings persist to discourage the "curious" and "weak hearted." The general idea is that if one cannot face unpleasant comments, they are not yet ready to move from "*milk*" to "*meat*," as said in scripture.

Kabalah, the mystical essence of Judaism, goes so far as to attempt to discourage people by discussing the dangers of heavy commitment to inner growth. It teaches that one out of four will receive enlightenment, one will turn back, one will become mentally imbalanced, and one will die ... such a warning truly serves to prohibit one from just "playing" with the teachings.

A spiritual emergency can be set into motion by any event, inner or outer, that wreaks havoc with one's "box." We each have a picture of "how it is" that we have gradually developed in our lifetime. It is usually somewhat like this:

– Our Beliefs (rather fixed as well) –

1. All good people go to heaven.
2. Politicians think of the people they serve, first.
3. All police are honest.

In Formation

Past – – – – – – – **Stable (fixed)**   **New Reality (more flexible)**
– – – – – **Future**

We are comfortable in our box until something more interesting comes along or something happens that does not fit. We may have a test or trial occurring and one day we cry "help, help." We get an unexpected experience. Let us say, an angel appears or a voice responds. Either of these could set off a psychic upset because it was outside our box; if we do not have a mediator, this "good, to some" experience can create an emergency. We suddenly *doubt* our rational mind and the *construct of our reality.*

Mentors or healers, ministers and counselors all need to know how to be of help in areas of special concern in our particular field.

The most common for many is *deja vu*, the momentary experience of thinking, "*I have done this before.*" Or "*I have seen this before,*" or some event about to off-center another. There is a respectful re-gard for this in psychic study, e.g., a replaying of a "prior-to-birth" memory which shows that one is as they should be in their spiritual journey.

One of the greatest "*opening or awakening*" experiences in the average life is emotional distress. Here, as spiritual emergencies make themselves known, we find certain pains in the case of physi-cal/emotional abuse or battering stress, as in trying to understand "why the attack," or such, when there is no simple answer.... And there are combinations of distress. Now, both physical and non-physical healing is needed, and trained healers are treasures.

Energy rushes often take one to the massage therapist. Similar to nervous leg syndrome in description, energy rushes are painful, scary, and keep us from sleep or rest. These often bring one to a physical therapist or healer to see how to resolve the uncomfortable feeling. We wonder: Is it a warning of something more wrong? Is this an unexpected happening of a psychic sort? A psychic open-ing, whether simple or complex, can occur as easily as sitting with another and picking up uncomfortable emotions or fears; or one can be "sitting with another and taking on their physical discom-fort," or receiving impressions as clear as "knowing what they are going to say next."

These are not dangerous, but unsettling when not understood. On the other hand, one finds this can be a problem, if they do not have a grasp of how easily personal boundaries can be crossed, even accidentally. Boundaries can be violated regularly, and when the most obvious ones are not well understood, they can be frightening.

The awakening of the "kundalini" can involve a unique ex-perience of body tremors, tears, sounds, and actions quite unlike one's normal behavior. Physical body phenomena are natural, even though they seem unnatural, as the experience of kundalini consists of some unfamiliar body movements or actions. These experiences can be quite scary if not ever experienced before, as the etheric body becomes over-stimulated and stirs in ways one has never experienced before. Mayans claim they gave the word to the Hindus and claim it means "ku," meaning "the god within form." *The New Dictionary of Spiritual Thought* defines kundalini as "the evolutionary force within humanity" … literally, the "serpentine power," defined as an electric, fiery, occult, or fohatic power. Some part of this primal energy of the universe lies coiled, as potential, at the base of the human spine.

When this energy flows upward through the body to the brain, it stimulates the etheric centers, which is sometimes associated with the state of enlightenment. As this powerful spiritual energy awakens from dormancy, it generally rises gradually along the spine, activating the chakras, igniting change, stimulating life activity. The process of conscious spiritual evolution awakens with this mystical force, which leads toward final union with the Divine. Enclosed and at work in matter, the feminine energy blends with the masculine in unique ways—the kundalini is stimulated, and together they facilitate its ascent. There is little known or understood about the unique development the psychological nature undergoes when an active kundalini arises.

Thus only a few, other than knowledgeable spiritual students, can be of help in this type of spiritual emergency or urgency. Manners of assisting this behavior are limited, but assistance with the process is becoming more available. This "transpersonal energy" lies dormant in all humans and is designed to help us evolve. When one does not understand the reactions of one's own body, the experience can become scary, but remember, this is a natural energy and is a signal that a natural process has begun and one needs guidance.

Another "spiritual experience" that has been recognized in the last fifty or sixty years and which can be both a real emergency and an enlightening one, is the "near-death experience." Of course, a real emergency opens the door to such an experience. The danger of nearing one's death may trigger an inner experience of meeting a light being. Such a powerful experience frequently changes one's perception of the nature of physical reality. Many times an NDE, as they are called, is accompanied with a revelation of important information or a remembrance of making a choice of whether to return or not. This experience usually ushers in a new stage of consciousness. Scientists have validated similar type of happenings.

A variety of NDE happenings, with each transforming one's picture of life in the after-world, are happening; the lasting effect is that people live their physical life differently. The NDE is a near relative to the Out-of-Body experience in which one becomes aware of differing surroundings and, while thinking something dangerous is happening, one unexpectedly comes to the realization one is without his or her body. Most often, this occurs by looking down and seeing one's body lying on the bed. With these types of experiences, the first fear one must face is that of mental derangement or of a psychic break.

Dr. Eben Alexander, who has spent more than twenty years in academic neurosurgery, including almost fifteen years on the faculty at Harvard Medical School, had a profound experience of watching his own cerebral cortex shut down. His book, *Proof of Heaven: A Neurosurgeon's Journey Through the Afterlife,* was published in October 2012.

Reading a review of this book, I was impressed with the explanation Dr. Alexander gives of the way he observed his brain activity as it shut down. It reminded me of the explanation given in *My Stroke of Luck* by Jill Bolte Taylor, Ph.D. and her observations surrounding her stroke. It is wonderful to have such persons share their experiences with us. *Proof of Heaven* by Dr. Alexander is a wonderful confirmation of Near-Death-Experiences and their validity. We have had heard enough of these kinds of experiences to confirm that there is something more than we had realized happening here on Earth, and such assurances of ongoing life is a giant comfort. We recall the important work of Dr. Raymond Moody when he published *Life after Life* and how it resounded throughout our culture. It produced an almost audible sigh of relief.

On certain occasions, individuals will have some other types of experiences with a former embodied being that one knows is now in the non-physical reality or meeting someone known as a ghost or spirit. This is called "meeting a discarnate" or seeing or sensing a deceased person. Such stories and experiences attract a lot of attention in the spiritualist community. The Spiritualist Church began in the USA with the Fox Sisters (March 31, 1848), who developed a code of knocking that proved they had contacted an unknown something or another reality.

The well-known story of the Fox Sisters had created excitement and strengthened an interest in afterlife. When interest waned in the USA, spiritualism grew rapidly in England and the British Isles where there were many older towns and establishments. Later, another wave of interest returned Spiritualism to the USA, and the interest in survival after death remains of high interest.

Some persons experience visions or mind pictures, either awake, or in meditation. These are a part of the visionary human make-up, usually when in an altered state of consciousness or any time or place the energy can combine to trigger a mental picture in an individual who is rather visionary. Such persons may develop a reputation as a visionary, a term attached to the religious especially. Sometimes a vision occurs and it is only recognized later. Visionary dreams are more common and they provide us a framework to understand the visionary experience better. Altered states of consciousness have proven that it is possible for events to occur or be revealed out of the usual workings of time and place.

Similar experiences bear witness to the appearances of angels. These spiritual beings that make contact with humans, or provide information regarding our well-being or the well-being of others, are another kind of phenomena that can occur. Historically angels have been with humanity through the ages as recorded in scriptures of most all faiths. As such, life in other dimensions has aroused great interest.

We also see other information in the news regarding aliens, the study of unidentified lights, space ships, vehicles, and other kinds of beings as well as angels. Interest in these things is high and has drawn much attention in the last several decades. It is understood that our planet supports many other life forms than our own, some of which living on dimensions we cannot yet see or perceive. Interest is high these days regarding space visitors, sometimes called meta-terrestrials, and extra-terrestrials, who may be visiting Earth, and this is part of becoming open to outside or unexpected phenomena.

Women seem to be more sensitive to spiritual emergencies than the average male. Perhaps this is because they are subject to more changes and periods of shifting change in their body during pregnancy and childbirth. They experience a wider range of physical periods within a normal lifetime than males and this may contribute to their strong sensitivity. Emotional and bodily changes, such as the many shifts from maiden to mother, may play a part in the emotional flexibility changes women experience. This flexibility may allow them to more easily open to new filaments of consciousness, while a certain amount of psychic distress often accompanies these experiences.

While often "poo-pooed," most women experience varying degrees of change due to hormonal imbalances, and mood swings are common during these months. Often the birth of a child produces a psychic experience in one of the parents or both. Many mothers actually do open psychically during pregnancy; fathers may, as well. For many there is a pure ecstasy accompanying the pain of the arrival of a child. Love consumes the inner Self during the birth experience, and it often seems the new state of consciousness can be stimulated easily.

We often do not understand some major changes that happen in the mother's newly awakened state. Fathers can have triggered experiences as well at this delicate time in life. In addition, surgery, serious injury, or some type of medical emergency can trigger distress that often shows itself as shock, distorted feelings and unnatural fears. Medication can combine poorly with some difficulties, even as care is given. Any and all of these experiences can trigger spiritual emergencies.

Similarly great **losses, such as divorce, the taking away of one's children, or losing** one's sense of wellbeing is such a tragic loss that it can upset one's view of life. A disturbed sense of self may result in the need for specific care or counseling to provide a dependable support to walk with during such a time. Assistance may help them regain their stability or balance to continue living in a renewed way.

Seen as a trial or a test, the "Dark Night of the Soul" can be another trying time in the life of one deeply involved in spirituality. We may find ourselves cut off from the normal support system, friends or spirit helpers. The loneliness is miserable and one suffers much isolation in this kind of spiritual test. Even as one reaches out, they cannot seem to connect with the help they need, either on this plane or in spirit. One must learn that he or she can stand alone with his or her own strength of character; it is part of the growth process and is very emotionally painful.

The discovery of a "possession entity" or the finding of an attachment within your nonphysical body can trigger other spiritual emergencies. Certain conditions, such as these, require a capable psychic worker in order to be of assistance to the troubled one. These generally occur when the involved individual has experienced some situations making it possible for discarnates or entities to attach themselves to him or her. In some rare cases, the attached entity will fight the builder of the body for control over his physical, emotional and mental bodies and can at times achieve it. Other entities may have no desire to hurt or hinder, but attach themselves to another with a desire to help or because of their love or need to be loved. Either and all of these conditions result in weakening the physical person. One should consult an exorcist or person knowledgeable in psychography or another specific technique.

Spiritual emergencies or psychic distress is always present in losses of an extreme magnitude. It is beneficial for anyone to have some specific training in the steps of death and dying as these can be applied to any great loss. A great loss is quite similar to death in many ways and just as pain-filled. One needs a dependable support to walk with them during this time to help regain balance. In addition, few realize the psychic injury often done to an infant prior to birth by the attitudes and emotions of persons close to the pregnant mother. With no ego to protect baby, many happenings imprint the fetus and need healing later in life. An understanding of this will be more well-understood as consciousness expands and one explores one's past-life or prenatal life.

Obligations become complicated when vows are taken, whether serious or not. We make vows to a superior power, civil or spiritual, to witness or affirm the value of what is spoken. These registered upon us spiritually, whether made either to society or to God. An oath explicitly states to whom one's loyalty belongs and binds the participating individual to the role one is committing his or her self to fulfill. To add God's name makes an oath stronger and more ethically binding; this is to make stronger the commitment the individual is making.

Therefore taking an oath cannot or should not be taken lightly. The soul remembers to whom it makes pledges. The law of karma applies in a more binding way whenever the name of God is included. Likewise, vows can be to one individual or to a group, but vows are binding until the intensity or sincerity of the commitment is completed.

- Vows are quite likely to invoke God as a witness. Vows between individuals are entered into with the law of karma standing as a third party to the arrangement. Marriage vows are an example.

- A Vow of Poverty has a spiritual meaning—"*gives all and expects nothing*"—a promise taken by those who choose to own no material property. One claims no worth other than the true value of one's own Soul. A monk or hermit—male or female—is an example of someone who seeks a state of absolute non-attachment.

- Poverty of Abundance needs to be included here, as well … "*for what does it profit a man if he loses his soul?*" The Christ asks this question in our hearts, even today. We must figure out "what is worth what" to our overall life journey. Do we want material riches? Can we grow into being one who establishes his or her independence from the value systems around us? These values are not just about money; they can be for fame, or doing things for reputation or acceptance. Many make critical decisions about time or talent, then find themselves spending their lives in activities that leave them unfulfilled. Poverty of Abundance addresses this illness of the soul; when the commitment in life is to fame or false values, we may not realize our sorrow until late in life.

- A subordinate takes a Vow of Obedience in spiritual life in return for initiation or admittance into a desired tradition or lineage. This pledge is binding upon the chela and the initiator until both agree to dissolve the oath or when spiritual development of the "younger" has developed to a degree that both realize through guidance or higher consciousness the time for release has come. Many continue to respectfully love and obey long after the formal need for allegiance has passed. The initiator carries the spiritual responsibility for the chela's development and answers to the inner world while the vow is intact. The Law of Karma charges the wiser one for errors in instruction that the chela follows. The compliant chela remains free from error.

- Various vows or commitments spoken with intensity and fervor are difficult to resolve: celibacy, poverty, service, etc. When the commitments are not resolved in the life in which they are made, they can be carried forward until a lifetime when such can be fulfilled.

- **Group Vows** are those to a country, lodge, or organization and are binding to both the group mind and the individual. Here the commitment is to the cause one is to serve. The passion with which one commits his or her self matters, as does the value the group mind puts on the vow. Either this makes the vow a blessing or it does not. It can be a blessing to both. Remember promises, commitments and debts can be to business, society, individuals and to one's self as well as to an authority. Certainly, the dignitary has vows to fulfill regarding right use of power in the name of state, church, or corporations etc.

In the Bible we are discouraged from making oaths and vows due to the realization that most do not know what challenges or changes the future may bring. Later they may not satisfy the vow, or even want to. One may be a part of a formal agreement or treaty between individuals, or even countries to make certain actions. Individuals may be committing themselves to a bonded circumstance. Examples are friendship pacts, covenants, treaties, or formal agreements to keep faith with one another. The one making the vow may grow and change his or her picture of life in some manner not realized at the time of the vow. The "intent" is the glue that is to be dissolved either presently or in a later life.

After such attention to vows, and pacts, it is important to look at the seriousness of a curse, again established by the use of personal power or energy.

- **A Curse** can be directed toward a single person or to a group. It is the conscious projection of negative energy toward another or others. Curses are more effective against those who have an underlying belief in such acts, as they have opened themselves by belief. Such acts are especially harmful when accompanied by destructive words, thoughts, or visualization. Spiritual laws warn about the use of destructive or harmful intent against another, which incurs karma for consciously setting harm into motion. One who does so damages one's own energy field and will attract a return of the same energy to his or herself.

In Christian teachings, it is written, *"Seek ye first the kingdom of God, and his righteousness; and all these things shall be given unto you"* (Matthew 6:33).

To seek the kingdom of God or Higher Consciousness one must be willing to become a seeker by aligning one's inner values to high priorities. The seeker's dedication pulls on the Soul energy available to oneself to aid him/her. In addition, the seeker receives blessings that are made available to those who commit themselves. This does not apply to denominational changes because these are considered "the natural growth of one's spiritual path." One in this circumstance is strengthening the dedication one has to his or her personal *path of initiation*.

The mystic knows to accept painful moments in their walk, for these are a part of the natural growth process, but they know also that, to write or talk too much about their challenges, can be an obstacle to others. No one wants to be a hindrance to another or to keep another from embracing their personal walk. This idea suggests discernment on the part of the one who seeks to share.

It is part of the "feminine nature of the senses" to be able to hold two points of view at the same time. We can be intrigued by something and scared of it at the same time. This often causes others to think *"one can't make up their mind,"* when it is really that both have value to us. Contemplation over time will ultimately lead to the wiser choice, recognizing that the essence of everything is Sacred, but the expression of everything is not. He or she of the Christ or of the Holy Consciousness looks for the sacred—beyond good and evil, beyond duality—in the midst of everyday life.

Master Morya of the Agni Yoga teachings presents a challenge by introducing the question:

> When have you become less through sacrificing? By making yourself sacred? Nothing is sacred, except what we make sacred.

Agni Yoga or Ethical Living is a rather new pathway that comes from a blend of Christianity and Buddhism. Considered "new age," this path is not physical like Hatha, but places value on "fire and light," the path of purification. A series of themes and virtues (rather than rigid dogma) are adopted to build an ethical life.

The writings were transmitted through the Russian Christian mystic, Helena Roerich. Few teachers are available in the U.S.A. because the first translations are very difficult to follow; however, a larger following is producing more instructors.

Torkom Saraydarian (1917–1997) is the best known and his written material is excellent. A dedicated practitioner of Master Morya and Agni Yoga, his work is readily available. As an Esoteric Christian, I consider this my path. One advantage to this path is that it can be practiced with the religion of one's choice or without a religious commitment. It fits well with the independent nature of many in today's society. The goal is to make your character sacred and offer yourself to the higher reality.

Sacrifice is derived from the Latin words *sacer*, meaning sacred, and *facere*, meaning, "to make." These words form the foundation for our term *sacrifice* that means, "to make sacred." The term comes from the Latin word spelled "*saq*," meaning a bond, a power, a restriction, or a commitment. It is the intent we make as we charge something with our life force or life-giving energy, for we are giving it a value that comes from our own self. A commitment is a restriction on what we call freedom. When we make something sacred, we rein ourselves in, we get into focus, we charge an object with some specific kind of energy with which we intend to charge our life, an article or an intended action such as sacrament, i.e., baptism, communion etc.

This can be the blessing of a rosary or any object. When we take an article and bless it with the intent to make it sacred, we are charging it with a particular kind of energy; we invest this energy to stay with the article and support the one to whom we give the article on his/her journey; now we call it a *sacred item*. We bind our energy both of intent and of blessing to the article. When we make ourselves sacred, we are binding ourselves to purification, dedication and focus, both in keeping to our intent, and the right use of our life energy in keeping with its designated purpose.

When we come to understand "sacrifice" as "to make sacred," we begin to understand all areas of our life can be made sacred. The wisdom teachings tell us that each kingdom—mineral, plant, animal, as well as humanity—is in the process of sacrificing itself to the higher. Let us look at this in a simple way:

> *Minerals are broken down and absorbed (sacrifice themselves) for the benefit of the plants. They, in fact, feed (are absorbed by) the plant kingdom, the birds, insects … even people help them in becoming a "higher vibration."*
>
> *The plant kingdom then feeds or is broken down by the animal kingdom (including humans) for food. Whatever a higher kingdom absorbs is uplifted to the higher vibration.*
>
> *The animal kingdom absorbs or eats the plants or weaker animals to transform them to energy; whatever is taken into the higher body can then vibrate at that level of consciousness, and through the sacrifice of the lower, it has earned the right to do so.*
>
> *This is where we so often hear: the little animal becomes a wolf, the wolf becomes a wild dog and then the dog becomes a German Shepherd, a protector and friend of humanity … it is a concept of sacrificial lives.*
>
> *The minerals serve the plant kingdom; the plants serve the animals, the animals serve the humans and the humans are learning to serve "holy ones or the higher kingdoms, angels, spiritual teachers" etc….*

This is ageless wisdom … you do not just kill the carrot; you help it on its way. If your consciousness is taking it with respect and appreciation, you are helping the younger kingdoms to evolve. This is what prayer is about in a simplified way. Native traditions have always recognized this and now we are. The point is to recognize the power of the divine invested in our nature and come to appreciate whatever life is serving us.

In the very near future, the fifth kingdom is to emerge. That is what the One Humanity concept is to fulfill. The Kingdom of

Souls, as it is known, is to emerge upon earth; the Bible uses the term "Kingdom of God."

The human kingdom is to give itself to the will of Spirit. Now change the word *absorbs* to **serve**, and this becomes easier to grasp. We are making sacred our lives as a way to evolve and to render respect, love and appreciation to the Higher for the gift of life. In the Christian tradition, we are told, "to serve one another" and this is why.

Now we can see that "sacrifice ... to make sacred" has a far greater meaning than usually understood; it is an important thought to contemplate. This is the reasoning behind the warnings against oaths or vows, etc.; they often have to be worked out in later lives when not completed in the original lifetime when we made the commitment. We now can expand these concepts into other sacrificial understandings.

We are learning to think in terms of one life, the One great life of the Soul. We are becoming aware of how we can contribute to the life of the Soul (who is really our self). We hope to live our life of this lifetime wisely. Each lifetime offers our soul opportunities to learn different lessons and have chances for greater refinement or higher awareness; rarely can one become "perfected" in any one lifetime or opportunity.

Perfected ... Not Perfect

Misguided thoughts about mystics confuse humanity about the nature of initiates or disciples. People have come to think they are all to be *"perfect."* That is not true to the wiser teachings. The Bible verse *"as my father in heaven is perfect"* is not esoteric. The goal is "perfection," to purify and perfect the possibilities of our own nature (all that exists inside our ring-pass-not). As a Soul we have acquired raw materials to refine; we are to transform the crude character, self-centered as we are, into a gracious piece of art. The perfection of our nature is to make it sacred.

A lovely therapist shared the following with me some years ago and I always remember it when I think of walking the path. Human beings are not the only creature that has to change repeatedly to satisfy its transformational impulse.

> *There is a remarkably unattractive insect whose gills force it to live in water for one to five years. Twelve or more times it sheds its skin; each time it remains water bound.*
>
> *Eventually it crawls from the muddy water to the top of a reed or up on rock. At last, after the final shedding, what it is to be has come forth.*
>
> *Emerging with a long slender body and gauze-like, iridescent wings, it is the beautiful dragonfly. A completely new life-style is now possible. It breathes air, feels the sun's worth and flies.*
>
> *This graceful flyer comes from the ugliest of bug; repeatedly it sloughs off the outer armor that is no longer appropriate. It then needs to pull itself out of the mud and water to a new life. Unless it does, it cannot use the power within. Had the dragonfly tried to cling to the old limitations; if it had refused growth and change, if it had waited for someone else to free it, it would never have emerged to fulfill the promises of its birth.*
>
> *Until we move beyond that which keeps us mud bound and waterlogged—until we lay claim to the creative life force within – until we honor our life experiences and patterns –we cannot fly free!*
>
> *Life Energy is always with us. It ultimately comes from the Universal Spirit, the Source. Life Energy is there for us when we open ourselves to receiving it. It calls for a heightened awareness of the interconnectedness of all life and represents our capacity to take responsibility for our growth and evolvement. The use of Life Energy can make for the magnificent work of transforming self and humanity.*

Disciples can be working within spiritual traditions and not be mystics; initiates can be living their faith; becoming a mystic is not their goal. The goal of all on the path is perfection, but mystics more acutely seek to "know" God in an intimate personal relationship. They want experiences in the other dimensions that witnesses to a more personal scheme of things than most. That is the major difference; one can be a disciple or an initiate and not have awareness of their inner life. The mystic does, at least to a certain degree. He or she has tasted personal love with the Divine … and rejoices living in this reality.

"To be perfect" each of us would be measured against the same model, as we think of a master or holy one, with each of us measured to that one. Thus, each of us would be exactly alike. Some have tried to use Master Jesus in this way; if so, one would have to pass through the tests, trials, and circumstances, the same as Jesus. Since we do not live under the same conditions as Jesus, our tests are now within our setting; we do not have the same society or eat the same food, walk the roadways, etc. In these modern times, our tests are also "physiological," in that we have to contend with a different environment as the collective mind of humankind creates new experiences and challenges for us. Since humanity is continuously evolving, humanity will continue to have greater capacities with which to meet its challenges.

Ethical principles and spiritual laws still apply, but how we understand them or how we apply them or penetrate to their truth is different. We could think of these as the esoteric meaning of the Ten Commandments, or of the Sermon on the Mount. These are concepts that have led the Master's disciples for centuries. We attempt to glean the deepest meaning possible to these words; we then attempt to apply our understanding to our life as wisely as possible. These teachings still have relevance, but now we quest for the deeper or underlying meaning that will help us live with the most integrity possible. These requirements produce new and different effects than when we originally heard them. When we are less mature, the requirements are easier when they can be understood literally. However, as we advance, so do the expectations and demands on initiates. We are to learn to live "up" to our own higher awareness.

The earliest meaning of *"be ye perfect"* was *"be ye perfected"* and this is still the goal for all holy ones or those who hope to achieve initiation at this time, as well as all humanity in due time. We are to take the raw materials of our nature and refine them into *"perfection"*… the best combination of potentials we can make of them.

Coming to understand occult studies, such as The Rays, Astrology, Graphology, or any other so-called *study*, are merely tools to help us figure out what makes ourselves *"tick."*

We are to discover the ingredients we contain and perfect them. An example is: We discover we have lots of will and make of it a great strength. We can persist, endure, and at last use our will power in a very strong manner, but at first, it owns us. To bring "will" for example, to perfection, we must also learn self-restraint. To use our own will power to restrain the force we have developed is the rest of the test. We must be equally capable in either the use of will or self-restraint when needed.

Self-restraint is a huge lesson for humanity as we reach for its higher nature. We need to become aware of what exists in the many levels of the inner world. The astral world is a reflection of wishes, desires and feelings as well as conflicting thoughts generated by humankind since the beginning of time. Humanity began as a primitive animal seeking to become more. This creature had all the instinctual capabilities of the animal-self, with additional levels of mind ready to start development.

This creature, called a humanoid, was ready to begin the journey of refinement. It was *"made in the image and likeness"* of the Creator, but could not utilize its creative potential wisely as it was. Therefore, it received growth opportunities and choices. In Ancient Wisdom, we are taught that in the beginning the first evolving animal-humans did not have the developed brain that could carry the *"mind" charge* until it was touched three times. Twice more it had to be touched by this energy before the evolution of the highly developed *animal-human* could adapt its instinctual unconscious to the new influence so that it could now cope with the implant of *mind potential.*

The powerful insertion was too strong until the physical instrument could be refined. It had a crude brain as a physical organ to build upon; we must be aware the mind and brain are different. The brain is the instrument; the Mind is the translator of the frequencies used by the brain. Both are still evolving. Earlier we reviewed how the mind has mastered the three brains that exist today, and how now humanity is evolving yet another. Remember this as we speak of mysticism. The work of the mystic-to-be is to sensitize his or her brain capacity to accept the vibration of Divine Mind in an increasingly perfect way.

In *The Mozart Effect*, Don Campbell, founder of the Institute of Music, Health, and Education (I consider him a friend, and he is excellent in all endeavors), lists the benefits of using your voice to enhance mood and memory. He says that all forms of vocalization, including singing, chanting, yodeling, humming, reciting poetry, and simply talking can be therapeutic. "Nothing *rivals toning*," he concludes. The word *toning* goes back to the fourteenth century, and means "to make sounds with elongated vowels for extended periods." *Ah, ou* (as in *soup*), *ee, ay, oh,* and *om* are examples of toning sounds.

Campbell writes that when people tone on a regular basis for five minutes a day:

> I have witnessed thousands of people relax into their voices, become more centered in their bodies, release fear and other emotions, and free themselves from physical pain ... I have seen many people apply toning in practical ways, from relaxing before a dreaded test, to eliminating symptoms of tinnitus or migraine headaches. Toning has been effective in relieving insomnia and breath, reducing the heart rate, and imparting a general sense of well-being.

Campbell reports that in his experience certain sounds tend to have certain effects on the body and emotions:

Ahhh   immediately evokes a relaxation response

Ee or *ay*   is the most stimulating of vowel sounds, helps with concentration, releasing pain and anger

Oh or *om*   considered the richest of sounds; can warm skin temperature and relax muscle tension

Try toning for five minutes a day for two weeks to see if this is of help to you (especially recommended to those desirous of a mystical mind!).

Here is a printout of the Oms that we use that we've found pleasing to work with. Rev. Roberta Wilkes wrote the music for us. The line is usually repeated four or five times. Roberta has served years as our music director and musician for other spiritual activities.

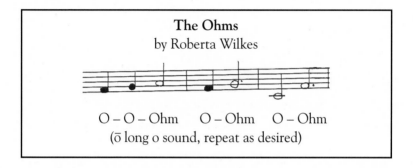

The Ohms
by Roberta Wilkes

O – O – Ohm   O – Ohm   O – Ohm
(ō long o sound, repeat as desired)

Also be aware, there are old hymns that are very mystical that we should learn, hum, and sing like affirmations. You may already be familiar with them, but if not, these might remind you: *"Be Still and Know"* and *"Trust and Obey."* You may know others but have never thought to use them in this way.

> *In a similar way, humming can also make a positive difference in mood and memory. Mozart hummed as he composed. Children hum when they are happy. Adults often hum tunes that go through their minds, lifting their spirits and tuning their mind. Consciously focus on humming during the day. As the sound activates your brain, you will feel more alive and your brain will feel more tuned in to the moment.*
>
> —*Change Your Brain, Change Your Life*
> by Daniel G. Amen, M.D., pp. 204-05

SEVEN

Restraint Versus Gratification

HAVE YOU EVER CONSIDERED GOD'S SELF-RESTRAINT? Having struggled with my own self-restraint, knowing my personality, and how little ability each of us have at times, we pause to observe what one human does to another, seemingly over the centuries without interference. Think how patient the Creator must be to allow Divine Law to let the Law of Karma administer itself. In our humanness, we struggle to wait nine months for a fetus to develop; what does it mean for Creator to wait thousands of years for humanity to mature? This is real self- restraint.

We can contrast self-restraint to instant gratification. We strive to have our wishes and desires instantaneously granted. It seldom happens in the way we desire. Nevertheless, to progress on our path, we also must have self-restraint. We must learn to ponder as we learn patience. Pondering is turning a thought over repeatedly in the mental mechanism to see how it appears from various angles. The underdeveloped kind of human being begins to produce emotions and actions that are self-serving and crude; today we speak of them as *"involutionary"* energies. They were the best energies one could produce in past times, and yet today humanity has evolved into a much more wise type of being. Insight, pondering, patience, and trust lead to self-restraint.

Just as the earliest humanoid had to have several touches of the fiery mind to prepare it to function within such energies, likewise, we may have to have several profound and difficult interactions with this Divine Mind to move from adolescent to adult. It seems most probable that, as we see some individuals move easily to adulthood and others, less mature, "suffer" to achieve maturity of mind, humanity's collective will have to do likewise.

Using Master Jesus as an example of a mystical teacher, we strive to be the disciple learning how to build a relationship to the higher world. We attempt to find our way amidst the wordiness of scripture, commentaries, mentors, and our own perceptions. All of our spiritual endeavors focus upon our need to perceive God's Presence in the immediacy of the present moment, as we see in John 14, verses 26 & 27:

> But the Comforter, the Holy Spirit, whom my father will send in my name, will teach you everything.... Peace I leave with you; my own peace I give you, not as the world gives, I give to you. Let not your heart be troubled and do not be afraid.

Just as we have a physical heritage, we have a spiritual lineage. Just as we respect the parents, family and karma of our physical lineage or DNA, we are to offer regards for our spiritual care and our spiritual family. Somehow our inner awareness awakened; some way we earned spiritual care, direction, and exposure. We remember the commandment, *"to honor thy father and mother,"* and see how it can apply to those who parent our spiritual life. We see this in reference to calling priests *"father"* and congregations *"sister,"* subtle remnants of the truth of heritage.

Our spiritual lineage reaches from Gnostics of the past to the disciples of today through various avenues. Most Christians who come to a Gnostic perspective do so through the lineage of Christ Jesus, knowing him as a Kabalistic Mystic who left behind a set of teachings. Some versions are open to the public through the traditional teachings of the earlier organized church. The various orthodox and catholic branches preserved the more mystical meanings. Fortunately, for us today, Esoteric and/or Mystical Christianity has become more openly discussed.

Many do not understand, especially in the U.S.A., that there is anywhere between seventeen and twenty-two other Catholic Churches besides the Roman Catholic actively doing their work throughout the world. Many are small chapels and churches in the U.S.A, of which the Roman Church is the most fundamentalist. As more open acceptance of esoteric teachings and additional material previously preserved in underground teachings comes to the surface, the group mind is enriched.

By the persistence of humanity's quest, these teachings continue to emerge in a more private manner. This more veiled tradition, emerging now along with this quiet work, is the *Sophianic*. By grace, both the Esoteric and Sophianic remain hidden here and there. They wait like treasures for us to search out when we are ready; and eventually persistent ones of a more mystical bent will find them.

One set of the Gnostic writings I have studied and enjoyed is the Gospel of St. Thomas. Verse #22 reads:

> Jesus saw infants being suckled. He said to his disciples, "*These infants being suckled are like those who enter the kingdom.*"
> They said to him, "*Shall we then, as children, enter the kingdom?*"
> Jesus said to them, "*When you make the two one, and when you make the inside like the outside and the outside like the inside, and the above like the below, and when you make the male and the female one and the same, so that the male be not male nor female, and when you fashion eyes in place of an eye, and a hand in place of a hand, and a foot in place of a foot, and a likeness in place of likeness, then you will enter (the kingdom).*"
> (Gnostic Gospel of St. Thomas by Tau Malachi)

In response to these words preserved by the Gnostics, I have held these words in contemplation and formulated a personal response. Here is what I made of this:

> *Make the duality within yourself one, and make the inside be your outside life; the outside life is to perfectly reflect the inside, and the "above" (the soul) to become our everyday consciousness. The active and the receptive become one and the same: the active is no*

longer the active and the receptive is no longer the receptive. When you fashion inner eyes instead of the viewpoint of the ordinary human, and when the hands are used in service and tending, and the foot walks its true path and not the ways of the world, then our likeness as a Soul becomes the real likeness, and then we can enter the kingdom of God (of Souls).

Fascinated by these wisdom words, we study them to perceive the wisdom locked within. The mystic either perceives the meaning or discovers other thoughts that awaken from the inner nature. These values become a part of ourselves as we hold them to be precious, and thankful that someone shared their treasure with us. Now you and I can have the good karma of living by such principles, and when ready, sharing them with others. We have to earn the right to hear the teachings, and take the opportunity to share them.

This regard for wisdom, and for wisdom carriers, affects your karmic pattern into infinity. Good karma means riches of awareness can be yours. Doors will open; ways will come in this life and others. Each is to respect how the teachings come to us, and to hold the lineage (of which one is a part) in high regard. Be conscientious. Your time will come and you will be able to pass on your gift to another. You are discovering a kind of grace. Do not cast it before swine.

Blessed by Grace

We have little understanding of grace; it is a great and mysterious subject. It is, indeed, a kind of soothing liquid poured out upon us. Stories of saints tell us that there is more to life than karma. We may or may not understand or even believe the tales we hear, but they do make us wonder. We hear of grace—the grace of the higher worlds that moves to meet and affect human life. When we study the history of humanity's journey, we discover it has been a very painful process. The miraculous stories in the lives of some reveal that another movement takes place as well: it is God's search for the hearts of humankind.

The clever or learned have active brains and knowledge of books. But books, to one lacking the inner sight, are as spectacles behind which there are no eyes."

— Sadhu Vaswani, Krishna devotee

As we ponder the power of Grace with all its meanings, we confuse it with the importance of an honorable life style and goodness. If we do not feel we are good, we tend to believe grace is not there for us. The influence of a particular ethic or culture—even the culture of an office—influences those who come into its midst.

Grace likewise has its impact. While hard to define, grace is commonly considered to be an outpouring of higher energy or spiritual power that lifts the consciousness into new and less-restricted awareness. It is important to realize that we do not necessarily earn it; that is why it is taught to be a gift from God. The word "graceful" comes from a certain freedom from rigidity that a particular individual may seem to have. The term likewise comes to mind when a particular **grace-filled** moment brings an unknown bounty to flow into our lives in such a manner as to **bless and set us free.** There are two points we must consider as we follow the teachings: first, *what is grace,* and secondly, **can we recognize it?**

"Let not your heart be troubled, neither let it be afraid." As seekers, we become aware we are in a process of building trust. Grace is a response to that trust. Through the power of grace, we will be drawn into a trusting relationship with the higher world. As we learn to see it work clearly and often enough in and through our daily lives, we come to rest in trust/peace. This is the promised peace of one's spiritual walk.

We build a faith—not a belief, but a trust—in which we sense a certain kind of security, assuring us the Universe loves us.

Grace arises from the fact that God, or the Universe, has already freely chosen to associate humanity to His/Her Self. This act of sharing in the bounty of the Divine is grace. It brings a flow of energies, qualities, and events into our open heart/mind that we can hardly imagine. It sets humanity free from the limitation of humanness.

Gratitude is one of the first steps in shifting from a worldly view of life to a more expanded or spiritual perspective. Responding with gratitude to everything—whether our personality likes what is happening or not—is taught as a beginning step. Each of us has to find a way to deal with this guideline. As we face it, we begin to tap into this stream. In the beginning, we tend to turn it off and on, but eventually one just keeps producing the flow of gratitude from within.

Saints are the revealers of the Spirit—the builders on Earth of the kingdom of Light and Love. The world around us is struggling through the midst of miasma or distortion. The consciousness of humanity is evolving from a primitive state, having emerged out of the animal kingdom and having formed the new kingdom of humanity. There is violence in this kingdom, but the Kingdom of Souls is on its way.

Torkom Saraydarian says,

> Grace is the essence, the content of the chalice. It is your savings account, accumulated throughout centuries … it is yours; it is paid from your savings account at the right time and in the right place." (*Becoming One's Self*, pp. 68-69)

Grace is an outpouring of spiritual power that frees from restriction and lifts the consciousness into a new state of awareness. While we cannot make grace happen, we can embrace certain qualities—love, freedom, beauty, and joy—to invoke grace. This shift of consciousness lets us experience the higher/lighter vibrations that dissolve the restriction of the lower reality. This shift precipitates droplets of fiery substance from the higher planes. These droplets act upon the underlying levels of our self to burn away some of the distortion we find within.

We cannot ever really say just how this comes about: we call this mystery, Grace. It brings healing, freedom from restriction—

perhaps physical, but not necessarily. We may not have any idea of how blessed we are until after the fact, but something protects us even from ourselves. Outer events may change and/or, as so often is the case, changes us so that we experience life differently. In some manner through grace in whatever disguise that it enters our life, we are made new.

A battle ensues between the "pride of personality" versus the outcome offered by the higher world. Gradually we begin to build openness to the idea that the outcome offered by the higher world may have value for us, even if different from how our ego level of self wanted it to be. There must be openness within us for us to receive. Here we confront the boundaries of our ego and adjust to the concept of a Superior Nature. We have all heard the jokes about God saying, "No." The truth is God or Universe, however we choose to say it, as the Source, does deny us certain things and we do not like it. We have not "earned" them, whatever that might mean, or we are being protected from our ignorance.

We have a rational mind that has a picture it believes to be so. Our emotional nature has an outcome it wants (desires); and there is a slight nudge at the heart-mind, which points towards the highest outcome. Yet, we are "made in the image and likeness," and our creative power allows us the "free will" to choose which level of our self will chart our course.

At moments, we find ourselves muttering, "This could not have come at a better time." We experience a recognition that comes at a particular moment and expands, perhaps transforms, our understanding in such a way that we know we are blessed, a divine child. "There but for the grace of God goes me," we say.

Two significant points can be grasped by this realization:

1) "I have done likewise and escaped the pain and damage that could have been," and

2) "Somehow my life escaped a fate others have suffered and I have no idea how I did so."

As the Lord Buddha taught, "*It is not enough to cease to do evil; it is time to do good.*" He acknowledged the reality of choosing the good and then, when ready, stepping into a higher role. Buddha was born about five hundred years before Jesus. He was preparing humanity for the coming of the Love Principle unto the planet. We must remember we can be *negatively good, meaning we obey the rules* but do not become *actively good*. We can do what is right by the law, but not by the spirit, and be exceedingly judgmental, very rational, and committed to following conventional wisdom to the letter.

This is a particular state of being, prior to the expansion of consciousness and the opening of the heart. The way of the Christ energy is to open the heart and allow lots of vital energy of the higher worlds to flow to us and through us into the human condition. This prepares the way for grace to visit humanity.

Throughout the ages, certain adventures of heroes inspire us. We have all leaned closer to hear, "Once upon a time...," the telling of miraculous events our rational mind could not fathom, yet over which our heart rejoices. We are all touched. Oft told and retold is the record of the little understood march toward God that is going on every day through human lives. Some children grow up listening to the stories of the saints and their struggles to know God in personal ways. Others grow up in the presence of seekers and do not understand the importance of the happenings they witness daily. They reduce it to commonplace.

Someone fed the simple baby food to you so that a new understanding could develop. Your lineage brought invisible grace to you, so you became capable of taking stronger and richer ideas into the expansion of mind you were building. A disciple becomes a link in a chain of wisdom and is grateful for those who preceded him or her. Likewise, he or she, or you and I, will come to realize how karmically linked we are to the tradition into which we are born. We, or others who may not like this, or who may find this remark very appreciated, must come to know we do not have a choice; it is a karmic pattern. Some may have longed for a religious tradition and had to search one out. We may end up doing battle with the faith into which we were born, or as many are today, broadening our tradition to be more "whole or holy." Nevertheless, ancient wisdom says there is a karmic tie and we best know this.

My favorite grace and karma story is true and wonderful. It comes from England, published in 1999 as a part of the uplifting stories of National Friendship Week. I call this a favorite story of grace, not just friendship.

> *His name was Fleming, and he was a poor Scottish farmer. One day, while trying to eke out a living for his family, he heard a cry for help coming from a nearby bog. He dropped his tools and ran to the bog. There, mired to his waist in black muck, was a terrified boy, screaming and struggling to free himself. Farmer Fleming saved the lad from what could have been a slow and terrifying death. The next day, a fancy carriage pulled up to the Scotsman's sparse surroundings. An elegantly dressed nobleman stepped out and introduced himself as the father of the boy Farmer Fleming had saved.*
>
> *"I want to repay you," said the nobleman. "You saved my son's life."*
>
> *"No, I can't accept payment for what I did," the Scottish farmer replied, waving off the offer.*
>
> *At that moment, the farmer's son came to the door of the family hovel. "Is that your son?" the nobleman asked.*
>
> *"Yes," the farmer replied proudly.*
>
> *"I'll make you a deal. Let me take him and give him a good education. If the lad is anything like his father, he'll grow to be a man you can be proud of."*
>
> *And that he did. In time, Farmer Fleming's son graduated from St. Mary's Hospital Medical School in London, and went on to become known throughout the world as the noted Sir Alexander Fleming, the discoverer of Penicillin. Years afterward, the nobleman's son was stricken with pneumonia. What saved him? Penicillin.*
>
> *The name of the nobleman? Lord Randolph Churchill. His son's name: Sir Winston Churchill.*

As it has been said, "what goes around comes around."

What, we might ask, is the greatest value of the mystical experience?

- It confronts the arrogance of humanity, making channels of Grace of each.

- It gives backbone to those suffering rejection of faith.

- God represents our highest potential instead of a sense of guilt, weakness, or failure.

- It marries the lowest parts of our nature to our highest parts, the God Consciousness.

The great task of making a mystic is to bring the highest potential of the invisible world down to confront the fear of unworthiness that exists in humanity. We know today of the damage done by telling children they are *"dumb, ugly, or not loved."* There is the same damage done by telling God's children they are *"sinners."* We all need to know the healing power of love, forgiveness, and blessings. We need reassurance when we make mistakes in judgment and errors in our ways; we need to have a trust in the Higher Power, whether we call this God, Allah, or by some other name.

Mystics come to know the real meaning of *"I AM THAT I AM."* Rocco Errico once spoke of this to our group saying that the mystic has to be 1) Self-saving, 2) Self-supporting, and 3) Self-caring. This means they cannot look outside for the solution to the dilemmas of life, because they have come to know that **the answers lie within.**

A mystic traditionally has insights that challenge others; **they gain their knowledge through their personal subjective experience.** Therefore, they cannot be very objective about their inner knowing. They particularly get into difficulties with outer authorities and with traditional defenders. They challenge faith ideas to expand the concepts of science or human rights, religion, or law. They offer ideas which often venture ahead of their time, and are rejected at that time, but for which they are noted later. This is equally true for renegade scientists as mystics, because the bright light of a blessed mind travels ahead of the collective.

Few understand the transformation that is to occur here on earth now and in the not so distant era. Spiritually awakened ones are striving to bring in this new kingdom, not by outward signs, but by turning inward and anchoring it first in their hearts and minds.

They give merit to **Sophia, the Holy Spirit of Wisdom** and the acts of dedicated ones down through the history of humankind who sowed the seeds of higher consciousness. Wise ones seek to know in similar ways and, from time to time, a breakthrough occurs that allows them to see through the veil, to perceive or to experience expanded moments. Grace descends into one life or many and, although not understood rationally, it is witnessed. **Grace makes herself known.**

Although it seems to be the nature of females to be more open to "right-brain practices," we cannot say with any certainty there are more female mystics than male. If so, historically women have not been as noted as males. Perhaps since women were not educated in the same manner as males, this may have helped them to be more "*in tune*" or more right brain. There are many who think so.

A number of saints are mystics. In centuries past, Hildegard of Bingen (b.1089, d.1179) is a noted one; Julian of Norwich (b.1342, d.1416) is another mystic becoming better known in our times. As women's studies are advancing in popularity, we are learning the long-hidden history of women. Convents were homes for persons of delicate or strange temperament who did not feel at ease in the societies around them. Women, who sensed a call to serve God in some personal way other than what their society offered, frequently chose a religious or convent life, although there is no recording of them as mystics.

An interesting side note about Hildegard is that she was a brilliant person with multi-dimensional skills: art, music, homeopathic medicine, author and advisor to many, as well as the establisher of a number of mother-houses. She left a body of spiritual inspiration that is being explored in depth today … a definite mystic and person of genius. In her art, she depicted Sophia in a manner similar to what others had used centuries before. She realized she was in touch with God's Wisdom and called her Sophia … at a time when few did.

Theresa of Avila (1515–1582) has received a lot of attention in our times for having recorded her journey in notes to her confessor, and the sisters of her lineage have had access to much of this inspiration. She also writes in a modern manner, which seems to speak to a public interested in experiences beyond the usual. *Entering the Castle* by Carolyn Myss is one of the recent books about the mystical life of St. Teresa where we can learn much about exploring experiences of the inner nature.

We also have the modern stories of Mother Teresa of Calcutta (1910–1997), and Mira Richards (1878–1973), best known as "*the Mother*" of Auroville in Pondicherry, India. Mother Teresa revealed a great deal about the power of one mystical experience to carry her through a lifetime without the personal satisfaction of frequent contacts. Few realize the significance of one powerful visitation.

The Mother of Auroville left much material speaking to the potential of the evolution of humanity, with details for the encouragement of both Eastern and Western minds, and the contributions of each in the transformation of the **new-mind-being.**

The stories of male mystics are legend; St. Francis of Assisi (1182–1226) may be the best known, loved for his peaceful nature and love of the natural; Jakob Boehme (1575–1624), a simple Protestant cobbler, left a great deal of writing about Sophia. An excellent book for an introduction to the history of devotion and recognition to Sophia is *The Sophia Teachings* by Robert Powell, and another offering a variety of teaching is *Sophia Sutras: Introducing*

Mother Wisdom by Carol E. Parrish-Harra. Other mystics come to us from different traditions and times. Recall Mahatma Mohandas (1860–1949) of India, often accredited with ending the rule of England without a war, and Sri Ghose Aurobindo (1872–1950), whose ideas ring with modern terms as he investigated the DNA of consciousness. Sri Aurobindo is quite different from most older Hindu gurus in that he has a clear concept of modern psychology and so requires less knowledge of Eastern concepts in order to read his works.

When we speak of love, forgiveness, and healing, we are speaking of the feminine energies of the Creator Consciousness beamed on humanity currently. In some cultures, it is easier to understand as the alignment of Father Sun and Mother Earth, or the Galactic Alignment. A better understanding of this Native American concept can be gained from *Touched by the Dragon's Breath* by Michael Harrington, especially Chapter Ten. The Native American cultures have preserved valuable information in both prophesies and calendars letting us know what powerful shifts are forthcoming. Note the word "powerful" not fearful, to help us regain an awareness of the great universe in which we dwell.

From Hunbatz Men, Prince of the Maya:

> One of the main reasons so many are drawn to sacred sites around the Earth is that sacred sites exist on all dimensions at once. When we move into the next reality, sacred sites will remain, but our modern society built of skyscrapers and superhighways will not. This is because sacred sites have a thread of energy that ties them to all the dimensions.

From the Mayan Popol Vuh:

> Let there be light!
> So the dawn shall rise over heaven
> And the Earth.
> There can be no glory, no splendor,
> Until the human being exists
> As the fully developed person.

From Stephen McFadden, an author, journalist, astrologer, gardener and ceremonialist who has worked with groups in both corporate and private settings for a good many years:

> According to Hunbatz Men (Mayan Prince), we are now participating in a new cycle of the Mayan calendars, which synchronize the cycles of time with human beings. This is the time when the Maya believe they must work with others to reopen the schools of ancient knowledge—to teach the first stage of understanding.

From, native North American spiritual teacher, Oren Lyons:

> When we walk upon Mother Earth, we always plant our feet carefully because we know the faces of our future generations are looking up at us from beneath the ground. We never forget them. In the absence of the sacred, nothing is sacred. Everything is for sale.

Truthfully, there are more natural mystics in all probability among the indigenous people than in the educated classes. These people are more loving within their own people and are attempting to be open to **all people,** in spite of the fear of others that they have built from past experience. Those within humanity with more judgmental attitudes will keep themselves closed off from their own heart. This new incoming energy is to help all of us to open to one another. When the native people began to accept outsiders, they were letting down their barriers. When we begin to accept the ones we have labeled unlovable, we begin letting down our barriers. Native people have shared with us one of their wisest mystical truths, "**All my relations,**" yet many do not get it.

With the acceptance of mixed marriages, relationships, mixed-blood children and leadership from others, we are crossing the line into accepting a humanitarian collective. We are freeing our hearts to open to the "*others.*" We have observed this kind of progress all over the world during this "*change of the age.*" It is still frightening to many, but it is the salvation of humanity and the collective well-being of humanity. Persons who see themselves as ecologists or join animal rescue forces are leading the way through their love of nature and love of any living life.

When the terror of our lives is such we can no longer meet life with terror, one begins to look for love and how to love ... we are to master the assignment the Masters give all of us, to "*love one another.*" All of this begs the question, "Do we really choose to be a mystic?" If the answer is "*yes,*" what are the steps? While this entire writing is about the making of a mystic, where do we begin? Remember the mystic knows that the world is painful, but agrees to love it anyway. Here are some suggestions in seeking this consciousness:

- First, desire to be One with God and humanity ... however the Creator of all life appeals to you. This kind of intimacy is passionately important.

- Secondly, it is about stimulating your heart, learning to love. In time, as you move from personal love of God to impersonal, then from impersonal love to unconditional, you learn to give love to all.

- Third, forgive those who have hurt you, or those of whom you are scared. Few realize that the "fear of another's ability to hurt you" is part of not being able to forgive. There is still a desire to protect one's self from this old pain, so we keep holding it, hoping the other will hurt just as badly. Then things will seem to be more even.

- Next, work toward the idea of unconditional love, because Personal Love causes the heart center to be protected. Show yourself pictures of suffering as well as tender pictures so you can feel your heart open and shut, until you can begin to control the closing off. The mystic does not want to bounce up and down, but to hold to their serenity in all situations. They wish to meet the pain of the world without losing their peace. Love it anyway. Give yourself a picture that helps you; mine is a picture of the planet with the words "**love your mother.**"

- Avoid occasions of pain as much as possible so you can live more openly. Give yourself a pep talk before interaction with those you fear so you can meet them more openly. Learn to resist fear of the other should you find yourself challenged.

- Use affirmations and music; poetry is a wonderful therapy. If you do not enjoy reading the writing of others, write your own.

- Have some friends you can really trust to visit with … this may be your spiritual mentor or best friend … as long as you are not afraid of betrayal. If you have had a lot of betrayal to struggle with in your journey, write or read positive materials consistently, daily.

- Keep these steps up. Mystics are "*cooked*" day by day for a period of growth. They are like diamonds built under pressure from the Higher World. Include exposing yourself to pain and pleasure until the line between them disappears.

Living in the Here and Now—Agni Yoga

In Agni Yoga, we meet ideas of art, science and religion leading each field to seek to lift humanity toward the Higher Realities. Nicholas and Helena Roerich, the founders of Agni Yoga, said that Master Morya, an inner-plane teacher and Chohan, stated that art, religion, and science all lead to the same Source of Life. The rapport between presentations of Djwhal Khul and the work of Alice Bailey is quite harmonious with M.M., as he is more commonly known, and many who enjoy one find the others' dictated work quite acceptable.

In the United States, Russell Paul Schofield established a number of Schools of Actualism using the Agni Material but they never really caught on. Culturally Russian teachings from the Roerichs were very acceptable until the Communist Revolution occurred. Their story is an interesting one. Suddenly America was afraid of Soviet ideas, and all things Russian were assumed Communist. This struck a blow to both the work of the Roerichs and that of Madam

Blavatsky. Should any of these have been in Russia at the time of the Revolution, they would have been killed with the destruction of the Russian Intelligentsia.

Each field—Art, Science, and Religion—inspires us to look at Life from a higher or expanded perspective. Each ignites our imagination (a part of our creative consciousness) also known as the "*image-making ability.*" Each can serve as a map for the study of truths not well understood by the general populous. Sophia (wisdom) is the companion of the "inner-directed person," as the new contemplative is called. As consciousness expands and the dialogue with the God Within comes forth from the hidden resources of the inner life, She, Mother Wisdom, walks as a companion to those who pursue the journey of transformation.

> **When we step from the path of religion
> on to the path of spirituality, it is into Sophia's care
> that we render ourselves.**

The study of Agni blends well with the mystical approaches to the divine as taught by both Kabalah and Esoteric Christianity. All these studies have aspects of mysticism. Judaism is the name of the religion; Kabalah is the mystical aspect. Christianity is the traditional approach while Esoteric Christianity presents a deeper picture with yet another presented by the Sophianic. Islam also has an inner teaching—Sufism—with which we may be somewhat acquainted.

This is true of all traditions. We know them as worldwide and respected outer identities. Christianity traces much of its tradition to the Old Testament and recognizes that the origin of the Christian faith grew from its roots in Egyptian teachings (see *The Egyptian Origins of Christianity* by Lisa Ann Bargeman), and also from Judaism and the Kabalah. Agni Yoga is quite a modern path presented by the Roerichs in the twentieth century as a blend of East and West, with touches of Christianity and Buddhism visible.

Art is a feeling science, not just painting and drawing, but a way of sharing emotion through picturing and color, poetry or drama. There is also the art of speaking and nurturing. A study of the hospice movement shows it to be a blend of caring and comforting. Also, let us recall the efforts required in the field of social work. All of these are seeds lying in the human collective that Aquarian energies are now stimulating. The "Possible Human Theory" and the increasing awareness that is today flourishing are needed for humanity to advance rapidly during this period of choice. Humanity as a collective is to aid this "new possible human" to flourish in a positive way and we begin to look at the different qualities of expressing this new awareness.

Helena Roerich, for example, lived mostly as a contemplative. She shared her insights with her husband, family and a few exceptional friends, largely through letters, as she was seldom in a location that provided her in-depth relationships. Nicholas Roerich was an artist and self-made archeologist. Both of the Roerichs were intellectually gifted. They offered ideas and practices that helped them to guide others to see the wholeness of life. Their master guided them, encouraging them to share the teaching they received. Due to their influential nature and the international contacts they made, we have come to know these teachings as Agni Yoga, which have been delivered from the higher world in the twentieth century to be a modern path for those who choose to add it to their personal practice. Simply, Agni is often called "Ethical Living."

In addition to offering a simple way of pulling together the teachings of East-West, we find both psychology and religion woven in, enriching mere "religion" with some deeper inner work—esoteric psychology—to birth the holy, the sacred, that lives within. It is alchemy, transformation, and the path of initiation, interwoven to assist one regardless of which approach we choose. It is exciting and meaningful to see this kind of teaching made available. The terms "*Agni and Indra*," meaning fire and light, i.e., gender shifts (first a life as a male, next a female, etc.) and tender wisdom—all unify in one body of teaching. In addition, it is clearly stated that the Age of Aquarius will be the Age of Woman.

To understand the Agni approach, one must do some investigating of the culture, nature, and personal ethics of the humanity out of which these concepts have grown … and add to these ideas a dash of archeology, astrology, and cosmology. Each topic provides guidelines to enrich our awareness and contribute new perspectives which are introduced to humanity to prepare it for opening to a more global view, or at least a cosmic orientation that we have not explored much in the past. The original founders of the wisdom teachings had this global view (some study of the Sumerian Culture or Zacharia Sitchin's writings will add to your overall perspective).

Agni Yoga suggests that stimulating high creativity is the goal of human life. A life is lived based on honorable themes that are to be built within oneself. Perceiving the differences between vices and virtues is emphasized, as well as the use of meditation for purification, so that one can enter higher consciousness without being disturbed by distorting thoughts.

Agni Yoga means "union with the creative fire," the *fohat* of creation, the fiery mind of God. Yoga comes from the Sanskrit word, *yug,* the same word from which we acquired Jesus' concept of yoke (Matt.11:28-30). That is, we invoke union with the creative fire, Agni (God), as the source of life. It is a dance to the Sun and a recognition of the gifts of nature. There are others who teach somewhat similar approaches. Solar Yoga or Actualism both have similarities. In Bulgaria when I was there, the Paneurthmy or Pan Eurhythmy Groups (spelled either way) held a practice taught by Peter Deunov that is quite similar. I feel there is much that is familiar in most of Ageless Wisdom.

All these approaches vary some, but the basis of all is the idea of union with the Solar Lord of the Universe, the sun (light and fire). We must stimulate the inner fire and practice purification to gain "*light.*" These more advanced pathways are not well known as of yet, but they may be "the Way" for some who have studied and tried to find a temple, church or religion, even a philosophy, in which they can practice a more eclectic approach designed mostly from within, or from the inner view.

An important concept to recognize is that when fire burns fuel, it creates smoke and cinders fill the air. When the personality begins to seek expansion of consciousness, the passion burning within creates smoke and cinders to be purified. As the fire burns hot enough to be bright and clear, and it burns away the debris of the personality (the glamours and illusions), we become white hot or smoke-free. Such is true for the disciple, who at first must burn away the debris and purify his or her self. When heart and mind are clear, the individual stands forth like a bright light.

We are acknowledging and utilizing ancient concepts each soul has experienced … everything we seek lies hidden deep within. We each have gathered much to be purified and as the smoke clears, we find a unique path waiting to be walked. If we have been a disciple of numerous paths in the past, we have many rich experiences to integrate into the fullness of our soul's journey.

Our unique path cannot possibly fit into any one defined mold, but each experience contributes to the total picture. This is what makes inner-directed persons so ready for some variety of mysticism. I also see that the concepts of Agni fit nicely into the general teachings of any ecumenical approach, as there are few, if any, dogmatic "*have to's*" to obey. In the idea of Living Ethics or Agni there are few or no rules, as such, but guidelines that provide a *light structure* for those ready to evolve, or best said, respond to the transformational impulse from within with the help of a wise mentor or analysis.

Religions always have difficulty with prophets and mystics. Probably no tradition has caused more suffering than Judaism, which is known for having killed their prophets whenever one was doubted or seen as "*false.*" Kabalists all received some rejection and harsh treatment; they lived with both respect and fear as do many psychics, disciples, and mystics of today. What is the relationship between people of today and those prophets of old? Let us remember the utterance of Martin Luther King Jr. who has now earned a celebrated day of his own in the U.S.A. Dr. King, Jr. was a critic of American society and was called a "*Jeremiah raging against society.*"

While he was not so adequately appreciated in his lifetime, Martin Luther King, Jr.'s death rocked our conscience and, like most prophets, he became highly regarded afterwards but *not in his lifetime.* Today Dr. King's contribution to social justice and the progress of his people is highly honored, as well as his futuristic vision. Mystics and prophets master the ability to shape their anger into a loving compassion that, in fact, is both transforming for themselves and a guide for others.

Sacred writings, as we refer to them, are scripture that becomes sacred because it is an accurate description of a reality at a certain level at a certain time. When people can see through the fog to a reality that needs acting upon by the many and points to the well-being of all, the prophet becomes a guide. There must be some way these words remain porous enough for the light (truth) held within to be relevant when we become light (mature) enough to perceive it.

The experiences described in early scriptures and their truths form the basis for collective knowledge for a time, and then new inspiration adjusts the collective perspective. The new reality, as it becomes public, may trigger anger, fear, or curiosity. Anger comes because the idea espoused is different from how things have been, because people have gotten safe with the old view and are now frightened by the new. They may be curious and just want to see the new concept, but each of us has a style that reveals how we meet new experiences.

Ecumenical conferences began in this country when a body of people, free thinkers, was ready for New Thought. They spoke up and began to reveal themselves. Liberated, enlightened or illuminated people have more responsibility, not less. With their new awareness, they have more responsibilities to live their truth: **To whom much is given, much is required.** These people led us into a social revolution, but also set a more open mystical tone for others.

Now mysticism is much less hidden because social issues are high on the agenda.

People have begun to speak more openly about intimate contacts with the Divine, causing modern day mystics to begin to share how such is possible. Help is invoked for individuals and the world; inspiration is ignited due to the pain of the many challenging situations humanity must face. Limited views do not work any more; new understanding is emerging and beginning to lead humanity into ways that are more peaceful. Humanity has much cleansing and healing to do, and methods are emerging to assist it in this process. A new consciousness is bursting out all over. Mysticism is quite simple; it becomes complicated when we explain too much, even as I am doing right now.

The Silversmith

He will sit as a refiner of silver, and purifier of silver: and he shall purify the sons of Levi, and purge them as gold and silver that they may offer unto the Lord an offering in righteousness. He will purify … and purge them as gold and silver that they may offer unto the Lord an offering in righteousness.

—Malachi 3:3

A group of women in a Bible Study class came across the above verse and it triggered a lot of curiosity about the words *"He will sit as a refiner and purifier of silver."* Being puzzled they wondered how this statement could be compared to God. One women took on the pursuit of how silver is refined and what was the true meaning of this verse.

She called a silversmith and arranged to watch him at work. As she watched, he held a piece of silver over the fire and let it heat up. He explained that in refining silver, one needs to hold the silver in the middle of the fire where the flames are hottest so as to burn away all the impurities. Of course, the woman thought about God holding us in a hot spot … of course she thought about the words, *"He sits as a refiner and purifier of silver."*

She asked the silversmith if it was true that he had to sit there in front of the fire the whole time the silver was being refined. He answered, *"Yes."* He had not only to sit there holding the silver, but he had to keep his eyes on the silver the entire time it was in the fire. He explained that if the silver was left even a moment too long in the flames, it would be destroyed.

The woman was silent for a moment. Then she asked the silversmith, *"How do you know when the silver is fully refined?"* He smiled at her and answered, *"Oh, that is easy … it's finished when I can see my image in it."*

Let us compare ourselves to a silversmith or metallurgist and think about the purification of the self until the Divine can shine in us. This is a beautiful passage: the idea of the person working with silver, purifying it again and again until he or she can see his or her face in it. When it shines like a mirror and one can see his or her own face reflected, one knows it is pure. A disciple is purifying their life until there is no separation between themselves and the Divine within. The face of the Divine reflects in their personality … not literally, but spiritually. This is the alchemist's process and this is resurrection. Persistence in pursuit of the dedication to one's inner life leads to divine attributes.

Thinking about the purification of the silver leads to thoughts about intervention. There is a time to intervene and a time not to. This is a most difficult decision. Sometimes we do more good by self-restraint. Parenting naturally leads to great difficulties with this issue—when to suggest or actually intervene, or when not to do anything. This is where our guidance helps us realize there are times when the answer is *"no."* When attuning to our inner message, there may be some misery or reluctance when we get *"no"* for an answer, or an answer that is not what we want.

Sometimes we have to wait until someone else makes a move or some other event takes place; sometimes the answer is not as we think it ought to be. Sometimes we must wait until we can perceive what is happening or grasp a new perception of the situation. Perhaps we will never understand, but just follow the guidance as best we can. Even mentors need mentors.

A gentleman once said to me, "*If God had answered all my prayers, I would be married to up to six women by now.*" It was important to hear this from a man who was acknowledging that "*no*" was the best answer at certain crucial times.

So we begin our study of self-restraint or, said another way, "*wait and let the unknown, the Divine make the next move.*" In no situation is saying "*no*" more important than in parenting and addiction work. Many times, we cannot wait for the other to take the best course, as there is such fear involved. At other times, we provide support and it is "*enabling,*" when it would have been better had we not assisted. To be a parent or best friend or to be wise, we must sense the proper next step. In the practice of mysticism, we repeat this kind of discernment repeatedly on our journey to wisdom.

"Enabling" can be a very offensive term, especially to caregivers. Dedicated to helping causes the line to blur between when it is help and when it is hindrance. Persons do not grow their capabilities or potential if they receive too much help, and the rational mind can always find a way to assist. This wanting to enable another comes from our solar plexus and is a part of our cultural training.

"Closed-ness"—being closed—rejects grace; we break from faith and experience the limitations of our own power. **We struggle with pride**. We believe we can do it on our own and we think we know how it ought to be. We have **a rational mind** with a picture it believes to be correct. **Our emotional nature** has an outcome it desires, and there is a slight nudge at the **heart-mind** as it suggests a higher outcome. Yet, as we are "*made in the image and likeness,*" our **creative power** allows us free will to choose which level of our self will chart our course.

We try to do what seems right and helping always seems "*good.*" The real work is to follow our guidance when it is not what seems right in the eyes of others. Learning to be true to our own Source is hard work; it is how mystics become a force for change. It is much like protestors; one does not have to *do anything but take a position and stand strong.*

Racism, Materialism, and Militarism

Major evils of our society that are recognized by aware ones, mystics, and prophets are Racism, Materialism, and Militarism. These forces are sworn enemies to feminine energies.

- Sexism is a branch of racism and is just as dangerous as the separating power of the color of one's skin.

- Racism is the mistaken claim that one segment of the human collective is superior to others. Sexism believes half of all the creative energy of the Creator is flawed. Both genders and all races are to benefit the greater good. The entire collective is to assist others to do their greater work.

- Materialism is to deny that creation has other dimensions than what the five physical senses can explore. Spirit has created a dense or physical plane reality where life must struggle against experiences that would be more destructive on other planes. To deny that the other dimensions make contributions to our life experience is to deny the power of love, heaven and hell, and all spirit reality. We need to stop and give value to other ways of perceiving "reality" beyond just the physical.

- Militarism is the embrace of rigidity, following authority without questioning it. It is a clear "right versus wrong" point of indoctrination. It is the will of the authority versus human personal evaluation. Thus, we train persons to disregard the value of the individual human will.

- These massive thought forms and their dangerous power threatens to taint the collective vision and harden hearts so that the sacred cannot flow easily into daily lives. The time comes when silence is betrayal; we can live in denial no longer. As a society awakening to its higher nature, we have also to confront rage, addiction, and violence. Prejudices that keep us separated hold these negative forces in our reality and do not allow them to dissipate.

- Racism is rigid in its perspective of superiority. It claims one group of people to be brighter, prettier, healthier, chosen, or better in some way; and the others are inferior. Class-consciousness grew out of such attitudes, and regrettably, began out of religious traditions. Concepts as clean and unclean, caste systems vs. others had good intent as they originally evolved. Nevertheless, eventually they over-shot their marks and became evil without an understanding of their original values.

Ann Manser, the excellent spiritual teacher and author of the Shustah Material, used to say,

> It is nine times as slow here in the third dimension than in the others. Here we think a destructive thought, for example: I am going to hit another. The body gets the thought, has to arise and walk across the room and then hit the person. Therefore, we have time to withdraw the thought. In the other planes, thoughts manifest instantaneously and no re-thought or cancelling thought can occur. Here is the place we learn to re-think or evaluate our words and change our action.

Militarism is not just about war but a restrictive attitude toward *"this is the way it must be"* or we are quick to *"defend/fight"* in response. Based on flight-or-fight consciousness, the militarist position became more or less stuck on the power to control. Originally, to secure safety for self and/or others, control and maturity were seen as the best way to assure safety. Over-use, or the inability to see the difference, allowed the "desire to control" to seek more and more power until dictatorship came into being.

In reflecting on religion, especially Judaism, even with its Kabalistic inner teaching and other more traditional practices, women seemed to be of lesser value. However, a recent book called *The Receiving*, written by a woman, Rabbi Tirzah Firestone, provides a new and different viewpoint. Her interpretation of the Torah is to say that God favors women, granting them a different viewpoint than males because she lives closer to Divine will. A female performs a different work for the higher world and has a different role than males, as male and female do not need to follow the same rules and regulations.

Rabbi Firestone offers the idea that the feminine side of our nature does what it has to, when it has to, without so much mental calculation. One's duty is put right before your nose and in your direct path, therefore it is yours for you to do. Whether it is cooking, scrubbing, nurturing, or helping a neighbor, or having babies ... the female has no requirement to follow the outer laws of the temple. This requirement is for the males; women may choose to do so, as well, if they enjoy the devotion/occasion.

Kabalistic study introduces regulations for refining the masculine: Rules, study, building the rational awareness, and work in the world versus caring for the home. "*She*" remains the queen of her home and makes it her duty to put that environment first with her care and nurturing. No longer free, as when she was the honored goddess, she is now enclosed in her personal kingdom (her own home and to be honored as queen within her personal kingdom) to care for, and the controlling male knows that any children are his, if no other males are allowed in the vicinity.... *A golden cage is a cage, even if golden.*

EIGHT

Bridegroom Meets Bride

WE FIND THE TERM *"Mystical Marriage"* repeatedly throughout the mysteries of the Christian tradition. It begins as a hint toward bringing the masculine and feminine coming into right relationship within one's self as heart and mind ... to *"think with the heart"* and then *'love with the mind."* This is an admonition held before all. Our first glimpse of the importance of this guideline is at Christmas in the Nativity Scene.

There, we witness Mother Mary and Joseph kneeling by the crib, the Mother representing the feminine influence within one's self and Joseph, the masculine within one's self. This balance is equally important for the Mystical Christ to be born within. The esoteric view beholds the birth of the *Christ within* as symbolic, whereas the public thinks of the birth of Jesus more literally. Here is a valued and well known situation where we find that the symbolism of the language both veils and protects.

The first initiation begins with the **lesser mysteries**. Think of the mother as the soul within the Soul (there is significance in whether the word is written with a little letter or a Capital letter) leading us through the birth and baptism stages. When soul is written with a little letter, it indicates a noninitiated soul, while the word Soul with a capital letter indicates

a soul that has met many tests and is more advanced on the long journey.

Simple scriptures are clues to this stage of growth ... but little understood. The symbolic language: birth, birthing, and labor show us the correlation. It is the work of the outer church to care for the un-awakened and set them on paths that will aid them in opening to other dimensions later. There are many different approaches in Christianity and/or Mystic and Occult Studies; likewise most who are questing investigate and experience many differing faith traditions as well. For example, almost any Christian denomination quietly implies it alone knows the "true" way; in fact, each one will provide growth for a seeker for a time.

After the first introduction of the term *"mystical marriage"* within ourselves, we learn that this is the coming together of our masculine and feminine natures. We began with the purification of the personality levels, and now come to the *"cleaning up stage"* through the baptism or washing away of the impurities. We begin to clear character defects as we choose wisely to transform.

We again meet the term *mystical marriage* as we explore meditation and soul-infusion ... an indication that the soul born within has reached a stage that can carry the life of the soul in a more direct way toward its transformation. Now we think of this stage as the *Mystical Marriage of Soul and Personality*—the third initiation or Transfiguration. The "Son of the Most High" is the personality who is guided by Soul.

Now the son seeks the bride. The concluding lesser mystery takes us to the *"greater mysteries."* The Holy Spirit or the Bride of Christ descends from on high to walk with the purified and transfigured Son (or Daughter) of the Earth Mother (Soul) who has lifted the self upward. Here we are recognizing that "the Sons of Most High" is not a sexist label, but a personality that is masculine, and always in esoteric teachings considered such. Therefore, the term "son" is used. The root word for man is *manas* or mind in Sanskrit and means the being carrying the mind-stuff. This human being is therefore a man or son of the higher world. Soul is Bride and Father-Mother or (Creator) is the Spirit. At an earthly level then, we all begin as Son of the Most High.

My understanding of a good human marriage in the physical world is that we need a *"worthy opponent"* against whom we can push. Neither the male nor female must be intimidated in the balance of relationship. Likewise, this is the model for us as we grow in our Divine nature. We must have a balance in our masculine strengths and our feminine nature. We must be prepared to make the shift from one to another, as needed in the circumstances of our lives. This inner effort is not necessarily easy to do, but necessary to learn and then be capable of doing. The bride descends from the higher world to join the personality as he crosses the burning ground.

> *The Master sat silently as a group of disciples discussed religion and spirituality. A novice asked, "What is the difference?" Finally the Master spoke. "Spirituality," he said, "is like milk. Religion is like a milk carton, which only has value if it has something in it."*
>
> —Anonymous

What is the relationship between the mystic and the initiations? Silence, prayer, study and meditation are the major practices of the inner life. The mystic life-style technically begins at any point after the second initiation as one builds the inner view. All paths require will power and persistent application if they are to assist us in our development. Any practitioner may become uncomfortable with the process and occasionally one resists rules and does not obey the *"commandments or doctrines."* Rather, they begin to follow their personal will (not inner guidance) too soon, and this then makes them a false prophet.

The mystic—one falls in Love with God, and has no other God before him or herself—places his/her life on the line. We are not to love God in some situations and then put our families, our job, our culture, and our comfort first, but one who is in Love with God every day radiates the joy of being in love. To "*know*" God is to love God.

Recall the story of Abraham and Isaac in the Old Testament (Genesis 22:9). We glorify this adventure because God saved the day. We glorify this story because God stepped in and stopped Abraham from harming his son at the last moment. This is what we want for ourselves—a last-minute reprieve from the terribly painful experiences we face. However, this escape does not always come. Family members die, businesses fail, heartbreak occurs, and the tests come in unique ways, and we choose God or whatever it is we hold in that supreme place ... not understanding what we are doing; we have confused love of family and country with God.

Today, think like a mystic and say to yourself, "*God comes first in my life before* _____," whatever it is that has demanded your major attention. Does the job, family, child, education, food, etc., claim first place? This will change as you reach the highest goal. Not intentionally, but in loving with Divine love, it happens. Here we are retracing our evolving transformational impulse and have more chance of seeing it. We must look once again and see. We must be in harmony with higher will if God is to come first, and we become thankful that most of our blessings and challenges are not as hard as some others have been. Remember, the general rule is: challenges are designed for you—no less than you can take and no more.

The mystical part of Judaism was not available to females, so Kabalah became even more sexist and intellectual in its set of concepts. Women overall were not taught to read and study. Therefore, I think for students today, some part of our masculine nature is satisfied as we study Kabalah. It provides a wonderful structure as we form our spiritual concepts. The teachings suggest there is nothing we cannot hang on the tree when we grasp it all. I would not know, but it comes close to this, I would say from my experience.

Now at this point in history, it does not really matter whether we are male or female, since we realize each of us are truly both. We are to bring our feminine love of caring, loving and serving to blend with our masculine love of study and rational understanding so the heart and mind can come together. We see this in images and symbology. We learn to perceive the inner meaning behind the covering that serves to veil and protect the deeper meaning until we can penetrate it.

Rabbi Firestone provides deep insights rarely seen elsewhere. She also specifically tells us how various Rabbis supported their wives as courageous couples shared the teachings. Persons interested in Kabalah should read this to fill in some missing pieces. We come, in time, to learn Kabalah is not as sexist as it appears. In more ancient times, when it was displacing the feminine at the close of the Goddess Era, it began to be dominant. At that time humanity began building the rational mind and the rational understanding had to find ways to overcome the teachings of the goddesses.

However also, the further we got from the goddesses, the more masculine Kabalah became. Originally, Jehovah had a wife (Asherah), mate or consort much like the Hindu traditions of male and female working together. *The Hebrew Goddess*, by Raphael Patai with foreword by Merlin Stone, is a good source of this material, as is an excellent video on a website that I use from time to time. Most of us have had no exposure to this type of material although it is in textbooks.

The referenced power point presentation above is posted by Bishop Katia Romanoff at her website: http://www.northernway.org/presentations/godwife/1.html as is "The Absent Mother Returns" by myself at http://www.Caroleparrish.com. Each will offer you new ways to think about the divine feminine. Enjoy. They blend the ideas of Sophia and other feminine figures into "*her story.*" You will gain much.

To pick up the thread of symbolism, we need go no further than Master Jesus. Nobody really knows what Jesus looked like, but we have hundreds of impressions of him as the "*loving master.*" Therefore, whenever we see one of these pictures of what we perceive as a *holy one*, we call it *Jesus*. The same is true of the *Mother Mary*. What these renditions tell us is that there is a perception or personification of the "*loving master*" or "*holy one*" that we have created down through time. The devotion to such can be to a prophet, a guru, or a holy one. Perhaps it is a priest, a missionary or a mentor that brings another to the spiritual path. In the Christian tradition, in the more strict or narrow the denominations, we hear more about building a personal relationship with Jesus Christ.

In the Esoteric or Sophianic that is not so. We learn the dedication to the Christ or the Holy Consciousness that enlightens us. I do believe many of us begin by a love of Jesus as taught to us in churches or by parents, and then we come to know him as the Wayshower who leads us to the Holy Consciousness. This can be true of any faith. The inspired one leads us to the Holy Awareness that then fills us with higher truth. This is the "*inner voice of the Holy Spirit*" we seek.

We see that this "*effort*" does not always exist only in *ministers and priests, or the representatives of the Church Authority. The tradition of organized authorities* does not seem to hold much respect for the personality of the individual. It has more of a "*one-size-fits-all*" approach. The Western tradition does not support the idea of *a guru* as the Eastern approach has for centuries. The earlier Christian (especially Catholic) churches had confessors who guided individuals in the spiritual life in many traditions.

Today this mentoring concept is flourishing once again as we see the resurgence of the spiritual director position gaining significance. Most of us are realizing—with the psychological and spiritual understanding we have gained—the value of "reflecting together," either individually or in small group work. This is priceless. Many seekers today have some type of mentor to work with them. Even publicly more and more information is available to help others begin "seeking," even when they do not realize the steps they are taking.

We simply begin to "know ourselves." The age-old divine directive of knowing "your own nature" provides us with a sense of honesty about our strengths and weaknesses, our lessons and our learning. We can become more genuine now. We dare to love the Self Within and see the inner child as worthy of loving. First, we love the beauty around us, then we come to see the beauty in another, and finally, the unselfish eye opens to let us see the beauty within ourselves. Now we can have compassionate understanding of others making the same journey. We begin to understand that each child of the Soul—each inner child, others, and ourselves— deserves love.

We learn to face life courageously, especially when fear threatens to take over. We face the lessons of life, and although we would like to avoid them, we come to see the significance of the challenging moments that help us learn to shape a response courageously. Grief and loss, sadness and trials are a part of the human condition. The Wise have taught us that this is the place of sorrows. We came here to bring light, not by denial, but by taking the steps necessary to walk through the pain and the darkness, understanding that these are teaching moments, the testy moments of building the character of the transformed nature.

Suffering teaches us to see kindness, goodness in the smallest actions. Let these acts lighten the heavy heart ... bringing joy to others whenever possible. Be like the sun and shine on the just and the unjust, bring smiles to bear upon the human family as you journey on your own pathway. Enrich the lives of others because you have come to know your own *divine within.*

Foster thanksgiving in the heart, and forgive and release what would hinder you. Life is on our side as we transform; hidden within our nature are talents and treasures we do not know about. We hear *"follow your bliss"* repeatedly; we are encouraged to follow that which makes our heart sing. Follow the vision or part of the plan that calls to each from within, hidden from sight; it sends forth the energy to empower the response. When happy with our efforts, we tend to be open to others and share from this rich center.

There are specific values of the mystical experience. Evaluated by the **degree of change it makes in the life of the one experi-**

encing, we are changing. Sometimes the mystical influence comes gradually upon the devoted practitioner of spiritual practices, prayer, or meditation, and builds upon each practice in a gentle and progressive way. However, other times, as we now know, it can burst upon us and rearrange the furniture of our lives.

The birth of a new state of consciousness creates changes readily notable. These changes do not necessarily come in a specific order, but they transcend the material boundaries typical of rational humanity first, and of the psychically-open second. Thus we find the mystically inclined integrating this new consciousness on all levels of daily life.

The Role of the Sacral Center

Until we mature in our spiritual understanding, we place a lesser value on the Sacral Center than we should. What does this great energy center mean to our human potential? The **basic self** anchors the earth energy as a dynamic resource to aid us to mature into our potential. Truly most of humanity does not as of yet understand the meaning of *"made in the image and likeness of God."* The whole Creation story is full of archetypal imagery. In fact, most scripture or sacred literature is encoded. The idea is that symbols and archetypal terms both veil and protect until one is ready to understand. In this way the deeper meaning of a mystery is protected so it cannot be misused.

"Let us make man in our image, after our likeness." (Genesis 1:26) These words attributed to the Elohim are best taken to mean that each is made as an aspect of the Creator Consciousness, not to imply a human god. The Elohim gave to humankind the potential for each to develop his or her unique capabilities as they could through the journey of this dense world. Here, within this slow vibrating realm, each could perfect the use of their potentials with less danger to themselves or to one another—little understood, but true. Personalities are like blooms on a plant. They bud, bloom, give

of themselves, and die. Personalities are the "creation" or "child" of the Soul. When we know this as the Soul, a Solar angel, or a guardian, we are taught that some beneficent assistant guides, guards, and seeks to prompt this personality when it is ready for maturity; until then, it wreaks havoc just as the puppy or young child. In time, it will awaken and be ready for the soul to interact.

Before personality is ready to evolve, the Sacral Center serves as a power in human propagation. Little understood, this center co-works with the Sensual Center (second), and struggles with sexual and survival issues as one responds to gain experience that leads to the upward journey. The sexual passion that resides hidden here is the pilot light for future transformation. More information can be found concerning the role of sex, passion, and love in achieving enlightenment in my book, *Esoteric Secrets: Sex, Passion and Love,* which defines these differing powers and the part that each plays in our inner growth.

The basic self with its instinctual senses guides us into one experience after another with little regard for our likes, dislikes or any understanding of a higher goal. We do not resist its pull, and we gather more and more experience—delight and pain. In spiritual language, ecstasy and pain rule our lives. We enjoy being the "*drama queen.*"

The sensual energy itself changes gradually into more one of manifestation and self-centeredness, learns duality and its price, rebels or struggles to conform ... until its creativity and caring begins to break free from the judgment of right or wrong, and one begins to see the relationship between the two extremes. Shades of gray begin to emerge, and we come to personally love the unlovable; we take care of those who should take care of themselves; we believe the statements of outer authorities and know nothing of an inner authority ... until "*the coming of the sunrise.*"

The great adventure of the path begins with little warning. We begin to ask too many questions and are told to wait, be quiet; we are thrown into "divine discontent." We see discrepancies in the truths we have learned, and we want to disobey, rebel, or be concerned only for ourselves. We have found the path … or the *path* has found us.

It takes time and inner conflict to move ahead. We are speaking of years—as long as it takes—until the struggle between the powerful self-centered solar plexus begins to soften and the humanitarian nature begins to take form. Finally, the awakening heart begins to stir and it manifests more in acts of service, in personal love, and then in a more impersonal love, less intimate and more colored by understanding. The energy changes, gradually becomes less intense, and more objective. We begin to function more from the heart and we begin to picture how we would feel should we suffer the experiences some others do. This is the change intellectual folks, particularly, have not mastered; often emotionally they cannot walk in the other's moccasins. The plight of others is pondered; gradually it becomes a valid reality. This is a property of imagination: the "*image-making-ability*" and a use of *extended sense awareness*.

A space in the psyche provides one the capability to love others. Then we become able to have love for a Creator, to trust the Creator, and to realize our relation with this Omnipotent Universal Consciousness. These come slowly.

As we become sensitive, we can become more receptive to the pain of another, and to their joy as well. We can be happy for the other for their success and not desire it for ourselves. What we want for ourselves, we also want for others. We are evolving into more of our potential. Association with others who are exploring their inner nature and its possibilities helps us to learn about our own nature. When we associate with kindness, we tend to catch it; likewise, with negativity or with criticism. We begin to evaluate our choices.

Spiritual axiom: Like attracts like on the non-physical plane.

As we self-observe, we find that we are quite opinionated, even though not everyone else may point it out. Nightly reviews, group counseling, study, inner work, all are ways we begin to overcome our narrowness (errors, ignorance).

A momentary change of consciousness begins to allow a change of personal subjective boundaries, if this *aha* registers. We usually call this an insight; the momentary release of a rational approach to daily life allows an inner movement in how we perceive, see, and understand to emerge; thus, our reality begins to re-arrange. This can happen through the influence of dreams, guided meditations, or even new insights to an earlier situation.

When we begin to note our dreams and impressions with interest and respect, things concerning ourselves will become clear in a different way. A new sense of being, a new and different regard for the self will begin. This redefines how one perceives the greatness within the smallness of one's self. We redefine ourselves as we have a sense of Oneness with the All.

There is a disturbed sense of time as our new consciousness has its moments: timelessness, vast time, no time, time standing still, or a seemingly long time passing in seconds; also, we learn time can be full or empty.

An alteration of thinking often becomes noticeably more frequent as these happenings occur. Concentration can be diluted; memory and judgment may change. Rational thinking is less restrictive; one acts with more sense of knowing and less concerned with the opinion of others.

As consciousness expands, perceptional distortions of the rational world become commonplace; experiences are usually not frightening or strange to the individual. Experiences of imagery, subjective perception, or illusionary events occur. Light, color, and geometrical patterns all are sensed. All senses are involved, not separated into differences. The feeling is often quite overwhelming.

Loss of control bursts one out of the packaging of the usual consciousness as a new vulnerability develops with the surrendering of one's will. Powerlessness emerges as loss of opinion as one comes into alignment with a higher will. Finally, the ability to allow a higher will to guide life—some kind of expanded sense—is recognized, and changes in emotional expression begin.

The extremes of emotion—tears and fears—all surface, and if one can be assisted and encouraged to work through these emotions, they will gradually calm and a new kind of detachment is gained. Involuntary tears can occur or prolonged periods of sadness can be experienced during this emotional roller-coaster period. Psychologists have actually named this occurrence *"involuntary tears."* It is a less well known kind of healing, a releasing of unrecognized wounds of the past.

In time, this altered state of consciousness—perhaps entered through prayer, meditation, or visualization—consciously sought or not, becomes comfortable and, in fact, rejuvenating. The altered state becomes desirable for its sense of Oneness, of the Presence, or of the Embrace of the Holy that emerges.

As all this settles into the life of the mystic, the loneliness he or she has known diminishes and one realizes in a new sense that one is never alone. Wisdom teachings of various traditions share their collective wisdom. As we seek a higher state of awareness, we begin to find the way to improve our perception of the greater world in simple steps. We perceive them as simple, yet they change us as we adopt them.

Practices of the Wisdom Way, or disciplines which assist us to change, are enumerated in many writings. A very famous writing is the *Philokalia*, the teachings of the Desert Fathers. The *Philokalia* provides guidelines for a simple way of life. Concepts run from a sparse diet, plain clothes, no servant nor materialistic goals. Attachments to resist are: clinging to possessions, parents, social life, and adornments of the body while gladly bearing your challenges and tests. Since this is one of the earliest Christian writings we have regarding the early mystics and saints, it is a kind of model that has been followed by many traditions down through time.

Most teachings suggest that temptations to the spiritual life are appetites for excess, seeking praise, and desiring admiration. Duties to others are limited to prayer and invoking aid for the welfare of others. Each is encouraged to imagine for others what they cannot see for themselves. Never imagine the bad or unruly but know the power of the divine within. We would be wise to see that these efforts are intended to tame the personality and make it subservient to the Inner Self, while growing in ways of knowing the divine through regular prayer and meditation.

To *"know"* is to be intimate in a relationship with God, which includes intimacy with various levels of self, others, and the natural world in which we live. The sense of Oneness becomes a reality rather than a concept. As we recognize we are living in this dense world, it is essential for us to be ready to refine our physical, emotional, and mental levels of personality. Mystical experiences are expanding the previous ring-pass-not. They awaken us to an expanded reality and we discover larger truths within. This, in fact, is the way the personal ring-pass-not grows.

In the *Gnostic Gospel of Thomas, Verse 22*, Jesus is recorded as saying, *"infants being suckled."* He said to his disciples, *"These infants being suckled are like those who enter the kingdom."* They said to him, *"Shall we then, as children, enter the kingdom?"* We can only ponder what is meant.

Verse 51 reads, "His disciples said to him, '*When will the repose of the dead come about, and when will the new world come?'* He said to them, '*What you look forward to has already come, but you do not recognize it.'"*

What is being addressed here? Contemplate it as a mystic and try to discover what is being said. A mystic might spend all day trying to understand this.

Remember, "the dead" are what Jesus labeled "the ones that were not awakened" by his remark, *"let the dead bury the dead."* We can think this is foolishness; but he is really saying, *"Let those who have not become alive in their consciousness deal with their own. You have other work to do."* When we realize this, we begin to understand the stream of wisdom in a significant way. Those who do not know better can chance having false ideas or values, but those who know better have experienced the inner death of the false self and, like a newborn child, are blown open to receive higher understandings.

Change does not just mean, *"Change our goals, our costume and our outer habits."* It means that each level of our being will change. Our physical body, our emotional nature, our mind will change as we change from its old nature to a new. "Oneness with God" implies this journey, rarely explained to Westerners. Models usually used mention stages of development corresponding to the chakras. Enlightenment is the acknowledged highest of these stages.

Each center is to be refined repeatedly, and if contamination occurs, re-purification is necessary. This is where the idea of backsliding came from in the world of religion. As each progressive chakra opens, fresh energy washes over the lower ones bringing the lower into harmony with the higher.

Waves of damaging energy surround us. The group mind's fear and negativity, and our own personal negativity, hostility, and resentment, all affect and damage levels of consciousness, if and when we absorb them. Our resistance to the contamination assists us to maintain our higher consciousness. It is a part of the test of maturing into a more spiritual manner of living *"in the world, and not being of the world."*

John White, friend and researcher, as well as teacher, explains that, as these changes are occurring, we are, indeed, not just building a light body (as so often we speak of the change of the mental vehicle into the causal body), but there is another body that is deathless. Yes, we do have an etheric form that lives on in the lower worlds, but a greater life is in store for all of us ... and few acknowledge it.

It is the perfection of this more subtle vehicle into a body that *"has been cooked,"* as Torkom Saraydarian speaks of it, the kind of body that Lord Herekan Babaji uses when he comes and goes through the planes touching humanity, and which continuously energizes the evolutionary process. As our vehicles are being *"amped up,"* we can better understand the phrase familiar to Christians and sages, "the Communion of Saints," those before the Throne of God, the Celestial Hierarchy, or the Rishis of old in the East.

The warnings we hear about psychic development are true, because human beings do mistake the reflections for what is "real." We use similar terms to remind ourselves and others that psychism veils greater mysteries. As we advance to higher planes, some veils thin, or more correctly, we vibrate at a higher resonance where the former veils no longer exist. Then we see more clearly.

Each newly awakened vehicle vibrates at the appropriate frequencies for the plane upon which we are to do our exploration, learning, or work. In this way, each plane provides us learning experiences and in fact prepares us for higher frequencies that will serve us. We gradually penetrate veil after veil and establish an ever more subtle base of operations in the inner reality.

John White, in discussing the model, says transubstantiation is the next step. Here the culmination of the entire evolutionary process of higher human development comes together resulting in a deathless body of light, the perfecting of the human body-mind, and a significant step before the last step known as translation.

Since these are hard concepts to understand I hasten to add, "*think this way*": Our inner energies have to be amped up to the frequencies of the dimension we want to explore or with which we want to interact. As we advance into the higher mental energies of the intuitional, atmic, and monadic planes, we draw down the energies of those planes into our more dense vehicles. We are "*in the cooker,*" as Torkom Saraydarian called it. Put to the test, we see if we can enter the purer or more subtle planes. The more pure, the more intense … the hotter is the fire or energy. As we live in the cooker, the energies of our more subtle bodies or vehicles are alchemically changed.

We change as the seven divisions or layers of vibrations of each plane stir together. These energies or ingredients blend like the ingredients of a cake. First, they are thicker, then as they blend, the smoother they become, more fluid, thinner, or lighter. This changes the chemicalization of that body. As each body becomes harmonized and reworked, we change our vibrations, our abilities, and our realities.

Spiritualization or "chemicalization" as it is called in Spiritualism, is the adjustments the spirit worlds help us make as we are assisted from the inner reality. More happens in the inner world than we realize. Our dedication through our right use of will, more devotion through love-caring, and more service activity gives us the foundation for these shifts and changes that appear to be invisible. This is why we are encouraged early to get accustomed to these practices.

Remember, ice when warmed becomes water;
water heated boils and becomes steam, steam evaporates and
enters the atmosphere as humidity.

An important part of the way we are "*in the world but not of the world*" is to share from our *knowing soul-infused nature* our loving energy, both toward the world of spirit and to the earth reality as well. We connect to the higher self and bring spirit energy earthward to uplift the world in which we live. We do not believe the world as we know it, or that it is all it can be, but we believe it is up to us individually to be lifted into higher vibrations and together create a more sacred planet.

Our first steps are to bring spirit and matter together in our own awareness, in our meditations, and in our loving support of the kingdoms of nature. This is necessary for that important connection we are making. Also remember, many mystics make their first connection with the Great and Holy through nature.

Throughout scriptures there are expressions regarding "*the kingdom of heaven….*" and disciples asking, "*When will the kingdom of heaven come?*"

To which came the response, "*It will not come by expectation. They will say, see here and see there, but the kingdom of the father is spread upon the earth, and men do not see it.*"

The way we talk about going to heaven makes it sound like a separate place. It sounds like New York or some other destination, but it is actually a state of mind; it is a state of grace. When we stop and think about prospects gained from our different levels of understanding, even while we live in the physical, we realize not all people see the same beauty, goodness, or level of concern about the earth and the younger kingdoms. Some live in peace and harmony; some live in hell.

I think of some wonderful scientists and researchers who have lived among the animals of Africa, the wolves, and even Antarctica. Photographers have educated us through fantastic shots of nature, and lovely PBS films as "NOVA," and the views of the universe such shows give to us. They present new understanding to us. These, plus Animal World, have helped awaken us to the beauty of earth and her kingdoms. Yes, Father and Mother have placed us in the garden, if we can only see it.

There is a mistaken idea that a mystic lives on a mountain top within a world of peace and serenity. Somehow, the developing mystic believes this as well; it is a glamour to believe such—a glamour even for the one growing into a mystic. A world of illusion and hope keeps all striving toward the unreachable goal. Gradually it begins to dawn on them that the hectic upset world of their everyday life *is* the life of the mystic.

The mystic holds the peace that links them to the higher perspective. In this guarded place, they find the peace that passes understanding. However, the serenity they have longed for, worked for, and strived for, they cannot find. The hoped-for, peace-filled existence escapes their day. They come to know there truly is no peaceful place—none, save acting from the inner peace-filled centeredness which is strangely best found while in the turmoil of fulfilling one's daily duties.

We come to know that it is a sense of inner serenity, our own peace of mind and love, that *delivers to us that inner place* for which we have been striving. We begin by building tolerance and end up with love-caring. We give up wanting the imaginary and accept the "what is." We settle into a balance of "non-striving yet continuously striving," and we establish a tempo in which inner peace can be found amidst the complexities in which we live. Now we build the "comfort zone" that we have been seeking for so long.

Now, as a peace-filled individual, we settle into serving to help relieve pain of heart or mind, of despair in others. Using the word "*channel*" to describe our approach just exaggerates the illusion of a false self. Doing daily duty is the reality. We eat, sleep, serve, listen, and live a daily life from a calm, clear center wherein peace exists. Centered in daily life with tinges of great love filling our heart, with compassion for both the other and the self—the other can only be temporarily comforted—the inner awareness grows. The "other" gains a bit of heart energy with which to heal and be restored. Love itself is the repair work, the tool we use, as we "heal" (ourselves and) one another.

We come to know there is no need to escape the hustle and bustle of the world. It is all there, but it no longer brings discontent. It is the backdrop of life, the world of the Kabalistic reality called Assiah, the world of busy activity. Its tempo recedes, leaving us with a bubble of serenity (higher world energy) in which to live. Here there is another tempo, the one for which we have been striving. It is not the world but our own ragged self from which we have been fleeing. Many have tried to tell mystics this, but each must discover it again and for his or her self.

I believe it was St. Augustine who said, "All the way to heaven (higher consciousness) is heaven itself." This is what the Christ (the Holy Consciousness) tried to share with us when the One who lived it said, "I am the Way, the Truth, and the Life." The path we build is our path to this state of consciousness that can be peace here and now. In Buddhism we find this expressed as "the goal is the path."

Our outer life is but a staircase from level to level, lesson to lesson, as we learn "peace" in the midst of hysteria. Each demand, each duty, and each need that comes lifts us from one-step to the next. We wonder why, because no one else can tell us the reason for which we must bear the struggle we are carrying. We cannot lag behind our society; actually, we are the present-day creators of it. We must swim in it and be leaders to higher consciousness through each personal and social struggle.

Keeping our efforts up contributes to the collective energy of the mass mind until it advances to make peace with the realities of the new that is emerging. No longer are we troubled by such efforts—we accept that it is what it is, and we are what we are. Our society reflects the new awareness for which it and we have struggled. Now we become a calm, clear center in its midst and we have found our goal.

It is hard, when striving to realize the truth of the mystic, that it is in finally **surrendering** that we gain the truth of the journey. "Surrendering" sounds like giving up. This word does not do justice to the "act" of surrendering. Seeing surrendering as "aligning" has helped me, as it tells us we are no longer resisting, because the flower has bloomed. Like surrendering to puberty, there is nothing to resist. The world within us has done its work. It has polished us until the light hidden in each moment dawns.

This is the mystery, not spoken, but even when spoken, it cannot be heard. It sounds so simple, and it is. Yet it cannot be believed until the Spirit Within has been heated until vaporized and the inner understanding has been gleaned. Now we can live daily life as a "grain of mind" peacefully lying at the edge of the ocean and emanating our truth/reality. No more struggle and no more pressure from the ego self—it has died, gone, disappeared, dissolved, evaporated....

Now we, the true Self, become the driver of the Chariot. Appreciating the fine horses and carriage, we realize we must ask, who has been driving? We speak of "basic drives" within us: the drives of our personality, our ambitions, our restlessness. These many desires boil, twist, and turn to express and interact, to gain and to give and to receive ... and all have value.

Each level (each horse) has drives held within that must be spent, utilized or transformed as we stay in the quest. Each must burn itself up to come to rest, but then when rested, recovers and goes into daily life once more. Repeatedly, always beginning once more, until at last we realize that the "burning ground" has a direct relationship to our drives. We *will* finish them, settle into rest, and come to peace some day when our consciousness is clear. Now, awareness begins to lead, direct, and drive the team. We are the mystic, living the mystery, and knowing it to be so. We try to give it to others; we cannot. We try, but who can hear?

A particularly meaningful, yet simple meditation that is very good for us, and which we sometimes use for the closing of a class or ritual, is the "Soul-Star Connection," as follows:

Meditation: Bring Soul and Matter Together: Embracing Oneness

Focus your attention on the "Soul Star" over the top of your head. Hold it there for a few seconds and then begin to draw the energy of the soul earthward. (Hesitate for a few seconds; then proceed).

Bring the light from the Soul Star to the Solar Plexus; fill this area with the Light of the Soul that Light might shine into the rational mind and into the activities of the outer life. (Hesitate for a few seconds; then proceed).

Now bring the light down to the feet, that the light of the higher reality might truly be a lamp unto our path as we move through the earthly plane. (Hesitate for a few seconds; then proceed).

Take the light now to the center of the earth and hold it there, blessing matter and stimulating the tiny points of consciousness that exist in each of the nature kingdoms. We focus our light to awaken and stimulate the kingdoms of Earth that our planet might become a sacred planet. (Hesitate for a few seconds; then proceed).

We now begin the long stretch to link the energy of matter and spirit together. We move the Light once again to the feet ... then we move the light to the solar plexus ... and then move the light to the Soul Star position. (Hesitate for a few seconds; then proceed).

We move the energy of the Soul Star to the Monad in the more subtle planes as we seek that flame divine. We discover the fiery self that went on the long journey into matter. We find the "Flame Divine" and hold our attention here. (Hesitate for a few seconds and then proceed).

Now we once again begin the long movement toward the dense world of matter. We move our attention from the flame of the Monad (hesitate) to the Soul Star, (hesitate) and now let us take the Light of the Soul Star and place them together in the midst of the group seeking to re-create the Light of Oneness in the outer world.

We pause, holding ourselves peacefully centered as we seek to fulfill our reason for being and to affirm right relationship to all humanity. (Hold the silence for a minute or two).

Now let us place the Soul Star back over our head, opening ourselves to that "Light Divine." We welcome the down pouring of the Soul Star to fill our consciousness and give us the guidance needed for the living of our physical lives. Rest.

Now in your mind's eye, we see our beautiful blue planet floating in the indigo night sky, turning gently as it moves in its orbit. We observe as we see little lights beginning to come on here and there, in various continents, in countries from people here and there; lights are coming on as individuals come to know they are truly souls awakening.

As the earth slowly and easily continues to turn, we can see the lights in every country—all races, all nations, all religions, all ideologies—are building light, brighter and brighter. As the lights burn more brightly, they ignite other lights around them, and we begin to see clusters of lights around the world.

We see the clusters forming as study groups, meditation groups, healing groups, schools, temples, centers, churches—all beginning to do the group work that is needed for humanity to move forward in peace and harmony.

Now, using the laser light of our minds, we draw lines of light and love from cluster to cluster, and cluster to cluster, forming a grid of light and love all around the planet. We are consciously seeking to stabilize planetary life, as the old energies are withdrawing and new energies are bombarding the planet.

We seek the grid of light and love to stabilize the planet, as old energies complete their work and the incoming energies take their places of service. They pulsate, shift, and settle in places made ready. And the kingdoms of the world rest in peace.

We give thanks for the love in our heart and for having a role to play in this rich and meaningful time. We give thanks for having heard the call of silence and inner life, for the lessons we have experienced and the learning that has resulted. We give thanks for having a reason for being, a work to do, and a way to serve. We give thanks for the light and love that guides us day to day into peace, harmony, and the world of right relationship. Amen.

Let us say our closing prayer. Repeat after me please, line by line:

> My Lord, / Thank you for the joy / Of living today / In the spirit / Of beauty, goodness / And righteousness. / May Your joy / Radiate in other parts of the world / As the Sun / Disperses the night / And brings the joy of the day. / My Lord, / You are the joy of my heart.
>
> —Prayer by Torkom Saraydarian

Close simply, "Good night everyone. Shanti. Peace." You may choose a song to close, but keep the gentle energy you have built.

After such meditation work, we recommend that persons hold the silence for a while before resuming a lot of activity or conversation.

NINE

Awareness of Consciousness

PREVIOUSLY WE NOTED that in Scripture, we are discouraged from making oaths and vows due to the realization that one does not know what challenges or changes the future may bring. Some teach that if a vow is not satisfied in a particular life, it might be left over to satisfy in a later life. As well, the one making the vow may grow and change his or her picture of life in some manner not imagined at the time he or she was making the vow. Remember, the passion or the intensity of the "intent" is the glue that is binding.

This may account for the "inability to commit," something we see in ones who have a monk or nun archetype. In addition, ancient vows of poverty linger to limit resources when the internal consciousness is straining against an old vow and the riches of new opportunity. Vows of celibacy may be a reason some resent or resist healthy marriages … who knows? The Soul knows.

In Christianity, the Christ says to his people, *"Seek first the kingdom of God, and his righteousness; and all these things shall be given unto you" (Matthew 6:33).* To seek the Kingdom of God or Higher Consciousness, one must be willing to become a seeker. As one becomes the seeker, one's dedication pulls the available energy of one's soul earthward and focuses the blessings to help them advance upon the "path of initiation."

The mystic accepts painful moments as a part of their process, but they avoid conversation about these happenings. If we do too much of this, we may discourage others and that is not acceptable.

This is a part the individual's test. One who is a mentor or teacher of "accepted students" knows that they carry some of their students' burden to cleanse. One who acts as a guide or mentor pays a price for influencing others. In the Eastern concept, one may ask the guru to take away the desire for cigarettes, or pain, or resentment, but it still remains one's own responsibility to act. The good chela often uses analysis and psychological techniques to assist themselves along the way.

It is a part of feminine nature to be able to hold two points of view at the same time. Often we think of females as not able to make up their minds, but it is somewhat natural. This dichotomy exists in all people as the higher centers open and judgment is left behind. We can be intrigued by something and scared of it at the same time.

The Field of Consciousness

We will explore briefly this diagram of the Field of Consciousnesst. Here we see a simple but clarifying way to think about levels of consciousness; these straightforward ideas come from the "Huna Tradition," a Polynesian psychological and healing method. We will use the following Diagram A to help us understand the levels of self. Three levels of consciousness are our own to master. The Basic Self has its field of activity as do both the Conscious Self and the High Self. Understanding the Basic Self gives us clues about how to proceed.

The Qualities of the Basic Self are such that we are each masculine and feminine in the psychological nature. As we come to know our inner self, we find we are more inclined toward one way than the other. Is our natural inner style more masculine or more feminine? Spend a few minutes thinking objectively about *you*. Think about your manner of operation.

The Responsibilities of the Basic Self are to operate the physical body in such a manner as to fulfill its work through the body and the automatic nervous system ... it breathes, digests, sees, hears, etc. Our emotional patterns exist in sensations that trigger hunger, sexual needs, and emotional responses to the events of our personality and day-to-day existence.

Our survival nature or psyche protects us, helps us to feel safe or unsafe, produces warnings, impressions or attractions, through smell, fight-or-flight impressions that arise from within ... irrational urges, fears ... all the remnants of the old animal nature that has sunk below the level of the conscious mind. From here, the dream-maker can create dramas to prompt us to new understanding, if we learn his language.

Intuitive Faculties are different from the psyche. Any previous experience in other lives of intuitive awareness continues to be anchored within each of us. Prior development, or even prior development of the collective of which we were a part, abides within until reawakened. This awareness of inner knowing is the home of higher guidance that works hand and hand with the Soul as the higher senses come into play. Not all humans have had much experience with the intuitive, but the psyche of each is alive and well. Although psychism is not the goal for a mystic, the intuitive faculties naturally become activated as higher consciousness develops. The saying goes, *"all psychics are not spiritual, but all spiritual ones are psychic."*

There is a little known compartment in our nature, called the *Repository of Memory Pattern*, where we preserve deep impressions from previous events and the emotions attached to them, such as past traumas. Here are memories of past lives (not acceptable to all, but this is where that repository exists). As we grow in awareness, we learn to clear or balance the lessons of the past. Now as an aware one, we are tested to meet such experiences anew and face them with the new consciousness we have gained.

The Conscious Self is the developing part of our nature; here the ego houses our current life experience. We become trained, programmed, and educated by our society; we have a perceived social status. We attend churches and schools. This cultural reality is "maya" in spiritual terminology. Here we live within the hypnosis of our place and station of birth. The ego believes it has the greatest value and will wrestle until death to prove itself.

There is an old example of crab grass: it appears to have been cleared only to grow back. The garden needs constant weeding, but the weeds spring forth repeatedly. We pull up the sprouts of ego more than once; they return repeatedly just like weeds. Ego dies hard and seeks to fool us into thinking it has gone … only to appear once more.

Our High Self consists of the" ball of knowledge" we have built through our many experiences. We draw upon this available wisdom as we develop a higher ethic, better perception, and the awakening of our spiritual nature. Generally, this aspect of our self begins as "conscience," which is in fact the "voice of our programming." As we mature, we are able to discern a more subtle reality wherein our own Soul begins to prompt us regarding realities unknown to the conscious mind.

Following Diagram A we see also that we gather information from Akashic Records, our Karmic Pattern, as well as the Soul and Solar Angel. These are all subtle impressions with both blessings and challenges. We will be working on the challenges we have brought forward through life experiences, which will assist us to grow. From these inner lessons our life will emerge. Primary sources from which we will learn spiritual attitudes will be the High Self and the Soul, as these aspects come into harmony. In our journey, we will discover practices we can utilize, and we will find ourselves calling upon higher help during life experiences.

Here we can see how much of our consciousness exists outside our intellectual understanding.

Study this diagram. Here we can see that much of our awareness has slipped beneath our level of conscious capabilities. We see how various qualities and responsibilities reside within the basic self. We build the ego consciousness in each life and then carry forward additional learning to the next lifetime. As the human evolves, through our instinctual nature, with its emphasis on survival, its acute animal senses, and its fight-or-flight syndrome, there

Diagram A
The Impact of Spiritual Practices Well Done

Practices   **Results**

As prayer and
meditation begin . . . . new insight and awareness begin.
We see the Plan and know.
We find our inner guidance.
We penetrate the Cloud
of Knowable Things

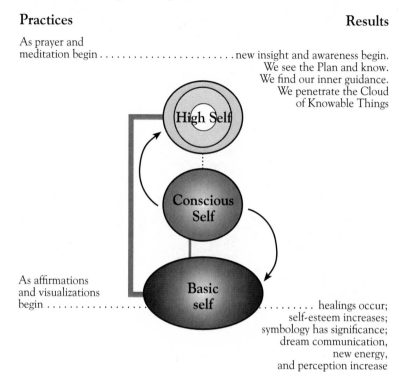

As affirmations
and visualizations
begin . . . . healings occur;
self-esteem increases;
symbology has significance;
dream communication,
new energy,
and perception increase

occurs a gradual shift where the animal self becomes a lower priority. However, as we learn in times of emergency or perceived loss,
or even sudden developmental spurts, our Basic Self resurfaces.

Our basic nature possesses capabilities we rarely focus upon
until we begin to "know thyself" in some new ways. The Basic Self
receives messages from our higher nature through codes that range
from dreams to stomach aches. The innate intelligence is inge-
nious at providing dramas and symbols to convey its information,
although we may only understand a limited amount consciously.

We do learn to communicate from Conscious Self to Basic Self
and from Conscious Self to High Self (higher consciousness) as we

Diagram B

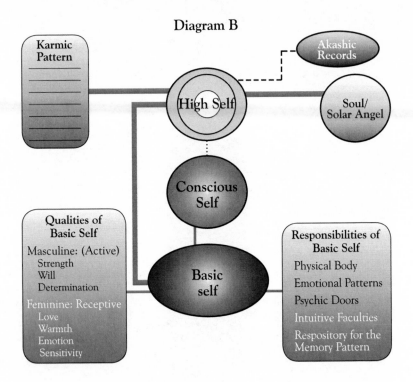

raise our consciousness. Early steps usually include affirmations and visualizations to communicate with the Basic Self.

We can see how we can use prayer and meditation as techniques for invoking the assistance of High Self and how it responds. Equally so, we see the assistance we receive using affirmations and visualization.

We dare to repeat: *"transformation"* itself is a process. In each life, one hopes to make progress in his or her own way and in his or her own time. Ultimately, the goal is to become all that one may be. Each one has levels of consciousness to evolve and transform. Each individual explores various spiritual practices as they seek to activate the conscious transformational process.

"Mystic" is the word used for the one advancing in the process, if, and as, they have experiences that open their own reality of a multi-dimensional view. This may happen gently for some as they begin their spiritual disciplines. Others may have a more dramatic experience. However, one need not have an astonishing experience to take this approach due to spiritual inspiration or a past dedication to the Esoteric or Sophianic approach; as they have found that which resonates to them, they become dedicated, and they make a commitment. Remember, "philosophy" means "*love of Sophia*" (love of wisdom). It is important to recognize that transformation is a process, not an end in itself or a product. The very nature of a "process" is that change is gradual and not always in measurable ways.

Remember, the ancient but time-proven formula to begin the journey to higher consciousness is to recall the four simple universal practices and stimulate the spiritual growth process regardless of faith. All paths begin by recommending these simple practices:

- Study

- Prayer and meditation

- Keeping company with others of high vibrations

- Tithing—practicing generosity

Each discipline or practice (called "Wisdom Ways" to me) requires a knowledgeable one to share his or her techniques; each may seem simple, but none truly is. Each teacher says to those he or she cares about, "*This is how I learned to do it.*"

Study and intellectual work stretches the mind and there are certain basics that one has to have to install a foundation for attracting broader concepts. The example I often use is to think there are dots in the mind that have to be connected, or that spiritual study is much like working a jigsaw puzzle. You get a few pieces together here and there. Then another set of puzzle pieces come together over there. In time, they attract your attention and you quietly work on them for a while until they begin to fit together and add new meaning.

Occasionally a set of pieces fall into place and it makes the entire concept make sense in a more meaningful way. It becomes necessary to think on these things, if you would be a disciple. The entire way in which you will see it takes time to build and it will continue to adjust as new ideas arise. Whichever path is chosen, or chooses you, determines which teachings and what parables you will be taught. While the verses or words may be the same or similar, the understanding will be different. The materials one feeds the mental body become very important. As we put high and holy thoughts into our mental (and emotional bodies), we apply the guidelines of "holy in, holy out."

A hard concept for some to accept but which has worked well for me, is that concepts are just like typewriter keys. There are sets of unspecified concepts, which when added together establish different concepts. This is somewhat like letters adding up to a word, or words adding up to a sentence. Now we can understand that concepts work in a similar manner to a typewriter key, with each key representing a concept. Your understanding gradually forms a "map"; once learned, your mind dances over these concepts like fingers on a keyboard.

Your spiritual patterns form designs that come together to give you a philosophy of life, it seems. Then when a new idea is introduced, you look to the "map" constructed in your mind and see where or if the new idea can fit with the concepts you have already found acceptable. If it fits, you add to the foundation upon which you are building. Test the principle and see if it is or is not usable for you. Study is like learning the keyboard to the piano, necessary if you are going to read music. Otherwise, you will fall for each idea tossed your way without discernment.

Prayer is a state of consciousness wherein one is expressing his or her self sincerely to God or to whatever concept of the Source of Life one happens to hold. In true prayer, one communicates with the Higher. The "lesser" is honestly bonding itself to a "higher" source. I like the expression "Higher Power" because it is a clear term anyone can understand. The concept of "God" has become a trap for many who harbor wounds or hostility, or even still envision a wise old man passing judgment on a little lesser person. We have to talk to God/Higher Power, the Mother or the Father without holding back our contrite self. If we are fearful, we must be able to say so, as truthfulness is the foundation for prayer work.

We learn to express our honest concerns, especially as this becomes even more clear. Especially so, if we believe the Divine already knows our needs. There may be a suppressed anger or hurt held within when we believe God knows our needs and withholds whatever. If we learn to understand the spiritual axiom: *"ask to receive,"* we know that whatever is for our well being will be given. The phrase, *"if it be the higher will"* can also be useful as we move ahead. The idea of God or Higher Power knows that: 1) our need is one of knowing that we are loved, and 2) that when we are de-nied, it is for our higher good, even though our personality level may not believe it. It is often hard to come to this understanding, especially after being wounded or seemingly rejected by whomever we consider *higher authority.*

An important truth is that fifteen minutes of prayer or contrite expression is not going to "make up" for twenty-three hours and forty-five minutes of arrogance. A part of adjusting to the role, when one is ready to be in relationship with the higher power, is to interact with the Divine, called by any name, with sincerity and honesty. This does not mean groveling; it does mean a respectful and often a repentant attitude.

There is a mistaken idea that when one has begun to meditate, one no longer needs to pray. One doesn't just listen; one must, with sincerity, express needs, wants, and wishes as if one is the lover of the other … it can be as a father, a mother, a devotee … but if you are approaching the Master or King of Kings, there is a natural demeanor of respect.

Meditation is a state of inner listening or of fixed attention, which can be experienced in many styles. There are endless ways and systems of "listening to the Lord" of one's life. Training helps one to discover a technique that works for one's self. There is a pyramid of approaches that work best from simple sitting still for a few minutes and learning to relax and "be still," to guided imagery wherein another leads and inner responses comes to surface. By following such a technique, or while listening to music, helps to achieve a very relaxed state wherein *just knowing* can happen.

An experienced teacher usually experiments with a beginner to help them find a methodology that will get one started. Different styles may appeal as one becomes more experienced. The goal of all meditation approaches is to be able in time to slow the brain wave activity down into the alpha range, and reach a state of spiritual guidance or awareness not available to the active mind in its beta state. Some approaches use mantras, some do not.

There are both Eastern and Western approaches, and many begin with chanting or a centering prayer to help one become free from ego and begin the adjustment inward. With practice we learn to create the higher vibrations needed to lift our spirit. Chanting or singing is a tool to celebrate the joy of higher vibrations. Either way, the practice is intended to benefit one in his or her spiritual or health practices. "He who sings prays twice," the wise saying tells us.

Some years ago, Swami Pranananda, from Washington University, U.S.A., advised our group to stop chanting in other than English. His explanation was that too often English-speaking, yet eager spiritual students, mispronounce Hindu words. He taught that without understanding the meaning of the words they spoke or sang, they could say "not-so-nice" words repeatedly. In effect, this becomes a negative affirmation and not beneficial. Due to these words of wisdom, our groups have used English only, or Latin words that they understand. Thus, it seems best to use your own language or words which are well defined.

Likewise, chanting and singing have different work to do. Chanting, particularly, is beneficial to create higher vibrations without concern for many words—easy to follow and easy to recall. Singing is more to create beauty and a field of energy with a central thought form to embed itself in the Basic Self. As one changes his or her approaches, they often have to update the awareness they have to a new understanding, and through singing the new "truth," one finds a quick and seemingly natural way to do so.

Tithing is a way of teaching us generosity, or gifting a share of one's resources; it is most commonly called "donations" or "gifting." The amount can be set or unset and the most common amount is ten percent from the Old Testament as proper to share with the Lord out of the bounty one has. If we give our gift or tithe with resentment, it negates the spiritual benefits, as tithing is truly a teaching to inspire generosity. The percentage of your gift is not the point unless one is measuring themselves to others in an egotistic manner; the goal is to realize that everything one has comes from the higher Source and we are only acknowledging that with an act of appreciation. Some teachers suggest another amount for a specific reason, i.e., the learning of a student. One soon comes to the realization that all abundance comes from a Higher Source of supply than one's own desire or will.

Tithing frequently helps one to determine the difference between prosperity and abundance. While tithing is being learned, I was once told, if you are going to give a dollar, break it into ten dimes, and practice giving ten times. Learning to give is the true consciousness we are to develop. While abundance and prosperity are similar, abundance helps us realize the need for health, friends, etc., not just money or income. Prosperity considers all of these in its approach, also. Disciples know that a share of their funds belongs to the higher world and they are privileged to distribute them responsively.

To figure out just how the master wants a disciple to serve in this way, one must learn **discernment**. Moreover, disciples are also taught that a share of their learning has to do with *what to give* and *to whom* without inner conflict. Major tests that go along with this learning process are those of pride and arrogance. While we are to have dignity in all that we are and certainly in this area, as we serve the Higher, we are tested to see that we do not fall into the trap of false pride or believing that our ego is capable of doing great things in our own name.

Keeping good company is a priority for anyone making a significant change of lifestyle. A person striving for higher consciousness comes to realize that he or she absorbs surrounding vibrations. This is a good reason for finding the correct group with which to associate. In time, each finds a significant group that is right for them and here they learn the discipline of shared responsibility.

Until one is comfortable with his or her own sensitivity, this is most difficult. Nevertheless, the first rule of *keeping good company* is a non-judgmental attitude. We learn to appreciate the exposure available to one's self. This is not a popularity contest, nor a social club. Here one is exposed to others with the warning that "like attracts like," so we begin the quest by using our own grasp of what is "good" as best we can.

We soon learn how differently we each perceive the world, spiritual subjects, and everything else. Soon we begin to learn lessons that add clarification to our studies, as well as our togetherness, discussions, and inner actions, for everything begins to teach us. This is in no way to say we are in the wrong group but more or less assures us that we have found a good group for us for a time. A new opportunity will appear to join others when it is right for us and we are ready to change. We allow our guidance to guide us.

When one finds compatible group interests, we interact with a number of personalities and group work begins in earnest. While many groups stay together with minor changes for years, others will seem to have a constant turnover, introducing concepts to many new persons. Some groups will not meditate with anyone but accepted members of their group. Some groups will be open to all and see this acceptance as a kind of service to humanity.

These latter groups see acceptance as expressing love and they seek to uplift visitors or others into their vibration. Others allow all interested parties to become a part of their regular routine. Either can be good company and either can enrich our journey. Practice your higher ethics combined with a non-judgmental attitude and stay open. The right group will appear. The rule is to remember always that the group energy affects us, and we, the group. Therefore, we must be selective. Groups have rules, as do, religions. Look before you leap!

Different cultures practice a wide range of **dietary disciplines**. Traced back to the early times when most disciplines were for religious or health reasons, it was determined which beneficial practices were to be accommodated. Today it is well known that dietary disciplines can be beneficial for either health or for practicing self-restraint in order to develop greater self-discipline. The practice of restricting or limiting either the amount or kind of food is fasting. Either practice can be beneficial for various reasons, but one must choose the practice to which one is going to dedicate his or her self and, if it is to restrict the amount of food, or certain foods are to be eliminated, understand that the reason you are doing it is for the strengthening of will power. Developing self-restraint or will power is a definite advantage and enables one to resist whatever tries to come into one's life that one would rather not give entry.

We discover that limiting the amount of food or substance taken into the body can be done for reasons other than spiritual growth. In fact, I think it necessary to realize what Jesus said: it is not what goes into our mouth but what comes out that is damaging. Different traditions teach different means of fasting. Spiritually, we come to know that everything taken into the body affects the chemical ether of this delicate vehicle; this leads to the approval or disapproval of certain foods. In relationship to health or healing, at times, restriction is advised to control habits or addictions. Some teachings are more restrictive than others are, but in the end, each one's effectiveness depends on the individual's cooperation/choice.

Sexual disciplines also are included. Practices of celibacy or periodic abstinence wherein one agrees to restrict sexual activity for a reason, spirituality being one, are well known. If partnered, the consent of the other is necessary since in committed relationships the partner has a say-so regarding personal practices that affect each. Those practicing celibacy often have a tendency to feel superior to others. This resentment is a distortion and most harmful to spiritual growth.

The study of dreams for personal guidance is often very beneficial. The practice requires the noting of inner awareness to impressions and actually helps us to become more sensitive to all impressions. The dream is a common way guidance is given. Some, we find, will have a better ability than others to capture impressions. This requires one to learn the language of symbols and to keep a dream log to identify dreams differing in symbols but similar in meaning. At some point, dreaming tends to slow down and guidance that is more direct becomes available.

A spiritual or good will practice is **service**, which is the sharing of one's talents, physical help, personal aid, or effort on behalf of another. As one realizes the bounty or blessings one has in their own life, service becomes a way to say "thank you" to the universe. Service is done for many reasons. One reason is to free one's self from feeling obligated to serve. This can be a spiritual act or just another way to build one's ego. As a disciple trying to do service, one desires to share, as an opportunity to gift a part of our bounty to others by lending our energy and/or resources to create greater growth and new awareness within ourselves (and others).

The training of a person in **visualization and concentration** has the goal of prodding the "psychic, unconscious, inner sight" to a more conscious level. Visualization, concentration and similar practices are disciplines to strengthen the development of mental powers. Concentration, or the ability to focus the mind intently in a powerful way, is useful for a number of purposes, i.e., for dealing with pain, irritation, or to make attunements to specific subjects or objects for the acquiring of impressions which can prove most helpful.

LOVE is the harmony that allows transmission or resonance with all life. We have learned there are energies on each plane; most teachings suggest seven levels exist within each plane. These seven levels must learn to work together (to harmonize) to create an abundance of vital energies on that plane— i.e., the harmonizing of the seven levels on the physical planes brings about physical health and well-being. Next, our seven energies of the emotional nature must integrate from our sense of personal survival to care for the survival of others. We refine our emotions and have a healthy regard for the feelings, hopes, dreams and wishes of others, as well as our own. We encounter these repeatedly. Mentally we have Maya, Glamours (Old English spelling used in esoteric/occult materials) and Illusions to dissolve. These terms all have special meaning to the spiritual teachings:

- Maya ... the agreed-upon hypnosis of our society

- Glamours ... emotional scar tissue that continues to distort our awareness of the experiences of the life we encounter

- Illusions ... false truths masquerading as real

As our personality— physical, emotional, and mental nature— becomes more refined, we become "integrated Personalities." Most occult material designates this stage with a capital P for Personality, while the next segment in our quest is "Soul Infusion."

A Healthy Self Is Our Gift to God

A critical point in the life of the ego occurs when it is conditioned to seek the satisfaction and happiness it desires and expects, and instead it finds unhappiness, grief, being blocked from goals, or powerless. Now one turns to seek relief, or some form of diversion. This may be to call on God with prayers, do spiritual practices, or seek out mentors. Just as often, one seeks relief through the underworld initiations: sexuality, alcohol, drugs, materialism, food, and other artificial satisfactions. This is a major crossroad for the individual.

One cannot give God what he or she has not built, so many of life's experiences are intended to build or grow oneself into the raw material which can become the catalyst for transformation. Some lessons are for the creation of an ego strong enough to be tested, and thus we often find we have more strength than we knew.

There is a natural struggle, no matter which choice, until one admits he or she is powerless to gain peace through temporary behaviors. The old behavior does not have to be condemned by one's peers or group mind for it to be destructive to one's Soul purpose. It may be fame or fortune, social status or power over others, but one must realize these are not helpful to the growth of the inner being.

Suffering is a teacher, just as all pain is, even if unwelcome. In time, it creates a change point in the personality. It assists the crossover from ego awareness to soul awareness, although this is probably not clear in the beginning. The submission to something higher begins in time. It may be relief or release, forgiveness or changing goals in a gradual, almost unnoticed manner.

Suffering is much more than *"bad karma."* It may be very much a part of the "good" journey to the higher world, but we cannot see it. The experiences we have are not to be labeled good or bad. The heavenly world does not work in *"good or evil"* ways. That is a judgment of the lower consciousness and is a limiting view. How many will say *"that was the worst experience of my life"* to only later say *"I could never be where I am if that had not happened nor as happy as I am otherwise."* Many wise ones know this to be a great truth.

A point that Asher Barnwell, author of *The Meaning of Christ for Our Age,* made in a paper entitled *"The Path of Process,"* is that transformation of the individual and evolution of humanity is not the same transformation. It is important for each intentional spiritual student to realize that their questing puts their current challenges into "speeded up action." Transformation of the soul—the soul growth that each individual must do—is fortunately the prototype for the species that has been modeled for us by Christ Jesus. We have other great ones who have achieved liberation as well, and we have a pattern to show us how it is possible. The Master Jesus gave us a model to follow; some traditions follow other models, but it is important that we recognize the transformation process outlined for humanity and follow the progressing steps.

In this way, each individual has an opportunity and a responsibility to make contact with one aspect of our collective future and to anchor that future in the present. Agni teachings suggest, *"catch a glimpse of your self as you will be some day, and be that now."* We must walk, and seemingly alone, on our own. Mysticism marks the route of a great many.

There is a relationship building between the One Divine Creator, called by whatever name, and the individual sparks which separate from this wholeness. The evolving spark descends and now must develop a personality and ego. Ultimately each must once again become a part of the Great Oneness with an awareness of the value and the meaning of that Oneness. When Soul consciousness is sought, liberation from the limitations of our humanness will come naturally, in due time.

The Higher part, the Soul, must interact with the human consciousness to help the human shift its awareness to higher levels of consciousness. The mystical moment is the inner action that builds the relationship. The transformational experience blends the two or lifts the lower to the frequencies of the higher. This is the "liberating path of initiation."

This union allows the higher nature to secure the experiences of the lower for soul growth even if the soul is not yet an enlightened being. All this becomes a part of the "permanent atom for future experience." The mystic comes to know *there is only One Great Life and that they are one with it at every stage.* All the many experiences of humanity are but individual opportunities for this One Great Life to acquire experience and become an even greater, richer, divine consciousness within us.

No Experience Is Ever Lost

As an individual seeking enlightenment, each of us must create a way to advance our own awareness, to keep refining and broadening our perspective or, we might say, "our box." I choose to think of this as *"our ring-pass-not,"* until we can comprehend a view far beyond our original limited personality, i.e. one made up of maya, glamour, and illusion.

Our advancement on our path depends greatly on our intentions. There are virtues and themes to help us build higher consciousness in all creeds. However, the evaluation of morality and the constructive characteristics we build must not become judgmental, noting that there are qualities defined as "good and bad" in all traditions.

We will keep reincarnating within humanity as we gradually learn to utilize the "mind." We are to become a thinker ... and begin to shape our own experience. We must learn "power of choice" and "freedom to express" in healthy ways in order to construct the experience we desire. In addition, each must come to realize his or her power to play a part in the collective human experience and does, in fact, have an effect within the greater group. This is the "mind being" becoming "made in the image and likeness" of the Creator.

We are to learn the power of prayer, as well as meditation. We must learn to talk to and to connect with the Higher Source and to direct energy through our mind with prayers for the benefit of others. We can—as loving, caring ones—invoke the higher forces to work for the "higher will be done," by strengthening and directing our own healing requests and the special intentions of others as we are asked. We are like additional little batteries amping up the power of good we can draw down and share upon the earth plane. This is a real work of the awakened ones as we seek to serve the higher world.

If you have not learned the power of prayer yet, **practice**. Prayer is a connecting and discussing in honest openness with the Great One of Creation ... and then becoming an outpost of this radiant consciousness. The work is to invoke and evoke ... be a co-worker of the Divine. We are learning the power of speaking "the word" from our own creative consciousness. Here we see examples that may be helpful.

Examples of Prayer

> *Dear Creator, Giver of All Life. Bless us this day as we invoke right resolution to the challenges we face. Provide for us the energies needed to guide our actions this day for the higher good, health and well-being. We give thanks. Amen.*

Another invocation for public:

> *Oh, Holy Breath of Life. No lips can speak nor tongue utter what You truly are; yet our hearts are not satisfied until they find rest in You. Our Souls hunger and thirst for Your Presence. Create within us a heart that longs for peace and harmony. Illumine our every thought with purity and love. Bathe us with Your Holy Hush and unite us in communion with the Saints, the unseen Hosts, and the Masters, as we offer ourselves to You in devotion and discipleship. Amen*

Prayers are Treatments, as well.

Treatments: A prayer or treatment is an uttering from one level of self to another or from one creature of God to another. We recognize the special energies of healing and hope, created and directed by our requests, whenever we are coming from our heart center.

This can be personal emotional energies for a friend or loved one, or an impersonal love, perhaps for an individual unknown to you … but you must pray or dialogue with sincerity. There is an unconditional love that we direct to a group, a city, a country, to a purpose or a culture. We invoke the higher good of an identity leaving the outcome to the Soul of the individual, group, or collective.

When a treatment is used, one is usually asking for help and relief in some manner for a personal condition concerning a known situation. It is more common to be taught in groups such as "Science of Mind" or "Religious Science" etc. Energies of the lower and higher planes flow into the etheric body of the individual for whom we pray, whether in a laying on of hands or absentee manner. There is little difference in manner; it is more terminology by different traditions. Often either is beneficial as we make an effort to dissolve the negative energies involved and assist in restoring harmony.

Idea for closing: An awakened one, an initiate, constructs a lifetime of directed action and self-discipline for his or her self. This is the simplest to understand: each one of us files a "flight plan with the higher world" and every day from that time forward, we must remember, **"It is the work of the world to pull us off our path, and it is our work to keep our self on it."**

The "closing of one's self" after doing spiritual work, prayer and meditation are spiritual strokes of importance. As we *return to the focus* of the outer world, we establish a practice often called *"tying the knot"* or closing off. The common signal ... with the Sign of the Cross ... is a conscious indication of the opening or closing of the heart, or the chakras. We may have our own term, such as "and we give thanks" which indicates to those present, if any, as well as to our spirit helpers, that we are ending the prayer or completing our effort. The most common term is "*Amen,* or "*So be it*" or something similar. With any of these efforts, intent is most important.

The Dark Night of the Soul

The "dark night of the soul" is a well discussed and frequently mentioned segment of the journey, wherein we move from the joys and blessings of Illumination to the difficult testing of a deeper segment; little understood, but of great importance, is this hard and seemingly alone experience. Evelyn Underhill is the much-quoted authority with an acclaimed study entitled by the simple name, *Mysticism.* Published in 1911, it is a royal rendition. The beauty of the writing takes a difficult subject, daring to put it into print with a scrutiny of discipleship while providing us with many opportunities to embrace or confront glamour and illusion.

Glamour invites us each to believe we are more "spiritual than we are, a great initiate, or living an excellent and loving life of discipleship." Illusion fills our mind with beliefs that we are "holy ones come to Earth for some outstanding purpose, living our concluding lifetime, and near perfection in all areas of life." The dark night of the Soul strips us of such beliefs and shows us our frailties, our sins, our weaknesses, and the errors of walking our day-to-day path. Here, stripped of the ego, we watch our glories die a painful death and see ourselves reborn to life with a new humility and reality.

At some seemingly critical time, we will find ourselves in a testing segment of life, reaching out for support and finding none. No matter what we try, we are cut off, it appears, from help. It is not there. This feels much like reaching for a familiar hand in the dark and not finding it; search proves that no support is to be found. This can happen and does happen more than once to each of us but this is a real time of doubt. It is important to realize there are mini-dark nights of the soul before the culminating event. These "small" periods of darkness are all we can endure at that stage in our growing process.

Most of us can review our lives to find we have had one or more of these trials in this lifetime. It is harder to realize we are not advanced enough to have had the great and final one. We have all kind of excuses come to us after each such time of trial ... as to why this or that was so, but the real reason for having such a trial goes little understood.

We may consider these mini-trials as preparatory to the final dark night of the soul, just as sleep is the practice for the great sleep we call death. Sleep periods are not only that, but they are growing times, real to the soul, when it is doing work on other planes. Likewise, the mini-dark nights are readying us for the "great aloneness" that will eventually come to show us we have all the necessary strengths and skills within us to undergo much more than we believed earlier.

Designed to strengthen us, these testing experiences are fashioned by our helpers in the inner reality. Ultimately, we discover there is more strength in each of us than we recognize. The wisdom we have been acquiring, the practical knowledge within us, the spiritual belief structure we have built is all tested. We learn by experience; we tend to give ourselves more credit than we have earned when the testing times come upon us. Thrown back on our resources in the midst of experiencing such, we become our real selves. We find our help "comes from the Lord Within." Although we have been growing, learning, and practicing, now the day has come, usually unexpectedly, that we must turn within to find our answers and our comfort. Only then do we begin to realize what our true resources are.

After one has experienced the real and final dark night of the Soul, there are almost no "psychic illuminations." There is a clear knowing, not much phenomena, unless this knowingness is so considered. There is a more calm balance between the "*states of pleasure*" and "*states of pain*." A quote from *Mysticism* by Underhill reads,

> ... the Soul after many a redoubled death, expires at last in the arms of Love; but she is unable to perceive these arms.... Then, reduced to Naught, there is found in her ashes the seed of immortality, which is preserved in these ashes and will germinate in its season. She knows not this; and does not expect ever to see herself living again.

The following paragraph grasps the purpose of the struggle,

> ... the soul which is reduced to the Nothing, ought to dwell therein; without wishing, since she is now but dust, to issue from this state, nor, as before, desiring to live again. She must remain as something which no longer exists; and this, in order that the Torrent may drown itself and lose itself in the Sea, never to find itself in its selfhood again: that it may become one and the same thing with the Sea.

Talk of the dark night of the Soul fills us with dread, as it should, but at the same time beckons us forward in our bravest moments. It will come when we are ready. We know that all the way on the path of initiation challenges will await us. Each experience is but one; now we walk courageously and calmly, knowing we can walk through highs and lows. Remembering the teaching of all teachers, to be spoken at our lowest moments, "*this, too, shall pass*" and similarly at the highest moment of recognition, "*this, too, shall pass*" … as we walk between the two towers of our path until we see the golden doors before us.

Longing for a way to create a relationship with the higher world, we often do not know how or what to do for the first step. Some teach to have "*gratitude*" for whatever comes to you. Torkom Saraydarian preached *Love, Freedom, Beauty, and Joy*. His thoughts were to prepare the consciousness for progress and the acceptance of the growth path, both gladness and struggle. Many others have wise ways and, with training, we can embrace them in theory and eventually in practice.

The mystic longs for the exposure to these grace-filled thoughts and secures them gradually by pondering inward long and hard. We often hear the terms "uphill and down" in relationship to the inner journey … the highs and lows have been harmonized, the illuminations have brought great light and joy, the dark night of the soul has burned away the dross and now harmony is found. One is one with the One.

For what does your spirit cry out? Speak into the morning light; speak into the moonlight. Invoke your need on the wings of spirit until you find your way. Invocation is calling down the power just as it was in ancient time. We call into our lives both lessons and learnings. We invoke daily by our thoughts and words of power. This is as true of our personal words as an invocation in church, meeting or gathering. All sincere prayers, memorized or spoken from the heart, are calling forth both the well-being of humanity and yourself. The Great Invocation is currently very popular as a call to the great ones to come and bring their assistance. We invoke the presence of the Higher and their energy into the human condition. Most often, we acknowledge this blessing as a gift from the higher planes.

The Great Invocation

From the point of Light within the Mind of God
Let light stream forth into the minds of all people.
Let Light descend on Earth.

From the point of Love within the Heart of God
Let love stream forth into the hearts of all people.
May Christ return to Earth.

From the center where the Will of God is known
Let purpose guide the little wills of all people—
The purpose which the Masters know and serve.

From the center which we call the race of humanity
Let the Plan of Love and Light work out
And may it seal the door where evil dwells.

Let Light and Love and Power restore the Plan on Earth.

TEN

Initiation ...
Beginning Again and Again

WE ARE THREATENED BY the greatest kind of divine discontent as we progress because our essence must become what we truly are ... even the Absolute is freeing itself from limitation, so a greater Love can flow. The Human Initiations lead to Solar Initiations of higher influences and they, in turn, lead to Cosmic Initiations, the endless assent back to the Godhead.

There is a statement from the early twentieth century mystic, Mable Collins, which goes something like this: "*We see the light, we enter the light, but we never touch the flame. It leads us on.*"

This helps to understand why priests, holy ones, and medicine persons teach that there is more value to "devotion." We feed our spiritual nature by receiving the blessings, or Eucharist, the blessed elements (the sacrament of bread and wine in Christianity) of communion, or prasad (a ceremony of blessed sweets or fruits in the Eastern tradition)—whatever is provided as blessed by our tradition. At first, we do it because we think we are supposed to, but as our spirit awakens, the ceremony and blessings, and our inner experience become the real food sought from the higher world for the Soul. We find it does something beyond understanding for us while we are clothed in physical form.

A part of what you may be ready for now, you may not have heard ... you may have gone to church, to communion, and did the best you could with whatever you learned. You experienced communion repeatedly, perhaps reaching a point when it no longer provided food for your hungry mind, so you felt dissatisfied. Perhaps you no longer participated in any worship, grew more discontent. Leaving the church behind; you had many questions and felt the answers held no meaning. This is quite agnostic and a most frequent modern entry to higher study.

Love Is the Evolutionary Force

The major step, remember, the mystic takes is to desire to be one with the Creator more than anything. We may begin by obedience to our culture, our family or our church practice, but the next step, a valued one, is working on our heart. Often a person feels guilty, for the Love of God draws us away from others as we cling to the experience of our devotion to the Divine. There is a genuine struggle with why we feel this way when others lay claim to our love. We accept this inner pull quietly as we deal with our family or friends' lack of understanding.

After a time we clear away the astral energy—the conflict and guilt—and find a real kind of devotion where the love we give to the Source goes forth and returns to us. We may not understand all of this; we generally do not. We just know, at times, our heart opens and we feel L-O-V-E flowing within and through ourselves. It uplifts us.

> At Catholic mass one day during the communion service, after the bread and wine were consecrated, the priest held up the monstrance. Looking at it, my heart filled with devotion, as the host flared up in seemingly fire and light, as if it were ablaze. The light filled the room and the fire reflected in my chest. As it was a Roman Catholic mass, I was kneeling. People started going to communion; I could not move. I stayed frozen in place causing others to climb over me. Mass ended, everyone left; I stayed, unable to move. The priest came out, patted my shoulder and said, "Go home now."

In that moment, I "*knew*" communion was more than I had previously understood. It is a real *calling down* of holy energy into our lives. It is the power of which Christ spoke, "*feed my sheep.*" In the Esoteric, we come to know that something more is happening than our physical nature perceives, until expansion of consciousness begins to share the secrets of the higher world with us.

We personally come to understand the meaning of Apostolic Succession—the tradition that goes back to the Last Supper where disciples witnessed the ritual of Christ Jesus for his followers. We usually have to struggle a bit with this understanding until we move into a deeper grasp of this teaching. Think upon this, **Esoteric teachings say communion, sacred blessings can be for you whatever you will let them be.**

This is a powerful truth. If sacraments are social events to you, that is all they are. If they are channels of spiritual grace for you, they are that by the power of your own understanding. If you accept the idea that the Christ of the Inner World is blessing and providing this sacramental food for you in the here and now, it will be. This is a part of the wonder of esoteric teaching: It is real. By the power of the spirit within you, the channel opens and the Higher sends forth.

A major part of the role of the mystic is to become the LOVE that never ceases…

Now you are at a different stage on the path of wandering, searching about, feeling you need more. For a while you received *milk;* this is the lesser … your needs were met, but now you have outgrown that and you have a need for *meat.* You are now ready for richer food; you are moving from the lesser path and ready for the greater and richer. This is the natural path for humanity … it is the journey to higher consciousness.

"**In mysticism the mind follows the soul.**" *That which is experienced, first as a spiritual reality is afterwards sustained by the mind. In ritual, therefore, interpretation follows internal stimula-*

tion. The purpose is to reveal to the individual his own capacity to participate in the movements of universal life energy. Nobility of character depends upon sublime archetypes residing in the psychic self. When man becomes beautiful internally, and discovers himself to be a creature of beauty possessing an internal insight greater than his external perceptions, he is converted to reality by the yearnings and longings of his own heart. His mind responds to the instruction of the wise, but his soul to the revelation of the eternal.

— *The Psychology of Religious Ritual* by Manly P. Hall

Most any dedicated mediator, group leader, or minister, as well as others with broader and wiser ideas, **serve to grow** themselves. To do so they participate in all kinds of groups by stepping down higher energies into that arena. If there is a group of individuals working together in a service, which has at least one illumined person present, the entire group is energetically uplifted. Remember that the Holy Consciousness (the "Christ" as Christians called this one) said, "I am with you always." This Consciousness is always *available* if one has the spiritual stamina to have earned it. He or she can then *step it down for oneself and for others.*

In a group, if the wise ones, be it ten or a thousand, know and are holding the energy for the group, **the "energy-will"** floods the group mind and blesses everyone present. These wise ones have to have **the intent and focus to serve as channels through which the blessed energy flows**. For this reason, knowledgeable ones are encouraged to go back to the unawakened and serve them in the ways they can.

Fundamentalists are merely ones who have found themselves to be more comfortable in the box than out of it. They cling to it as a safe haven. It is important to realize that for some it is the right practice at this time; for others it is time to challenge the rules of established thinking and move ahead on their individual journey.

The next step for those on the conscious path is the stripping away of the ego. This painful experience takes place so we will be able to offer a more purified vase to the more refined frequencies we are to contact in the future. We must dare to embrace the process as best we can. The harmonious beauty of the Intuitive or Buddhic plane allows the free passage of the sounds, tones, and colors existing there in their archetypal form … a profound vibration … to enter our reality. We each are to allow as much of this as possible to flow through us.

As the poet Rumi said, **"We are to be the reed that allows God to breathe through us."**

The question is, can we render the mundane holy … and bring through the dimensions the love needed on the outer planes? Love is the evolutionary energy itself. In time when we are "full" enough, love will burst the causal body/the chalice, breaking it apart so the next (greater) stage of love can flow through. Again, and again, love will magnify, breaking down the next barrier until the great love of the Monad will flow freely. If not now, some day.

> *Just as the flame of a candle increases at the expense of the candle, selfishness, self-interest, egotism, vanity and possessiveness must decrease and vanish so that the flame exists. A disciple has a flaming heart. A disciple is a candle who burns in front of a Great One.*
>
> —The Flame of the Heart, Torkom Saraydarian, chap. 10

For what does our mystic listen? From the time we begin to practice meditation, we are building a receiver set. We advance to a place where "the cloud of knowable things" registers within us. We acquire the words and knowledge of the Soul, if we dare call it that, by attuning repeatedly to phrases with depth.

But the mystic in his or her private relationship with the Divine knows there is more and wants this simple outpouring for his or her self. Now we are ready to seek the "Word" of God. The Word that went forth and set all Creation into motion; the mystic wants this to fill him or her. Moreover, in time it will.

Importance of Spiritual Food

The time will come when the mystic hungers for more than just knowing ... and gains a higher aspect of intuition ... with no words, no sounds ... "no-thing" but a vibration sent forth. Sometimes, the Source is called the No-Thing and this is what is being sought. The No Thing sends out a vibrational frequency such that many over the years have elected to arise early and listen for before morning sounds begin.

The Sound Current can only be heard in the deepest silence; here the Holy vibrates to invite all to be in harmony with itself. The silence is not just about "outside," but the silence that comes within the devotee when one knows that outside sounds matter not ... any longer. One has reached the Source and here one drinks of the vibration of the "Word" as it vibrates its own Current. It is the long sought "Word." It is being with the Light and Word at its highest. No more can be said.

The mystic seeks to be a living personification of his or her inner inspiration, allowing the energy or teachings of their "Master, Teacher, Guru or Honorable One" to flow out through them and into the world. In the case of the Christian, this would be the teachings of Jesus; other traditions would use their Holy Books.

A most important realization is to remember that **LOVE is the evolutionary force.** LOVE is the alchemical tool in the transformational process. This is not just a comment; it is recognizing the potency of the "lots of vital energies" that exist in the higher reality and which blend within each one of us in order for us to become whole.

Using the idea that we are all aspects of the One Made Manifest in the dense world, we can see ourselves as bits and pieces of the whole. See yourself as an aspect of the Divine and know ... so also are all others. When we love another, we "glue" ourselves to those for whom we care. This is why the Master says, **"Love one another."** ... Love is the glue that binds us together and, as all of us come into loving each other, we rebuild the One. **Love is evolutionary; it is the glue.**

We must come to know this is why the command **"to serve one another"** … means to care for one another. While we are each different and unique in our journey, we are each a "cell" of the divine. In our process of becoming, we have to overcome our separations and divisions. Our limited world teaches us false truths and we must remember, **"It is easier to believe a lie heard a thousand times than the truth heard once."**

Many of us are richly blessed and it falls upon us to lead the way to the best we can toward more acceptance, especially if we see ourselves as aspirants, disciples or initiates. A good Buddhist teaching is to avoid giving offense because it adds negativity to the world; to take offense does so as well. Let us remember to offer much forgiveness to others, as *"They may be just having a bad day."*

There are "simple, uncomplex" individuals on this planet who are very in tune with the higher world, yet they cannot even read or write. Down through time many of the uneducated, poor, farmers and woodsmen had no book learning to block them intellectually. They perhaps could not read and write but knew God through some other means … perhaps through "the book of nature," through family love, through kindness to animals, and respect for weather, and devotion to God, to Church, to moral decency … all expressed naturally in the lives they shared with others. They just knew the *magic of mysticism* by living daily in respect and with regard for the value of each human being.

Self-reflection or self-examination is difficult. Anything suggested by another seems trite or belittling. For this reason, teachers, confessors, counselors come to be a part of the path of the mystic or gnostic. The role holds value; we all know the pain of constructive criticism. We all have had this experience with hard-to-describe results. We have both tried to guide others and been critiqued by others.

Guidelines for your growth practice:

- Remember to say to yourself, "*do not blame, shame, or play the game.*" Watch this in yourself and you will grow immensely.

- Some things—which I have tried and/or recommend to others who are attempting growth work by their own efforts or with a trusted one—are listed below. They may trigger your own trials. Find what works for you and how best to proceed. Keep written notes; you will be glad you did.

- Make a vow to tell the *truth to yourself for a twenty-four hour period*; you may make it longer if you like. Nevertheless, no little white lies … the truth. Tell the truth, allowing your face to show your truth; it is time to let go of the poker face that has covered your truth.

- Realizing that you are vain when to yourself *you are denying being a vain person,* even as another level of self knows how vain you truly are.

- *Returning hugs falsely or when you would rather not,* even while knowing you are participating in a "social game" that holds no truth. Why pretend or actually attempt to mislead?

- Being polite while *lying because it was expected;* conforming to the games of the society of which we are a part.

- *Thinking you are living humbly* when you are really only embarrassed … wanting to be seen as humble.

- Believing you are hurt and *even have reason to be,* **while you really are angry,** but **do not wish to appear so** or perhaps have not admitted your anger to your self.

    Remember**, "*Only a lit candle can pass on the light.*"**

The first and consistent test for all of us is dealing with our ego. The best comparison is to return to the concept of the crabgrass. You pull it up and it comes back. You think you have pulled it up and it has only broken off. You find plenty of sprouts but you never get to all the roots. For the roots lie in humanness and as long as such exists ego will as well. These last vestiges of humanness are burned away as one crosses "the burning ground."

Another deadly trap is low self-esteem. Just as offensive as egotism, and sharing the need for self-review, is low self-esteem. The two, egotism and low self-esteem, are two ends of the same problem, or two sides of the same coin. Both will endure as long as does humanness. The adept must free themselves of these hindrances.

Moreover, humanness lasts until at least, according to most teachings, we finish the third initiation and one passes into a new stage aligning to adept-hood. An adept is lining up for the fourth initiation or pre-mastership. The preparatory stages for each initiation is strenuous. Writing about our feelings and the way we face our limited humanness, helps us to bring the unconscious into consciousness. We are now in a process that allows us to turn feelings into either love or compassion. We will have to do this a number of times throughout our lives, knowing we will gradually empty the bucket.

All we have learned about detachment, objectivity, forgiveness, working negative energy out of our self will help. Addressing pain, grief, anger, etc. ... instead of letting it live within ... is a major way to "empty one's self." I use the idea that each body, physical, emotional, and mental have to be 1) purified, 2) exercised and 3) fed daily. We get to pick how and with what we can do the job.

We understand the physical needs: food, bathing, exercise very well. Nevertheless, emotionally we need to acquire or feed ourselves positive emotions daily; we need to release our old emotions and give ourselves the means of acquiring healthy new emotions. Likewise, we need to exercise our emotions so as not to go sour: we freely love and care for others, we grieve for ourselves and for others, we cry with others and openly express our healthy exchanges of giving and receiving.

On the mental level, we need a ready supply of inspirational matter; we meditate and pray; we encourage others, guiding and explaining what we can. This exercises our grasp of other realities and yet steps them down into helpful tools as possible. We confront our fears and replace them with beauty, fine music, writing, projects that uplift our spirits. We can find these tools if we really want. Watch out when you begin to argue (even with yourself) or say, "But, I cannot because...." The "but" is a clue; you are avoiding or cancelling the first part of your own statement.

A mystic has years or lifetimes of pondering with which to struggle. Some examples of the challenges the path holds are easily seen. Most certainly, these are not all. Stop and ponder this list of ideas; take time to think or write about each of the below. These are the ponderings required for facing life with a mystical intent.

- Grief is to be recognized. See example offered in Chapter 3.

- Death of one who has been dear; this may be a physical death or separation from another with whom you have shared life or the death of an earlier stage of your own life.

- Loss of loved ones in many differing ways ... loss is loss: people, places, and things.

- Loneliness for others and facing loneliness because no one understands you.

- Fear of whatever you find yourself having to face ... something that suddenly presents its impact on you ... it may be spiders ... or it may be existing "without" someone or something who/ which we think we need.

- Your existing physical beauty is fading ... have you noticed? You are not as charming as you once were.

We must release all these in the process of discovering our inner nature. You might think of this as emptying one's self as one centers his or her self more and more within a total relationship with God.

The Nightly Review becomes a dear friend as it consistently makes us face ourselves. We will become more discriminating and more sensitive to the truth of situations over the years of practice.

A simple eye-opener can be practiced by asking ourself three questions: 1) Where was my blessing today? 2) Where was my challenge? 3) Where was my chance to do service? As we practice these, the challenge quickly comes clear; the blessing is the most subtle. There will be so many chances for service that discrimination is necessary. Watch this over a period and even suggest it to others. It changes us and can be one of the first disciplines we use; however, it deepens as we stay with it. Our inner senses begin to be quite alert.

Introducing Initiations

We have little understanding of the initiations. They are steps we will come to know more about after we have followed closely the previous efforts of advanced humanity (masters). Ideas of initiations are varied; there are many examples used to more or less present the same stretching and growing exercises Life holds for us. We have to become a new kind of being, and this involves clearing, stretching, and clearing and stretching repeatedly.

There is a familiar formula. Stated simply, to become a master of humanity, one goes through several stages—over a lengthy period of many lifetimes. (Think this way: there are really only five human initiations and we probably do not take one every lifetime; while it might be possible, it is not feasible.) This is the major basis for reincarnation and even teachings about numerous past lives. One of the reasons Jesus did not teach much regarding reincarnation is that most folks already accepted the idea in his time, and secondly, the Church, as it became a leader of society, wanted its people to be obedient and diligent in following its guidelines. Reincarnation was seen as a way to postpone getting diligent regarding the quest.

At a point where we come to see ourselves "doing our inner life" very well, then a series of tests generally come. We believe we pass through these tests at least satisfactorily, and if we do, then we receive the "blessed touch" or grace. But immediately afterwards it seems, all manner of upset occurs; this is the feared "unstableness" raising its ugly head as we adjust to the new frequency and "stay the course."

Said another way, in human life, it may take years of study and practices to begin to live a truly ethical life. One seems to achieve some manner of success at the inner level when tests arise at the outer level and attempt to pull one off the path; we are to hold strong. One feels strong in their faith, path, or journey and stays true to it when suddenly "all hell breaks loose." One may have an "infant dark night of the soul" to work through. One seems alone and unaided as waves of pain and sorrow wash over us.

Somehow, it subsides and one knows a new closeness to the Divine and has a greater understanding or awareness. One knows that what does not kill us, as the saying goes, strengthens us. We are more centered and whole in the peace that passes understanding. Here the mystic dwells.

There is an example often used by teachers that comes to mind. When there is a storm at sea, the waves toss and pile high but, remember, the water deep underneath stays calm. This is the way a mystic experiences life. Outer events and other people can go up and down and yet we shall live in the quiet and calm of the peaceful inner center.

After Human Initiations Come the Solar and Cosmic

Teachings challenge us to never plan or try to foresee an end to the path. We are to know that transformation will occur repeatedly on the endless path until the droplet that is, at present, our person-

ality re-enters the sea. We hear endless concepts of the path; after
Human Initiation there looms ahead the goal of Solar and Cosmic
Initiations. We look at them as forming the continuous path, but
remember, the goal is to stay in the present. Just as a pregnancy
seems endless as it is lived, it ends. The path that seems so endless
will end as well. With that said we look at some thoughts embedded in spiritual teachings that stretch our imagination and give us
cosmic insights.

We should try to know the meaning of the Solar Initiations,
with as much understanding as we can possibly gain from studies.
We venture to use our imagination to envision a higher world
wherein holy ones themselves take tests and achieve a most remarkable new perspective. We imagine our Soul and our solar
angels climbing a staircase to higher dimensions when we cannot
truly understand the transformation we are presently making in the
human initiatory path.

Here we know that our wise ones, our elders or unrecognized
saints are making progress even as they participate in the integration of the solar system. Souls, Solar Angels, Chohans, and/or Initiates from other planetary systems with names we may not know,
join to serve higher purposes than our own in our and other solar
systems and to continue endlessly in love and wisdom.

From *Gateway to Liberation* by Mary Gray, we learn:

> No one can escape, but the longer he delays, the greater will be
> his suffering. There is no escape through death, through denial; there
> is no oblivion. The Forces which created the universe are ever active,
> and (hu)man cannot evade the effect of Their action. He may delay
> and obstruct to his own undoing, but he cannot escape the will of the
> spirit to force him to the heights.

This is the growth pattern of the many lives, such as the inhabitants of the higher world (solar angels, angelic families, archangels
and any other inhabitants of our solar system), who learn to work
together peacefully and in harmony. Some day after we complete

the human initiation path, we will advance to Solar Initiations and take on duties we know little about now. This is the stuff Star Wars is made of … we shall see when we acknowledge other life forms … some day.

We know ever less about the Cosmic Initiation but believe there is an "advancing path" for our solar system and its family of planets, when all are sacred and all are ready to be a good co-working planet in the great cosmic sea.

Come back now to the work at hand. How do we become the mystic? By embracing the challenge of becoming the human "be-ing" and not the human "doing," we want now to discover what exists inside the folds of our own being. Are we really a part of something more and invisible? The onion may be ready for peeling. At least to a certain degree we dare to think so.

In religious approaches, we accept and believe we **have** a soul. In spirituality, we come to know we **are a soul with a human per-sonality.** The majority of humanity has developed the animal self but has little awareness of the real self, the Self Within. We are like a nut ready to crack or a fruit to be peeled.

We are certainly aware of the outside form: look at the thou-sands of dollars we spend on cosmetics, entertainment, foods and care of the physical. We groom, exercise, shape and perfume it to make ourselves pleasant and acceptable to others. No one but us knows what we are really like, and we do not want others to dis-cover the real us for fear of rejection. We want to measure up; we want acceptance.

Now if we begin to think **we are a soul**, how are we going to care for our very nature? First, the idea of our being a soul must become real to us; we must believe in our beauty and goodness, our own Light and the power of this inner power to express itself. We want to dedicate ourselves to the care of this invisible wonder that is our true nature, "made in the image and likeness of the Creator." We have to have appropriate boundaries for the care of this pre-cious one that we are.

In the distant past our human race was given ancient prayers as techniques for invoking help. Herein certain important words are affirmed. How to use them is significant as a beginning step to knowing ourselves in a new way. We expand our consciousness by meaning whatever statement we utter, not just learning a prayer or adopting a mantra.

We learn about "affirmations" to awaken us to new possibilities; we learn to use them to build a foundation for the awareness we seek. An affirmation is a statement used to change our awareness to another state of mind. For example, affirmations can be useful to help us shift our inner beliefs from one perspective to another, perhaps from negative to positive, or to affirm a new condition or reality.

We adopt affirmations to help us realize that we are more than we were told as a child or small developing personality. When possible, we keep our eyes closed and speak the words gently to ourself. As we speak these meaningful words to re-program our basic nature, we affirm the importance of the basic nature, the inner child, or whatever term with which we are comfortable. We are overcoming old programming, not trying to enhance the personality.

We are to greet **our personality** with an attitude of acceptance, as what we have to work with … it is ours, even as we strive to make it into a container for the true self, the Soul. We want that container to become, in time, the crystalline vase in which our Soul can express its beauty. We want to allow the Light of the Soul to shine through it as radiantly as possible. We begin by training the personality much like training a pet in our home. We use our will to bring it into harmony with higher will, and, as best we can, discern what that higher will might be. This "will- aspect" will change over time to respect and love.

A major first step in our quest is to explore "simplicity." The mystic has a goal of a deep personal relationship with God, Creator (or any such term as one might use), seeking a clear path directly to the Source of Life. To do so, we realize simplification is necessary, not just in everyday life, but in all areas of Life. All the "stuff" of ordinary life gets in the way, so clearing must begin.

To simplify our lives is different due to the various lives we live, but we are talking about every aspect—work, play, games, lovers, children, goals, and all our aspirations. Everything must be processed in consciousness and be completed and released. And in due time it will, bit by bit. We spend years sorting through wishes and wants, accusations and belongings. Simplifying our lifestyle starts a never-ending life practice ... not that a mystic cannot have belongings, but belongings cannot have the mystic.

One can have anything as long as it does not attempt to take first place in one's life. The commandment is "Thou shall have no other gods before Me." This means not your children, your favorite hobby, your spouse, or any personal goals. This requires vigilance and the sacrifice of ordinary pleasures. This is the first rule of the making of the mystic. And a great deal of contemplation must be experienced by any of us before we can truly say, "God or Higher Will comes first."

Each step is different on each of our paths. Karma has shaped our lives and new awareness evolves day by day. Simplicity means one thing at one juncture and a new awareness later will bring new issues to face. These shifts are subtle and often painful; it takes time for the little pieces to come together to shape new realities. Here we discover the path we seek and often go through "the valley of the shadow of death" as our hopes, dreams, and wishes vanish or fade away before us.

The tools that comforted us yesterday fail us tomorrow and we search again for assistance. Just as simplicity becomes a way of life, so does quietness. It is the silence of inner thought, first in meditation; then it is to learn to *live in the silence*. Without the distractions of modern life, the mystics of old sought nature and peace in it ... those gentle sounds soothed the spirit; in crowded cities, we have to find another healing agent. It may be gentle music, and it certainly is at times. Here too we learn that the **deep within** wants to have our attention and we learn to live in a more quiet manner. As thoughts dance through our everyday mind, we find random words of wisdom, write notes, capture impressions, meditate, and grow in the way of the inner life. We learn to listen inwardly and outwardly as we bring both together in our search for God.

To stretch humanity from the time of the "ape man" to the *humanus spiritus* has been our task. We think about the steps of initiation, but most earthly mystics are still discovering and processing the basic mysteries. They are not so much focused on initiations in a competitive way, but rather on advancing ahead, leading us in the march toward purifying the human initiation path.

Humanus spiritus reveals humanity's refinement. Humanity has evolved from the cruelty of the primitive being of the early stages to the finest sensitivity of our group consciousness today. As advancing human beings, we are to bring our human condition up to a fine toned pitch that is far more refined than most imagine. This is the state of fully human and fully divine that we seek to experience. This is a meditation in itself.

Being "fully human" indicates the perfecting of our human potential as the archetype, e.g., Jesus. While we are made in the image and likeness of the divine, we are to fill out our manifestation of the image with a polished and blossoming potential. In the likeness of the Divine, we are to claim our Creator capability and use it in a manner divinely inspired. We are to dream the dream of our Creator and bring it into manifestation.

Affirmations

May the wise ones encircling the planet come together and bless us. May each give and receive joy, goodness, and strength. May we strive to meet the needs of humanity and to protect the well-being of Planet Earth. Bless each of us as we seek understanding and clarity in our roles. May we serve wisely and may the holy ones bless our path to enlightenment. Amen.

Thoughts to Ponder

Here are some mystical thoughts that we should all develop and claim our ability to ponder—from *St. Mary Magdalene: The Gnostic Tradition of the Holy Bride* by Tau Malachi,

> Mary (Magdalene) spoke these words in private. She said, "The body and blood of the Lord is like fire and light and the power of the Mother Spirit is in it. There is fire in the bread and light in the wine, and the Holy Spirit passes in between them and joins them. So are the Bride and Bridegroom joined, and it is for this reason it is called a wedding feast. Understand that the body and the blood are not the image on the cross. They are the image of the Risen Savior, so that, consecrated, the power of the Risen Savior is in the bread and wine. What is the image of the Risen Savior? It is the image of the Groom and Bride united, called the Second Adam." (109)
> … Mary said, "The spark must become a flame, and the flame must become a blazing fire. When you shine like the sun, you will be complete."(210)

Ponder these thoughts and see how you are led to think. Repeat them to yourself and even take a few words at a time and work with them. Use this set of seed thoughts that come from the writing:

> *Body and blood is like fire and light*
> *For this reason, the Eucharist is a wedding feast*
> *The image of the Risen Savior is in the bread and wine*

Could this be code for the masculine and feminine in us becoming one? On the other hand, could this be telling us that the Love within us must become one with the mind that is to open to blend with it?

See Where Your Thoughts Lead

Mystic Mabel Collins wrote hundreds of wonderful things. You can find her work and her story in a piece called *The Inner Life of*

Mabel Collins. I offer a couple of excerpts for you to work with in your new pondering technique. See below:

- *"No one is your enemy, no one is your friend, and all alike are your teachers. Your enemy becomes a mystery to be solved. Men, Women, persons, must be understood. Your friend becomes a part of yourself, an extension of yourself. A riddle, hard to read. Only one thing is more difficult to know, your own heart."*

- *"Not until the bonds of personality have been loosened can the profound mystery of your self begin to be seen. Then and not until then can you use all your powers and devote them to a worthy service. Within you is the light of the world. The only light that can be shed on the path. You must receive from within yourself. There is no point in looking for it elsewhere."*

In these words, we receive Wisdom from a wise one.

Honor the idea of *"pondering"* because you are discovering/arousing your own thoughts that are triggered by the resonance of another: you can choose a mystic to emulate. This need not be a famous or dead person. It may be a poem sent to you. If you reverberate to it, it can become a doorway inward.

Resonance is very important. It is what draws us together without our understanding. **Birds of a feather do flock together.**

You are doing many things to advance your consciousness (vibrations) so that you can be in the company of the holy ones (both on the physical plane and behind the scenes). Reading material of higher vibrations and resonating to it is a way to make progress. It assists us by opening the door and revealing the treasure within.

St. Thomas Aquinas, when he had a deeply rewarding spiritual experience, said, **"I have seen that which makes all things I have written about and taught look small. My writing days are over."**

You are decreasing the identity of your powerful personality and declaring your new and true identity as you repeatedly remind yourself, *"I am the Soul."*

I am the Soul Mantra

I am the Soul, and also love am I.
Above all else, I am both will and fixed design.
My will is now to lift
The lower self into the light divine.
That light am I.
To where that lower self awaits,
Awaits my coming.
That which desires to lift
And that which cries for lifting,
Are now at one.
Such is my will.

Namaste
by Rajender Krishan

This simple word
uttered with a gesture of folded hands
is among the finest salutations
humans have ever been able to vocalize.
It simply means:
I honor the place in you
In which the entire Universe dwells,
That place of Love and Light
And of Truth and of Peace.
When you are in that place in you,
And I am in that place in me,
We are One.

Here is another version of the "*I Am The Soul*" meditation that some may prefer. I did, after I was ill and wanted to become more integrated with my body. I realized I had never paid ample attention to the body ... I had just demanded service from it as I needed it. A stroke gave me new appreciation for the body and a great desire to achieve a cooperative relationship with my body. Then I found this version adapted from Roberto Assagioli, M.D. He was founder of Psychosynthesis and most respected in the spiritual field, especially Agni Yoga.

I Am the Soul
as adapted by Roberto Assagioli

I Am the Soul.
I have a physical body but I am not my physical body.
My physical body and my senses are parts of me,
I Am the Soul and I am Whole.

I Am the Soul.
I have an emotional body but I am not my emotions.
My feelings and emotions are parts of me.
I am the Soul and I am Whole.

I Am the Soul.
I have a mental body but I am not my rational mind.
My thoughts and opinions are parts of me.
I Am the Soul and I am Whole.

I am the Soul.
My physical body, emotions, and mind are parts of me.
I am greater than these.
I Am the Soul and I am Whole.

I recognize and affirm that I am a center of pure self-consciousness. I am a center of will, capable of mastering, directing, and using all my psychological processes and my physical body.

A Closing Salutation

The mantras above are intended to move the consciousness from one level of perception to another. They are used to invoke our identity or a higher energy to help us. The reminder concerning *Namaste* is merely that, a reminder of the simplicity of the wisdom of the Eastern path. Sometimes another suggests a mantra or you may suddenly find your own thoughts developing into one that is right for you. I have used one for years and it evolved from within. No one "gave" it to me; I think it grew out of my study. I love it and value saying it; my mantra is, "Sophia, lead, guide, and direct me all the days of my life." It is short, easy and meaningful to me. This is what a mantra should be, I believe.

As the Mayan say, "*Remember to remember*"; and as Buddha taught the importance of "*right remembrance*," we complete this review of all the things we already know deep within. Our real heartfelt desire is to be in the Presence. We are sitting with the Presence; it has its scent, vibration, and love, and it is folding its arms around us. The highest potential is within us. As we hunger and thirst after righteousness, the high and holy potential stirs us to move to carry our gifts and talents out to the world—outwardly, as gifts for those who are unhappy, and for those who do not know about the inner stages of growth; we seek to lift them gently toward **the reward**. We may never speak our piece, dance our dance, or share our picture, but we vibrate it out every day to those around us. It is our gift to give; *we are in the world but not of the world*. Remember the assignment to pass along the vibration of the Presence. It nurtures us as we are to nurture the world. It is the life of service that enriches us, and as it happens we can enrich the whole of humankind. Therefore, it is....

An Exercise for Manifestation

Step One:

- Visualize two circles ... one gold (4 or 5 inches in diameter), the other silver, same size), and begin to bring them together until they overlap.... The overlapping part is called a *vesica piscis* (literally, "a fish bladder"). Color it indigo blue. This is the color of the deep night sky.

Step Two:

- Learning to use the Creative Point

- Lift hands to the prayer position as if to capture the Vesica Piscis. Visualize a small rotating center (clockwise) within the field of deepest color. This represents the dark light from which all is created.

- Allow your fingers to touch lightly (in a prayerful, creative mudra position) as we lift our hands to the Third Eye area ... the fingers form an energetic connection. This Ten Finger mudra serves as points of contact to lift our requests to a higher level, connecting our personality strengths with the power of the higher center.

Step Three:

- Creative Breath

- We will take a series of ten deep breaths inhaling smoothly and exhaling through the Brow Center (same center … in and out). We use the power of intent and imagination as we do this. We are clearing away the glamour and illusion that forms around humanity's distorted picture of the plan; this is the plan that is held by the Great Creative All.

- Ten breaths smoothly but strongly … inhale and exhale slowly and rhythmically. As you do, you are stating to the Creator Power Center, "I bring my energy into alignment with your greater plan."

Step Four:

- Second Hand Position

- Bring your hands, still in prayer position with rotating center within, directly over your mouth with thumbs resting comfortably under chin. At this Creative Center we are creating, at this present moment, and we must come to realize that our words and actions are always sending forth creative power to help build, as well as unfold, our life experiences.

- We affirm that our personal actions align with the Great Creative Power. Once again, we take ten breaths, this time inhaling and exhaling with "*intention.*" Have your intention in mind, knowing that you, the Divine Within, are blowing the breath of God's Creative Power through yourself as a "*reed*" into your life and the collective life. As you breathe, you are working as one of God's instruments, and all these enlightened breaths become One.

- Now we do the creative breath, inhaling ten times in through the Third Eye area and out through our mouth, our Creative

Center. We align with higher mind as we set our intention into motion.

- Do the ten inhalations and exhalations slowly and strongly ... breathing into manifestation your intent.

Step Five:

- Third Hand Position

- Now bring your hands (still in prayer position with its rotating creative center in the Vesica Piscis) to the Heart Center. Bring unconditional love for the world into your consciousness as you breathe in through the clear Brow Center and exhale through the Heart Center. You serve as a human instrument through which the Love of the Great Heart can manifest into and through the human experience.

- This series of breaths creates a circle within ourselves as we complete our exercise. Imagine yourself breathing in through the Vesica Piscis directing unconditional love for the planet and all life upon it.

- Do the ten inhalations and exhalations slowly and strongly, invoking clarity and unconditional love to the planetary experience.

Step Six:

- Closing

In this exercise, we connect our heart, mind, and creative power. As we close, we send forth a prayer of gratitude for the opportunities Life provides for each of us to have a relationship with the great All-That-Is.

*****

We long for heaven, or wherever God is, but we learn we have it in our power to be in heaven with Him at this very moment. Being happy with him now means:

> *Loving as s/he loves,*
> *Helping as s/he helps,*
> *Giving as s/he gives,*
> *Serving as s/he serves,*
> *Rescuing as s/he rescues,*
> *Being with her/him twenty-four hours,*
> *Touching her/him in her/his distressing disguise.*

—Mother Teresa of India / adapted

ELEVEN

New ... Not Just Different

There is a legend that men, clearing the foundations of an old temple, found beneath it a secret room wherein there burned an everlasting lamp. In this room, also, was an altar to God, and secret instructions for the restoration of the temple. This again alludes to the search beneath surfaces for those enduring principles which have been hidden from the beginning of the world. Through long and weary ages, men have been born, have suffered, and have died. The long record of the human search for reality is part of humanity's Heritage and exists within his own nature, for he is the child of all that has gone before. Thus, there is available to him all that he needs for his growth and improvement, if he will seek sincerely and labor unceasingly.

The resurrection of the spiritual from the material, and the restoration of the Golden Age are not only the dreams of poets, but sovereign realities, possible to man when he understands his own origin and destiny. The Greeks liked to think of the day when the entire world would prosper under the government and wise authority of the philosopher-king. This august and glorious person was in reality the Hierophant of the Mysteries. The Golden Age comes to each and every human being when the divine self within him is the ruler of his mind and body. When the superior part of man governs the rest, there will be no further conflict or contention within the soul or the flesh. United in all its parts by the noble resolution of the spirit, man is a self-governing empire, dedicated to truth, and obedient under law. Then neither his thoughts nor his actions will *escape from the circle of his virtues, and he will stand in the adit [entrance] of the everlasting house.*

—*The Psychology of Religious Ritual* by Manly P. Hall

SYMBOLISM IS THE LANGUAGE OF MYSTICISM. We have come to the peak; we have been climbing after a long and tiring walk through the darkness. We have embraced the Light; we are trying to live "A Life of Adeptship." We cry out like Job, begging for an understanding, and then one day, we will "*know*" the purpose of it all. It has been seemingly like a birth canal. We stand and stretch; we now are different ... we know we cannot turn back. We begin to grasp the reasons behind our experiences. We can be more comfortable with both others and ourselves. We surely are *wiser* in the core of ourselves. We stand at the peak of a mountain and look about; there is light here for today. We delight with inner peace and satisfaction. All the trials and tests seem to fall into place. We rest.

As we are resting, we look around and discover other mountain tops looming even higher in the distance; they, too, are to be mounted. The peaks loom so far above our head. We hear and perceive the call of the heights. We look away and try to rest; we pray and absorb the trials of the route we have travelled. Then, after a time, we know we must go forward toward the awaiting slopes. Each ascent beacons higher than the last. *The voice of Job rings in our ears.* We remember the Twenty-third Psalm; we know we are in the world of the dead ... *let the dead bury the dead* ... the words ring through the stillness. We vibrate with the words, understanding the words anew.

The Lord is my shepherd; I shall not want.
He makes me to lie down in green pastures:
He leads me beside the still water. He restores my soul.
He leads me in paths of righteousness for His name's sake.
Yea, though I walk through the valley of the shadow of death,
I will fear no evil: for thou art with me;
Thy rod and thy staff they comfort me.

Thou preparest a table before me
In the presence of mine enemies:
Thou anointest my head with oil;
My cup runs over.
Surely goodness and mercy shall
Follow me all the days of my life:
And I will dwell in the house of the Lord forever.

The temptation to give up lifts; now is not the time to rest. I hear, see, and know the higher is with me. Water flows through the valley below a short way down the slope; it is still begging my presence. I go forward, knowing there is nothing for me behind. The past is over; the looming peaks beckon and I must go. No time to wander; eagerness fills my Soul, and I long for the higher peak, and the next.

Girding ourselves for the climb ahead, voices cry out, "*It is useless. You have done enough for this lifetime. It is not worth it. Call it quits ... rest ... relax.*"

What does this mean to a modern world? Knowing ourselves as disciples, we can never quit. Wise Ones have our allegiance; we have heard the call. As the wind whistles, strong inner voices call us to keep our resolve. Gentle inner words comfort, strengthen, and prod us to keep moving. Relief will come in its own time and way; events will allow pauses as needed, not as we want them, but as Spirit wills it.

We know Life is to be rich in learning, and every day a test. Knowing this, it is not as hard; each day is also radiant with the true light; it returns many times to lead us onward. Eternity waits. Walking among the peaks, we find no place to linger.

Flashes of Fire and Light

We struggle across the burning ground; the testing repeats it seems, spiral after spiral. In the early human life, the seed for the human family, the Divine within us, cries for transformation; thus, the *longing* for change is fulfilled. No longer able to cry, there are no more tears; the heart has bled until it no longer bleeds. In the midst of each journey, one utilizes all they have conquered; this is the process.

Feet are weary; bones ache. There is no bench for the weary traveler. Hold up the Light and *walk on, walk on,* for the journey calls and pulls you to respond. A pattern shows us the way forward and studies have prepared the mind for expansion; each lesson or challenge is to be faced. Repeatedly, we are presented difficulties to be resolved; something subtle arises to be grasped ... and then some attitude is released from which the self is freed.

We consciously absorb the inner work while holding close the holy vibration of "wisdom" within. For a moment, Shekinah whirls and dances, allowing glimpses of the mysteries to one's inner chambers. One's response is to be gentle, humble, and poised.

Having outgrown less desirable traits, good qualities have been cultivated. There are glimpses of beauty and times of grace. Hungering vibrations have morphed into lesser vibrations repeatedly. Now transformation continues and there are new eyes with which to see. There is no rest, only renewal; in the quest, there are no words, but the mind fills with sanctified thought. Others do not grasp your efforts but feel your absence from the earthly world; and you are.

To experience this love, freedom, beauty, and joy—which consistently brings grace to dawning—one must live on trust. In the inner reality, one hears the sacred tones that call the heart and mind to attention. The magic of this dawning delivers the sweet fragrance of grace, an indescribable freshness that renews the Soul and strengthens the body. No trial is too great to continue the quest.

The magic of transformation is a process of cells earning light by the fire of purification. The Magic is that we begin to comprehend the mystery of Fire and Light. Every tradition of true mysteries is in some way reduced to fire and light. The process begins by invoking Light; then discovering that we must embrace Fire. We learn that to get to the Light we must embrace Fire. The fire can be of willingness. Master once said to me, "*one does not need to be perfect, one must only need be willing.*" If we seek and are willing to listen inward, we will find the Light and the Fire.

The modern path is one of embracing ideas that bind an ever expanding collective of illuminated ones together. Seeing others as good, willing, striving, and honorable helps "glue" together the emerging collective of ones who care for the ascent of humanity. Ralph Metzner, Ph.D., a friend and researcher of spiritual techniques, once said, "*Heaven is experiencing high consciousness, Purgatory is being on the spiritual path, and Hell is getting stuck.*" It is so and, if we accept this, we go steadily through the purging our soul calls for.

When we "wake up" to new ideas and concepts, we begin to seek answers, missing pieces and further ideas. This period is identified as "digging fifty one-foot holes"; after satisfying our curiosity, if we enter serious questing, we will dig one hole fifty feet deep. This is truly the entry to new growth.

After World War II in France, at an extremely discouraging moment, Philippe Vernier, a C.V., M.D., Ph.D. in Developmental Research (in a number of scientific areas and advanced in spiritual teachings), spoke strongly and I have loved his words for years. Listen as he speaks to disciples:

> If you are a disciple of the Master, it is up to you to illumine the earth. You do not have to groan over everything the world lacks; you are there to bring it what it needs.... There where reign hatred, malice and discord, you will put love, pardon and peace. For lying, you will bring truth; for despair, hope; for doubt, faith. There, where there is sadness, you will give joy.
>
> "If you are, in the smallest degree, a servant of God, all of these virtues of Light you will carry with you.... Do not be frightened by a mission so vast! It is not really you who are charged with the fulfillment of it. You are only the torch-bearer. The fire, even if it burns within you, even when it burns you, is never lit by you. It uses you as it uses the oil of the lamp.
>
> You hold it, feed it, carry it around; but it is fire that works, that gives the light to the world, and to yourself at the same time.... Do

not be the clogged lantern that chokes and smothers the Light; do not be the lamp, timid or ashamed, hidden under a bushel. Flame up and shine before men. Lift high the fire of God.

In Hindi, the term Agni means "Fire" and Indra means "Light." They are as linked together as masculine and feminine. They each need the other; they create the fervor within us. The secret of the divine is dawning: by continuing our quest, we shall discover fire and light, Agni and Indra, within our nature, and the secrets of our spiraling upward and inward, of lights and challenges will become clear. We pursue the energy of transformation and the beauty at the end of the climb.

Once I heard a preacher say, "The message must be spoken anew for each generation in its own words." The teachings must be veiled but understood by the awakened and yet protected from the misusers. Fire is dangerous when used as a toy, as is sexual energy, or money to waste which is not earned, or power that exists in personality without sensitivity. These burn the user and destroy health, society, honor and bring the lessons that lurk in the Bardo.

Let us create an image of a spiritual student getting serious about his or her goal. We see this one sitting and contemplating. Awareness is dawning and this one thinks of many things. As the spark within is growing, fervor does so as well. Psychic energy binds the fire with a "material matrix," and the teachings warn that this energy-stream can stimulate illusions to dance through the mind … as do many glamours, of course. We see our thinker pondering issue after issue, sitting in front of the fire.

Imagine now that the thinker recognizes his or her unconsciousness and is deeply moved to quest with seriousness for a new consciousness. Thinking, pondering, and having communion with far off worlds stimulates psychic energy and the fire increases. When one is ready to surrender folly and to discipline his or her self toward a higher regeneration, the path of purification is embraced. All wisdom teachings speak of the fire of purification and its rewards. Thus the consuming of old encumbrances is achieved by fiery purification.

We see that the purification of Spirit lies at the base of all transmutation. The highest seeker is not a passive receiver, but a co-worker and co-creator. When the fires of life are strained, we use our sensitiveness to purify our self and burn away our burdensome layers of accumulations. The sensitivity brings out our fire and only this fire will set us free. Only the highest functions of intention and dedication can bring about such purification.

The time will come when the fire will be raging. A wonderful symbol that the Hindus have brought down to us that we can use in our life today is that the priest has earned the right to "put the logs in the fire." Now, let us go back and think about this. Only one that is seeking to grow spiritually is permitted to put a log on the fire—the sacred fire is kept burning, keeps burning by the ones seeking spiritual growth. The one seeking spiritual growth goes to the sacred fire and puts in something to burn. Think about all the releasing ceremonies, where you write what you want to release on a piece of paper, roll it up and put it into the fire. The person seeking to grow will release, dispose of, and transmute the impurities in their life. They feed the sacred fire that is a part of purifying humanity.

They put their own imperfection in ... to feed the fire that is purifying humanity; they put their own things in, but they only get to do it once they have committed themselves to the process of spiritual growth and change. It is no accident, the word "Agni" and "Agony" come from the same root word. It is useless for a non-interested one to put in anything, because if one is not sincere or doesn't mean to give whatever up, to release it, and embark in the struggle, there is no point. The other side of this is that only those in the process of transmutation can feed the sacred fire. Those in this process of releasing and changing maintain the sacred fire within the collective consciousness of humanity, whether they know it or not. Wonderful symbology!

Let us picture each flaw or fault we would cleanse from our self as a rumpled piece of paper or a log to throw into the fire burning before us. As the glamour and illusions, misperceptions, and judgments are surrendered to the fire, smoke fills our eyes and lungs, clouding our awareness until the dross burns away. How greatly does the mind shrink from such a task; it can only be driven to this assignment by an intense desire for purity and great love of Creator. Every effort leads to a greater harmonization with the universal energy that lies at the base of all Life. This purification brings change to our consciousness with support to advance us on our quest.

This is a personal message to each of us to inspire us to take time to make an honest examination of consciousness at each opportunity, to be willing to go slowly, observing carefully our own nature. Knowing that there is a universal message as well, the more disciples and awakened ones who participate aid the human group mind, and our planet as well, to advance in their collective process.

When we speak of psychic energy, we speak of the same Sophia of the Hellenic world, of Saravati of the Hindus, the creative Adonai of Israel, and Mithras (ancient Persian god of light and truth) and his dynamic of solar power. We think of the power of the Holy Spirit of Christianity, and certainly no one doubts the fire of Zoroaster. We face now a new step, defining the turning point of humanity toward a new manifestation for this decisive and affirmed Aquarian age. We often see references to Agni and Indra, the fire and light of creative inner play. We see the flashes move between Light and Matter when Creativity is at work or play.

Each of the logs that are put into the fire are those items, articles, conscious thoughts—whatever that, in fact, are put into the fire ready to be purified, that are ready to give themselves into change. The fire is used as a symbol because it consumes itself. It consumes everything that comes into it, but as it reduces all to ash, the ash itself is the purest of all matter. **The disciple puts himself into the fire, consciously, willing to embrace the powerful energy so they themselves may become pure by dealing with, working with, and struggling with the fire that they ignite and feed.**

The Light of the Creator is not the light of the sun like daylight, but the light of the mind that was created by Father-Mother God long before the sun and the moon. This is the Great Light we found as Sophia, Wisdom, in each of the kingdoms expressing the innate intelligence of its Self. Here is the Light that enters into Darkness and is consumed. The Light needs matter or something that can reflect it within the world of matter. We are unconscious (in the dark) until we become conscious.

Terrestrial fire is the tool of higher consciousness. The energy of fire gives off heat, heat changes the property, but what happens when something is burning? When it creates smoke? The Light descends upon us and in our nature; it creates insights or the fire which in turn creates illusion and disillusion. It, as it works within us, begins a process of change that has an effect that often binds or veils. It is designed to veil, designed to mislead us and to produce illusions until we are wise enough to see through the veil. During this period, we struggle with much karma and lessons. Nothing is ever lost; our growth continues, but we now gain understanding, or we say, "clarity." We have many names for this illusion or veil: perception, reaction, misunderstanding, shadows. We can see this in our own walk.

Kundalini

In the story of the Garden of Eden we read of a serpent that entices Eve by saying that eating the fruit of this tree can make her "*as smart as god.*" The East uses the dragon in its symbolism, while the West tends to use a snake or serpent. There is no simple translation of this, but think this way—"be as wise as the serpent and as gentle as the dove" (Matt. 10:16).

Most often, the serpent is a reference to the Kundalini, the god within arising. It can be confusing as it is also used as a reference to the initiate of the feminine mystery cults who cared for the serpents. The point is that each individual who has a mystical experience is destined to grow and change many times along the way. The similarity is that we grow, pop our skin, and have to grow again. This we will do many times on our way to enlightenment.

People have assumed the serpent means "snake" ... not necessarily. It can mean "dragon," "shadow," or "water beast that is moving about on the ground." The Mayans often picture a huge serpent with an open mouth and the head of an individual emerging from within. Let us ponder this for a moment; the "feathered serpent" of the Mayan Mystery tradition represents the earthbound part of each individual, with the feathers representing the ability to fly into the less dense world. The feathers have meaning in this culture just as the thousand petals of the Lotus do in some others. The idea is that an initiate is at home on both earth and the inner worlds.

The term "water serpent" comes from the word "*hydra*," from which also our word hydrant comes. It acknowledges the intense flow of energy contained within. Each is to become the serpent that grows, pops his or her skin, and must grow again. Likewise, this is for each of us our work … and this is transforming. With each new awareness, we birth a new level of consciousness, then outgrow it, and once again repeat the process. The serpent is not a snake, but a modern distortion we have inherited.

> The transformation force is often called "serpentine power" or in Hindu, "Kundalini," the sleeping energy of evolution waiting to awaken. Due to the healing power of spiritual force and transformation, the serpent became an integral part of the caduceus, the physician's symbol of two serpents (one black, one white, entwined about a central column and rising to its height). The duality represents spirit and matter in cooperation, the column—evolution, as well as spinal column—and the top, the highest level of consciousness possible within the world of duality, reconciliation of duality. (*The New Dictionary of Spiritual Thought*)

Drugs are no means for inducing mystical experience. Some have hoped this would work; some have achieved phenomena experiences or altered states, but they are poor substitutes for the real arousal. Often serious damage is done to the physical body or mental mechanism when the body is not ready or the experience is forced. While the process of awakening does vary from person to person, it has a value, and during this time, doing the subtle work that is needed gains one the attention of the inner world. Without

purification when there is forced stimulation, there occurs serious physiological damage as well as psychological. Go slow, learn
patience, and do the work guided by mentors, and then later your
inner guidance. Impatience is the enemy of the modern day path.

In Phoebe Bendit's writing about the "Sacred Flame," she says,
*"The keynote of the path of return to righteousness is increasingly that of
becoming conscious of the processes of mind and the sense of direction
that light gives to consciousness."*

In spiritual teachings, there are three particular forces that are
all called *fire* for us to discover and utilize.

The first kind of force we become aware of in spiritual thought
is called **rejuvenation.** This is where new, spontaneous igniting
caused by the duality of the body regenerates and reproduces energy
within the physical body to spring forth.

The second force is friction and this friction is constantly
being created in our life to produce change. We call it friction,
conflict, and change. It is experience. We have conflict any time
we have male and female, hot and cold, up and down. Any time
we use the lower three chakras, we are working with friction, and
these dualistic aspects come together to move us from experience
to experience. It is out of experience that we ultimately begin to
move to higher levels. Ultimately we say, "That is all the pain I can
handle. That is all the struggle I can take...." When people go to
the peak of their career, whatever that is for a person, and when
one says, "I am not striving any more," it is then that they begin to
go over to the next level. They desire to settle down, to be more
comfortable and enjoy the fruits of their labors, however they put
it ... but they make a shift.

**So, with that change of consciousness we begin to talk about
creativity and the use of passion at a psychological level.** When
we talk to these creative people, they will say, "I had an insight,"
"a flash," "it just came to me." Creativity has a dualistic aspect and
occurs when what they know and what they do not know come
into right relationship. Think about an artist, a musician, a writer:
they have a discipline, that is what they know; but in the moment

of using it to the utmost, a flash happens (that is what they do not know), and these two come together. Born out of that flash they have the "creative insight" or what we call "inspiration."

People who are highly creative live in that psychological place where they play between what they know and what they don't know. Professor Douglas Dean, as he did work with successful companies in the U.S.A., reported that the most successful companies are directed by persons who are very intuitive, because the higher you go in an organization, the more it has to be guided by the unknowns instead of the known. The president of a company is dealing with unknowns all the time. When you are trying to anticipate what is going to happen in the future and integrate it into the known, you have to be more and more directed by your intuition than by knowledge.

Shift back to everything you have heard about mystics. They do not know the future. Mystics press against the unknown with the fire of fervor and the waters part for them; at a last incredible moment, they know. They do not claim to know; they claim to do that which they receive as guidance or believe is right to do, revving up the fire that is within themselves, even up to the last moment, and then all of a sudden they are given what to do. The answers come; they have their answer, subtly, for that which is to be done.

The final step is that when enough fire, agony, purification and trust is created in Life at the Soul level, the veil itself dissolves. The illusion, the smoke, has burned all the material. The smoke diminishes and one sees the face of God. Another way of saying this is, "Looking into the light, Indra is seen." Indra flashes: "You are the Light of the World." Agony is the path to the Light, producing the intensity demanded. It is said we must get to straight knowledge … to get to the Light … to become the Light … and the realization dawns at that moment.

Grace and Grace-Filled

As we travel around the spiral of Life, at each turn there comes renewed hope and joy. At the same time we are encouragement for others walking behind. Looking ahead, shadowy figures of others appear trudging on *their* way as well. We are grateful and longing for their company; efforts deepen. "Friend Silence" walks close by and lifts the effect of weariness. Hope floods the heart with new riches as the mind quickens. The rush of lives past is felt and so is the challenge of letting them fall away. We will not be trapped here.

The far vision of the future comes in bits and pieces requiring attention be kept on the now ... for here, no evil can touch one, but delay, distractions are everywhere. The *temptation* to turn back falls away, dissolving into an eagerness to charge into the next cycle; there is a great rush onward.

Seeking to understand "*Grace*" is seeking to understand a major aspect of the nature of God ... Allah ... The Ultimate One. Embrace the Light and seek the flame. Knowing how to receive grace is a new experience; each fold contains its own blessing. The heart is so full. Mind cannot hold on ... in the arms of Grace, sleep comes.

In both Eastern and Western spirituality **Grace** is considered a great mystery. To many, grace is experienced as the result of almost "*no*" thought, and it works for each in its own way, according to the need of each. As grace embraces and is embraced, the natural uplift brings healing and faith. Answers to unasked queries nurture the willing one, and the response to situations, not processed, emerge. No wonder it is called mystical and magical, for there is no rationale ... it just is. While only a glimpse is revealed at a time, the true path beckons us forward.

We see the evolution of humanity and ourselves as the challenge of moving from unconscious, to less unconscious, to more conscious, and then to merging with the Divine Consciousness. Standing at the brink, we trace our "*knowing*" state as grace-filled ... a kind of *Holy High* that allows correction, change, adjustment, and new realities, unexplainable and non-verbal. We *become* the very silence we have entered. The importance of the changes that emerge as one walks the Path of Initiation or the Pattern of Becoming is unveiled. Each lesson presents a challenge ... first, a difficulty, secondly, something to grasp or understand, then some attitude from which to free ourselves—to embrace holding ourselves in a positive and open manner. The formula gradually emerges.

Gradually, even our bodies are different and function freely behind sleep. We weary of the heavy vibrations of each day and long for the lighter dimension. To make physical life tolerable we try to capture the notes of heavenly sound, sparking impressions, translucent colors, and poetic thought. We now carry more capably the weight of daily life and walk through stresses, knowing that these strengthen and do not defeat us. To share what one has learned presents the challenge, yet how to share what others have not experienced is our difficulty. To attest to the broadness of Life and to share its depth forces growth. Here we learn to put into words the wonders of expanded reality.

Here we become aware of an inner tone, the forever-occurring song of the universe, delivering *Grace* and its new kind of freedom, one aspect at a time. Living life between the worlds, with a part of us within each, reveals the challenge to those evolving. The spirals leads us, illuminating the steps needed to complete the pattern, that is, to bring out from the inner the higher frequencies which are needed to cleanse us. This is our duty, but not without loving ourselves. Progress may be slow, yet grace comes to open hearts that *can* be filled. Minds which are unblocked can *perceive* freely, even as the human psyche searches for a new way.

Words fail; symbology delights the intuitive and gives hope to grieving ones hungry for an inner life. Often, "*grace*" and "*light*" are used interchangeably by the teachers of inner truth. The East always *feeds* grace (darshan) to the people by radiating higher frequencies. The West tries, but rarely knows how; instead, it *gives* words. Often, words are so restrictive that no one awakens. By releasing the frozen intellect and trusting the intuitive heart and inner knowing, Wisdom embraces her growing child-being. He/she learns and then activates inner knowledge of times past, so all experience merges into a river of flowing thought which is not known in the everyday world. Inner reality becomes the teacher; guardians of the Lighter Worlds guide us.

Master Morya says, *"As a lever sets the wheels into motion, all understanding leads to the light."*

We recall the three paths: short, long, and Bardo. Here they blend into the One Great Way, rich with insight. Releasing the heaviness of *distorted devotion* brings rapid healing of the anguish each has experienced. Bliss results—not thought—and we see everywhere, in bits and pieces of reflective light, the truth we have met over the years ... in Kabalah, in the Old Testament, in occult training, Eastern study, in Ancient Wisdom, and in the Christian New Testament.

Mary Gray in her serious occult writings tells us that we are but reflections of the sun and moon, which have occult (hidden) relations to the earth besides the physical one. The sun represents the creative mind, and the moon, Kundalini, creative fire. She reveals that the moon arouses sexual energies (feminine mysteries) and the sun stimulates the mind. She clearly states that we are to bring together within ourselves the fire of the earth and the fire of the heavens; as we do, the divine in each one arises and a new, natural force field is awakened.

As Mary Gray states, *"It is the whole sympathetic system that is the product of the action of Kundalini, as the cerebro-spinal is the product of the brain. The sympathetic system is not controlled by the brain, but by the solar plexus, with merely a secondary reaction on the brain."* We learn that the impulses of Kundalini arise from basic instinct. Only at one's individualization does the mind undertake to guide the personality through the brain. Thereafter, the fire of earth (feminine, she who dwells in matter) and the fire of sun (masculine, son of spirit) begin the enlightening interplay.

The long-hidden formula emerges within the Self as it stimulates the potent desire for Oneness. The caduceus is formed within the body temple, the heart-mind awareness flashes, and life is lived from inside out. Inter-control allows life to be moved to the point of balance, either active or passive. This moment is much like the critical point of a see-saw when poised in stable balance. The use of energy determines what is "*appropriate to the moment and appropriate to the situation.*"

Most of us have mistaken ideas regarding kundalini. In truth, there are two energies, the fire of the earth (kundalini) and the fire of the sun (spirit) that have to connect within us. The human body, we gradually learn (She Who Dwells Within), contains the earth fire energy, and the fire energy from spirit has to descend to meet within our higher consciousness.

Simple and clear portrayals of transformation guidelines are offered wherever we look: in Kabalah, Christianity, and Sufism. "Wisdom ways" wait, tucked here and there. Wonderful examples of this are preserved in geometric designs and reused as designs and symbols. First, we have the circle, as the Oneness that began to stir. Next, the circle develops with a dot in the center, followed by a triangle representing the Creator Consciousness: masculine, feminine, and the powerful spirit that flows as energy arcs between their polarities. The consciousness of the initiate meets the situation, and power is invoked with which to do the work of the higher, on whatever level he or she is focused.

The Square represents the Earth with her four directions, four elements, four worlds, and four levels in each world, upon which manifests the Father, Mother, Son, and Daughter (earth). Each of us has four parts to develop as well: our masculine, our feminine, our mind, and our heart. We recognize the four kingdoms that inhabit the Earth: mineral, plant, animal, and human. This is what is meant by "kundalini is Earth-born," for the human is a part of the nature kingdom—the very finest of the human kingdom. We have long heard, "we must build the heart in the mind and the mind in the heart" without a clear understanding of what all of this means. Presently we are striving to manifest "The Kingdom of Souls on Earth" as well. This is the emerging fifth kingdom for which humanity is working.

Some diagrams show the four kingdoms with a circle sitting on top of them acknowledging ether (the symbol of the new emerging fifth kingdom). This is the cause of chaos or, said another way, for the current struggles within the group mind, and the call for humanity is to "rework" all that is.

The energy of emotion and the physical body ground the bottom of the triangle that holds the animal kingdom grounded. The human mind stretches upward forming the mental point of the triangle. This triangle stabilizes the lower world, while a higher life triangle of energy, sometimes known as the Supernal Triangle, delivers energy downward to each individual.

As our initiate labors to climb to the higher planes, the personality forming the triangle from below strives to receive energy from above. By human effort, the physical and emotional energies live in the heavier energies (symbolizing lower planes) while the invoked higher energy delivers a down-pouring to it. The personality forms the earthly triangle and struggles to reach the down-pouring of higher energy. In time, the personality will connect with the inspiration of the higher world and the goal is achieved. The star of the perfected personality gradually forms. As work continues, the two triangles overlap to form the Star of the Disciple, with which we are familiar as the Star of David.

Modem teachings encourage using the Light of the Soul Star over our head in activating the higher centers. The Manu of the Fifth Root Race so influenced Zoroaster that he taught that nothing lasting is gained spiritually by concentrating on the lower centers; this led to the formation of a new Western yoga. The old practice is too severe and drastic to be attempted in this age, and it is utterly unsuited for the Western mind and body. Until the meditations are done consciously with full brain cooperation, the "Narrow Way" is not found.

From a simplified student guide entitled *Cosmic Fire Revealed,* one can gain a better understanding of Kundalini. Sarah Leigh Brown, a wise woman of my acquaintance and instructor for Sancta Sophia Seminary (when it existed), delved into this topic with all her expertise. I wrote the foreword to *Cosmic Fire Revealed* and am aware of its depth, so I delight in sharing some of its insights with you.

Information is dispersed very carefully regarding the kundalini and its arousal, due to various potential dangers that can be activated. On the other hand, the stirring of the kundalini is most natural when it is awakened by ethical living and dedication to simplicity, honesty, and clarity. In a way it is like puberty: it is natural, but can be a troublesome stage. Thus one finds transformation occurring naturally without any damaging events when a respectful life moves from one stage to another. But to force these energies—as a result of a promise of power, greed, or personal gain—is destructive and can lead to sadism and evil.

Three triangles of fire exist in the human body. The two lower ones assist us with health and vitality. We value the lower triangle for it provides sexual impulses and what I call "the pilot light of our nature libido." The middle triangle rests in the upper torso between the shoulder blades, the diaphragm, and the spleen, and helps us have a healthy caring for one another. There is a gap between these lower two triangles and the upper triangle which is gradually bridged by techniques of learning to "love-care for others" (humanitarian love), ethics (high-minded-ness) and the building of the completed *antakarana,* or internal inner fires of the body. One need not know this consciously for it to be taking place or happening. The densest energy begins at the base of the spine and gradually integrates the energy of the other two triangles into the energy of the head centers, the supernal triad. A healthy kundalini, with natural arousal in due time, is the goal for each of us.

Cosmic Fire Revealed by Sarah Brown states:

1. In the head, the fire circulates around the pineal gland, the pituitary, and the Alta Major center at the back of the neck.

2. In the body, the triangle of prana is made of the center between the shoulders, the diaphragm, and the spleen.

3. At the base of the spine, the three lower centers are composed of a point at the bottom of the spinal column, and the two major sex centers of either the male or the female.

When this bridge is completed, merging the two lower fires of matter with the fires of mind results in a tremendous energizing of the entire physical body. This accounts for the incredible physical stamina of the great geniuses of the race. Furthermore, the electrical stimulation of the head, heart, and throat centers invites the down-flow of Spirit, or monadic energy. The three fires of body, mind, and Spirit have met; the at-one-ment with the Ego/Soul is completed; combustion takes place, and the Spirit is liberated (fourth initiation).

Previously it was mentioned that the two lower triangles of fires blended long ago without harm or conscious effort. Today we are striving to blend the fire of the mind, but only about one-third of humanity has begun this step and a small number done so. Afterwards the three channels are now one, so we see the transformation of humanity changing from "the beast of the Earth" into a divine one in the higher world with a high consciousness that operates on many additional planes other than just the earth; also, we will see that distortions and false values are burned away. With a high consciousness to guide us, "legitimate procedures" are to be done safely through study and purification, meditation and service, and most urgently under proper supervision.

Two more sources of rare information comes to us in *Cosmic Fire Revealed*:

The information is new and needs to be sought out by sincere seekers and left alone by those who are undisciplined or just fooling with ideas, and not yet dedicated. The above books will tell you that, when the spine is ready, we move our focus to the head. This is a principal part of the technique shift: to pull down the energy of the Soul Star from above your head and wrap it around your head instead of trying to raise it from the base chakra.

As we focus upon the head, essentially the pineal gland and the pituitary body, the carotid gland, and the medulla oblongata, we find a new stage of growth occurring. The human brain has a fundamental resemblance to the human embryo; it represents the parts of a bodily form in miniature. The little form is hermaphrodite.

The pineal and pituitary represent the male and female elements. It is taught that the prototype of the new human embryo takes shape first in the head, and that the baby's little body grows as an extrusion of the inner brain form.

This little living form which composes the human brain is found to be hermaphrodite, male and female, in one. As a true hermaphrodite, it is able to give birth to a new being. In this case, the new being will be a spiritual entity capable of awareness and activity in the invisible world of causes.

The truth of this reality of a new entity in the brain of a human being is not new, but understood in ancient times. Civilizations such as the Egyptian, Indian (East), China etc., taught that this marriage in the head, between the two major glands, pituitary (female and physical) and the pineal (male and spiritual), takes place to bring about the birth of the Christ child. This is the true spiritual being that we long to be. Now the true Third Eye glows and the Christ Consciousness lives. The second is like unto the first.

> *Such achievement is the birthright of the real you and I and all others. That spark of the soul embedded in matter is your very self. When God said, "I will make man in my image," what did He mean?... The Teaching is that God divided Himself into Male (Spirit) and Female (Matter) so that, as these two fused, the result of such a marriage was Consciousness, the Son Christ. Man's ultimate achievement is to bear a spirit-son within his Hermaphrodite brain, and thus join the ranks of the spirit-world whilst still in bodily form.*

> — Paraphrased from *The Fifth Dimension* by Vera Stanley Adler

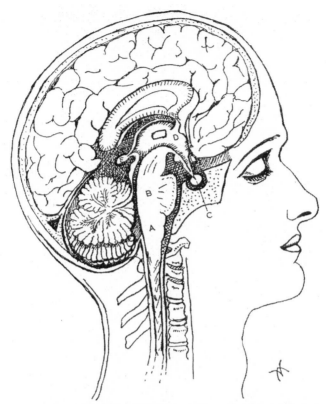

As the result of a dedicated life, transmuted energies rise up the spinal nerve channel, into the Medulla Oblongata, (A) through the Pons or Mid-Brain, (B) then pass down into the Pituitary Gland (C) (behind the eyes). The increasing Pituitary radiations finally pass through the Third Ventricle (D) (or air cavity) until they awaken the dormant Pineal, (E) and the Third Eye lights up between them.

(Drawn by the author from specimens in the Royal College of Surgeons, London)

Results of the Quest

When one becomes a wise one, under the guidance of the Soul, he or she serves by then stepping wisdom down to the world around him/her. Wise ones demonstrate their ability to create and find purposes for utilizing these energies. By employing "right use," they are able to handle inner and outer realities (balance the see-saw) with appropriateness.

The Mystic Bible, an East West Commentary by Dr. Randolph Stone, addresses past karma and the Master's Grace, including the effort required during mental concentration as we practice penetrating into what we have known "as the cloud of knowable things." We have been taught that meditation/concentration/contemplation each raise our consciousness internally to higher regions, as does the degree of humility and service we render to humanity during our lifetime. Of course, the manner in which we conduct our relationships to others enriches our inner progress in appropriate ways; in this way we demonstrate we have learned what has been taught.

We are not extricated from the mire of our karma by crying out to God; however, we are prevented from sinking deeper. We must grow into a desire to be liberated, and begin to direct our thoughts toward the higher world. We must seek to do our best in the ways we know and see … if we hear what to do to invoke a better way of Life. Every genuine struggle has merits, but transgressions must be worked off. Satan, as the ego-mind principle of the tempter, attacks all initiates, even as Jesus was tempted in the wilderness. We have to come to an understanding of the limited mind principle vs. the higher Mind that is our most trustworthy friend. We each have three faculties of our mind to struggle against: namely, our thinking faculty, our memory, and the ego. Only our higher Mind will hold steady during our trials, and thus we earn our freedom.

- Our thinking faculty can have erroneous patterns of thought.

- Our memory carries the "rights" and "wrongs" we had programmed into us by cultures past and present.

- The ego thinks up tricks as to how to get its own way. That is why the ego is sometimes called Satan.

All traditions' crowning teachings share the same truths in different manners. We practice love, freedom, beauty, and joy in our daily life. We meditate to build up our glands, gradually perfecting them as possible. We study to use well our intellectual powers and we do service to share with humanity the vibration of our quest.

One of the wise ones with whom I studied wrote the following:

> It is necessary to realize there is a difference between the functions of the visible physical body, the invisible electrical counterpart, the living emotional reactions, the varied mental activities, and the subtle abstract realizations and ideals.
>
> All these separate, living entities, as it were, each one trying to usurp power over the whole!
>
> A person can be a slave to any of his physical appetites. He can be galvanized into extreme activity either under emotional, mental, or spiritual stimulus. The uncontrolled emotional stimulation is exhausting; the mental stimulation is equally so.
>
> The stimulation which comes from the soul has a calming effect and feeds the nervous system with the 'peace which passes understanding—because, in fact, the understanding has been by-passed!
>
> We now come to a more mysterious part of our techniques. We have to bring our imagination into play and visualize the work to be done by stimulating the activities within others as well as ourselves, which cannot be seen. (*The Fifth Dimension* by Vera Stanley Alder)

These are valued steps to be utilized in building the Transpersonal Self, the Christ Consciousness or Soul Consciousness, and each are introduced as we start transformation. We are creatures of dichotomy: earth and sky, inner and outer, heart and mind, male and female. A major step is our commitment to become a Soul-Infused Personality. From there we need a mentor or guide of some sort.

Many resources and opportunities await all of us. The techniques of blending the understandings of various traditions are unique to each individual path, but enough alike to help us see the four principle steps involved.

1 Awaken to inner guidance and appropriate outer actions.

2 In Esoteric Christianity, Fire and Light are used under the guidance of Sophia, the Holy Spirit.

3 In Eastern Kundalini, the energies of Ida and Pingala wrap about the Sushumna.

4 In Kabalah, we find these Life Giving energies as three columns: male, female, and central; we come to balance them into the central column.

From a handout several years old and source-author unknown:

- *Although man is the highest product of evolution, the process of evolution is still active in him. This evolution is not confined to his mind alone, as held by Julian Huxley, Teilhard de Chardin and some other evolutionists, but involves also a corresponding evolution of his brain.*

- *This idea of the continued organic evolution of the cerebro-spinal system has not found general acceptance among scientists, so far, for the simple reason that the working of the brain is very imperfectly understood. Secondly, biologists are not prepared to accept the existence of a Universal Life Force, which is the architect of all forms of life on the earth.*

- *The reason for their attitude in relation to continued organic evolution lies in the anomaly existing between the thinking of biologists and the physicists about the basic realities of the universe. While for the latter, the observed phenomena cannot be entirely separated from the observer, the former continue to allow the same outdated concrete position in atoms and molecules as was alleged by physicists at the beginning of the twentieth century.*

- *The base of the spine is the seat of the Generative Force in man. It is the abode of romance and love. It is from this region that the Spark of Life is transmitted from the parent to the child. It is here that the Life Force exists in its most concentrated form. What is still a closed* book to the learned is that precisely at this spot the evolutionary mechanism is operative in the human race.

- *This vital fact has been known from immemorial times, but always interpreted in religious, magical or supernatural terms. The methods to activate the mechanism were known to ancient Egyptians, Chinese, Indians and others, and the image of the serpent has been the most common symbol used to represent this Force. In India, the evolutionary Force with the mechanism it controls has been known as Kundalini.*

- *The continued evolution of the human brain has a target, which is to carry the entire race to the same state of extended and blissful consciousness, which has been, time after time, experienced in Mystical Ecstasy by the Illuminate of all ages and climes. The remarkable similarity between the experience of one mystic and the other, separated by vast distances and long durations in time, has been mainly due to the fact that the target of evolution for all members of the human race is the same. Hence, all those who came, heard, or arrived at the goal witnessed an identical change in their inner being. Their recorded accounts, from the time of the Vedas to this day, amply corroborate this fact.*

- *Language is a direct product of evolution. So are art, philosophy and science. Man has advanced in all branches of knowledge and art because of the progressive evolutionary process. Were this process to cease or reverse itself, stagnation and decline would follow as surely as night follows the day. Ascendant nations of the past fell victims to decay and groveled in the dust because the evolutionary process ceased or backfired on account of the laws which govern it. The modern civilization, too, is facing the same crisis for the same reason—violation of the evolutionary laws. The main factors responsible for this tragedy are the ignorance of the laws, the materialistic tendency of the age and, the unbridled lust for power and possession rampant in the race.*

- *With the arousal of Kundalini a new man is born. For the first time, the ineffable World of Consciousness opens before his Inner Eye. For the first time, he marks the gulf between the normal and paranormal consciousness. For the first time, he delights in the Glory and Eternity of the Soul. This sublime experience gave authority to the great prophets and saviors of the past. It is this glorious Vision, which alone can grant authority to the elite of the future to act as leaders in every sphere of human activity and thought. It is only then that the race will abide in security and peace, immune to the danger, which threatens its survival at present.* (Author unknown)

The Path of the Masculine builds courage, will, strength, and daring; he has learned to defend those who need it. Bold and daring, the Lion-hearted can be as fierce as a situation calls for or as gentle as is needed. He can defend the weak and poor, the old and young. The same Will that is awakened to discipline the basic nature can now be utilized to show self-restraint; the warrior can be gentle and tender, share delicate love. In control of the qualities developed, Chivalry lives within the Self and emerges as needed. Herein lays the blend of Lord and Master, well aware he is to balance his every step ahead (and remember we are each equipped with both masculine and feminine energy and learning to use it).

Entwined with him is Lady of Love, both tough and tender; she is nurturing and creative. Receiving and outpouring, the Giver of life soothes and heals, giving birth on every level yet walking with death without dread or fear, easing transition by her presence. True to her guidance from within, she dances and plays, is enduring, and intuitive. As the companion, she shares all pain, but receives also the joy of the higher world and steps it earthward. The Lady of Love, known in the Mideast as the Dove, embraces the good and not so good, knows Love is her tool and touch is her way. She sprinkles delight; her joy brings forth her play.

Again, whichever body we wear, we must learn to use our masculine and our feminine resources in our daily life. In this way we become the Wise One.

Graceful and delicate, bold and powerful, is the caduceus that builds within our nature. It is a blessed spiral the serpentine energy creates, as each opportunity is well met and the *aware life* happens. It is not always as we plan, but by the response, we find we advance. Growing and glowing, we go on our way knowing we can enter the Light, but never touch the flame. World upon worlds await our embrace. Standing in the Light, we know we are the new being ... *humanus spiritus* ... and we shall pass this way again *being the Light.*

**Many blessings to you as you become
the mystic you are meant to be.**

Prayer to Sophia

In darkest night, when lights are dim,
And all in sight seems sad and grim,
I find you there; your arms surround me,
Your spirit fills me and it grounds me.

I look to you, Lady of Truth,
Most ancient One, yet eternal youth,
To keep me safe, protect my heart,
and with the wisdom you impart
Fill up my empty mind and soul.

It is you, Sophia, who can make me whole,
And that is what I need this day —
This is what I ask and pray.

—Author Unknown

High Creativity charms our heart and makes us glad. I share a dance I wrote some years ago. I make some suggestions to get you started; build on them and enjoy.

First step: Read it through ... use gentle music and imagination, and you have your tools. One person reads the words with expression ... slowly, carefully.

A dancer improvises the words as they are read by the other. This dancer is to be very graceful and nymph-like, wearing a light, flowing, loose garment and moving gracefully, working together with the reader. Allow the words to indicate actions. There can be simple props, no need for much.

Another way is to have several dancers dress in appropriate colors of the chakras and each one dance to the appropriate paragraph. Use the colors: red first paragraph, orange second paragraph, yellow for the third paragraph, blue for the fourth, then green for the fifth or for the heart. Indigo or rose (some groups use one color, some the other) for the throat with lavender for the seventh and highest chakra.

Closing: The dancers stand all together in a circle, raising their hands into the air. Begin to sound gentle OMs. Hands assume prayerful position (palms together) as they begin to sound the OM (or three OMs one after another), and together they lower their hands (in a gentle style) as they finish the sounds.

The Dance of the Soul concludes our study of the Making of a Mystic....

I am the Soul. Filled with a great desire to express herself perfectly, the Soul of Life, which is everyone, spoke forth and said, "Let there be Light," and there was Light. This was the first step.

CHIME

Thus the Soul, which is everyone, began its journey filled with great light and went forth to find experience. The journey led the Soul into great darkness and pain, but one day the Soul realized it was far from Creator's home and stood erect and dusted herself off and with rededication began to find her way. And this was the second step.

CHIME

On the top of a hill the Soul, which is everyone, could see far into the distance. This is past and present and future. At this peak point of awareness, Soul feels very wise and sure. The Soul names every experience, knows good and evil, and watches as they merge into a great drama creating the School of Life. The Soul, which is everyone, knows itself to be Power. It loves the feeling of strength and ego and is no longer afraid. It would always be right. And this is the third step.

CHIME

Life has gotten so hard. Every day is different. The journey is no longer fun or light or under control. The Soul, which is everyone, is so tender, vulnerable and sensitive that life hurts too much. Soul says, "I will hide away and I will pray and I will love the world from safety. Let them fight and struggle. That way is not for me." As Soul would hide, the hole closes over her. Soul prays. The message comes: "Do your service." When Soul cries, wee small voices cry out, "Please help us!" Soul weeps and this is the fourth step.

CHIME

Today, Soul, which is everyone, cares so much. Soul opens her mouth and the higher pours into expression. No longer so sure, but much more willing, Soul experiences Life, allowing the tides to wash over her. Soul loves, accepts and acts with new strength. The Eye guides her, the Ears hear the mysteries and grasp meaning behind meaning; the Forces of great compassion know her to be their servant. It is the fifth step.

CHIME

One day, Soul realizes all that is to be known, and finds herself looking at the Life from afar. No longer does the journey seem so important nor does "becoming" seem so fascinating. She takes a great breath and sees the sparkle of great light go from her nostrils;

she breathes in and sees the ethers create new shapes. She holds her breath, aware of her power to change and be changed. She relaxes, is filled with peace, and knows herself to be Life. For a moment, fear almost comes and then the energy changes to love. Soul knows her power and trusts Creator for having given her the journey that She might become all She can be. She knows this is the sixth step. She is home.

CHIME

Thus, heaven and earth become one, and the journey of Soul of Life, which is everyone, achieves its goal. Soul's perfected consciousness merges with the Divine and becomes one with the entire manifested universe. Now there need be no effort, for all is accomplished. Knowing truth, loving all creation, Soul comes to rest in a state of sanctified peace. This is the seventh step. Soul is truly blessed.

CHIME

Chorus sound the Sacred Tone together three times: OM, OM, OM

References

Alder, Vera Stanley. *The Fifth Dimension: The Future of Mankind*. Ryder: London, 1940.

Alder, Vera Stanley. *The Initiation of the World*. Ryder: London, 1939.

Alexander, Eben M.D. *Proof of Heaven: A Neurosurgeon's Journey into the Afterlife*. New York: Simon & Schuster, 2012.

Amen, Daniel G. M.D. *Change Your Brain, Change Your Life: The Breakthrough Program For Conquering Anxiety, Depression, Obsessiveness, Anger, and Impulsiveness*. New York: Random House, 1999.

Aurobindo, Sri Ghose. *Integral Yoga: Sri Aurobindo's Teaching & Method of Practice*. Lotus Press, 1993

Bailey, Alice A. *A Treatise on Cosmic Fire*. New York: Lucis Publishing Co., 1925, 1973.

Bargeman, Lisa Ann. *The Egyptian Origins of Christianity*. Nevada City, CA: Blue Dolphin, 2005.

Barnwell, F. Aster. *The Meaning of Christ for our Age*. St. Paul, MN: Llewellyn Publications, 1984.

Bendit, Phoebe. *The Sacred Flame*. Pasadena, CA: Theosophical Press, 1962.

Bucke, Richard Maurice. *Cosmic Consciousness: A Study in the Evolution of the Human Mind*. Eastford, CT: Martino Fine Books, 1905, 2010.

Butz, Jeffrey J. *The Brother of Jesus and the Lost Teaching of Christianity*. Rochester, VT: Inner Traditions, 2005.

Campbell, Don. *The Mozart Effect*. New York: Avon Books, 1997.

Collins, Mabel. *Light on the Path* and *Through the Gates of Gold*. Pasadena, CA: Theosophical University, 1949.

Collins, Mabel. "The Inner Life of Mabel Collins." Wikipedia.com

Dourley, John P. *Love, Celibacy and the Inner Marriage*. Toronto: Inner City Books, 1987.

Eastcott, Michael J. & Magor, Nancy. *Entering Aquarius*. Sherborne, Dorset, UK: Sundial, 2001.

Elgin, Duane. *Voluntary Simplicity*. New York: Morrow, 1981.

Ellsberg, Robert. *All Saints: Daily Reflections on Saints, Prophets, and Witnesses for our Time*. New York: Crossroads, 1997.

Evans-Wentz, W.Y. *The Tibetan Book of the Dead*. London: Oxford University Press, 1927, 1960.

Firestone, Rabbi Tirzah. *The Receiving: Reclaiming Jewish Women's Wisdom*. New York: Harper One, 2003.

Forman, Robert K. C. *Meister Eckhart: Mystic as Theologian*. Rockport, MA: Element Books, 1994.

Freke, Timothy & Gandy, Peter. *The Jesus Mysteries: Was the "Original Jesus" a Pagan God?* New York: Harmony, 2001.

Freke, Timothy & Gandy, Peter. *Jesus and the Lost Goddess*. New York: Harmony, 2002.

Freke, Timothy & Gandy, Peter. *The Laughing Jesus: Religious Lies and Gnostic Wisdom*. New York: Harmony, 2006.

Gibran, Kahlil. *The Prophet*. New York: Knopf, 1927.

Gray, Mary. *Echoes of the Cosmic Song*. Whitefish, MT: Kessinger Legacy Reprints, 2010.

Gray, Mary. *Gateway to Liberation*. Tahlequah, OK: Sparrow Hawk Press, 1992.

Gray, William G. *An Outlook on Our Inner Western Way*. Newburyport, MA: Red Wheel/Weiser, 1980.

Greeley, Andrew. "Fitness of Body and Mind," in *American Health*, Jan-Feb 1987, p.47.

Grof, Christina. *The Thirst for Wholeness: Attraction, Addiction, and the Spiritual Path*. New York: HarperOne,1994.

Grof, Christina & Stanislav. *Spiritual Emergency: When Personal Transformation Becomes a Crisis*. New York: Tarcher, 1989.

Hall, Manly P. *The Psychology of Religious Ritual*. Los Angeles: Philosophical Research Society, 1955.

Harrington, Michael. *Touched by the Dragon's Breath*. Susan Creek, MI: Susan Creek Publishing, 2013.

Harvey, Andrew (Ed.). *Teachings of the Christian Mystics*. Boston: Shambhala, 1997.

Isaac, Stephen & Phyllis (Ed.). *The Collected Works of Flower A. Newhouse: Volume 1 - Christian Mysticism*. San Diego: Christward Ministry, 2006.

Isaac, Stephen. *Songs from the House of Pilgrimage: The Biography of a Mystic and a Way of Life That Foretells the Future of Christianity*. Branden Press, 1971.

Keller David G.R. *Oasis of Wisdom: The Worlds of the Desert Fathers and Mothers*. Collegeville, MN: Liturgical Press, 2005

King, Thomas M. *Teilhard's Mysticism of Knowing*. New York: Seabury Press, 1981.

Krishna, Gopi. *Kundalini: The Evolutionary Energy in Man*. Boston: Shambhala, 1967.

Kybalion, The: A Study of the Hermetic Philosophy of Ancient Egypt and Greece. Chicago: Yogi Publication Society MasonicTemple, 1912.

LeShan, Lawrence. *How to Meditate: A Guide to Self-Discovery*. New York: Little, Brown, 1974.

LeShan, Lawrence. *The Medium, the Mystic, and the Physicist: Toward a General Theory of the Paranormal*. New York: Viking, 1974.

LeShan, Lawrence. *The World of the Paranormal: The Next Frontier*. New York: Allworth Press, 2004.

Levi, Eliphas. *The Great Secret or Occultism Unveiled*. New York: Weiser, 2000.

Maimonides, Moses. (Isadore Twersky, Ed.). *A Maimonides Reader*. New York: Behrman House, 1972 .

Malachi, Tau. *St. Mary Magdalene: The Gnostic Tradition of the Holy Bride*. Woodbury, MN: Llewellyn Publications, 2012.

Malachi, Tau. *The Gnostic Gospel of St. Thomas*. Woodbury, MN: Llewellyn Publications, 2012.

Malachi, Tau. *The Gnostic Tradition of the Holy Bride*. Woodbury, MN: Llewellyn Publications, 2006.

Manser, Ann & North, Cecil. *Pages of Shustah: Divination and Meditation Cards*. New York: Paragon, 1974.

Maslow, Abraham. *Toward a Psychology of Being*. New York: Van Nostrand Reinhold, 1968.

Maslow, Abraham. *The Farther Reaches of Human Nature*. New York: Penguin, 1993.

Maslow, Abraham. *Religions, Values, and Peak-Experiences*. Penguin, 1994.

Mead, G.R.S (Transl.). *Pistis Sophia*. London, England: J.M. Watkins, 1896.

Merion, Jim. *Putting on the Mind of Christ: The Inner Work of Christian Spirituality*. Newburyport, MA: Hampton Roads, 2011.

Metzner, Ralph. *Opening to Inner Light: The Transformation of Human Nature and Consciousness*. New York: Tarcher, 1986.

Moody, Raymond. *Life After Life: The Investigation of a Phenomenon—Survival of Bodily Death*. Mechanicsburg, PA: Stackpole Books 1976.

Mundy, Jon. *What is Mysticism?* Unionville, NY: Royal Fireworks Press, 2008.

Myss, Caroline. *Entering the Castle: Finding the Inner Path to God and Your Soul's Purpose*. New York: Atria Books, 2008.

Needleman, Jacob. *Lost Christianity: A Journey of Rediscovery to the Center of the Christian Experience*. New York, NY: Doubleday, 1980.

Newhouse, Flower A. *The Collected Works of Flower A. Newhouse Vol.1 Christian Mysticism*. San Diego, CA: Christward Ministry, 2006.

Pagels, Elaine. *The Gnostic Gospels*. New York: Random House, 1979.

Palmer, G.E.H. (Transl.) *The Philokalia: Sayings of the Desert Fathers*. London: Faber & Faber, 1983.

Parrish-Harra, Carol E. *Esoteric Secrets of Sex, Passion and Love*. Tahlequah, OK: Sparrow Hawk Press, 2011.

Parrish-Harra, Carol E. *The New Dictionary of Spiritual Thought* (Second Ed.). Tahlequah, OK: Sparrow Hawk Press, 2002.

Parrish-Harra, Carol E. *Sophia Sutras: Introducing Mother Wisdom*. Tahlequah, OK: Sparrow Hawk Press, 2006.

Patai, Raphael. *The Hebrew Goddess* (Third Ed.). Detroit, MI: Wayne State University,1990.

Powell, Robert. *The Sophia Teachings: The Emergence of the Divine Feminine in Our Time*. New York: Lantern Books, 2001.

Ram Dass. *Be Here Now*. San Cristobal, NM: Lama Foundation, 1971.

Roerich, Nicholas & Helena. *Flame in Chalice*. Whitefish, MT: Kessinger Legacy Reprints, 2010.

Rupp, Joyce. *Prayers to Sophia: A Companion to "The Star in My Heart."* Notre Dame, IN: Ave Maria Press, 1999.

Saraydarian, Torkom. *Cosmic Shocks*. Cave Creek, AZ: TSG Publishing, 1989.

Saraydarian, Torkom. *Cosmos in Man*. Agoura, CA: The Aquarian Educational Group, 1973.

Saraydarian, Torkom. *Love, Freedom, Beauty and Joy.* Agoura, CA: The Aquarian Educational Group, 1974.

Saraydarian, Torkom. *The Fiery Carriage.* Agoura, CA: The Aquarian Educational Group, 1973.

Saraydarian, Torkom. *The Flame of the Heart.* Cave Creek, AZ: TSG Publishing, 1991.

Shapiro, Rabbi Rami. *The Divine Feminine in Biblical Wisdom Literature.* Woodstock, VT: Sky Light Paths Publishing, 2011.

Sisirkumar, Ghose. *Mystics as a Force for Change.* Adyar, India: Theosophical Publishing House, 1981.

St. Romain, Phillip. *Kundalini Energy and Christian Spirituality.* New York: Crossroads, 1991.

Starbird, Margaret. *The Alabaster Jar.* Rochester, VT: Bear & Company, 1993.

Stone, Randolph. *Mystic Bible.* Punjab, India: Radha Soami Satsang Beas, 1956.

Taylor, Jill Bolte. *My Stroke of Luck.* New York: Penguin, 2006.

Trigueirinho, Jose. *Esoteric Lexicon.* Buenos Aires, Argentina: Editorial Kier S.A, 1994.

Underhill, Evelyn. *Mysticism: A Study in Nature and Development of Spiritual Consciousness.* New York: Dover Publications,1911.

Vernier, Philippe & Pierce, Edith Lovejoy. *With the Master: A Book of Meditations.* Fellowship Publications, 1943.

White Eagle Lodge of London. *The Christian Mysteries. Vol. III: Illuminations.*

White, John. "Resurrection and the Body of Light," in *Quest Magazine* 97, Fall 2009: 11-15.

Wilber, Ken. *Eye to Eye: The Quest for the New Paradigm.* (Third Rev. Ed.) Boston: Shambhala, 2001.

Index

About the Author

REV. CAROL E. PARRISH-HARRA, PH.D., long known as a "practical mystic," is the founder of Sparrow Hawk Village, an intentional community located in Tahlequah, Oklahoma, a small settlement in the Ozarks.

She currently serves as Bishop at The Chapel of Christ Sophia, which is affiliated with the Ascension Alliance, part of the independent Catholic movement, and Dean Emeritus of Sancta Sophia Seminary, a modern-day mystery school.

Carol has stimulated many to rejoice in their personal spirituality. Many find hope in her lucid explanations of how certain fundamental truths, which underlie all major religions, can guide us in these changing times.

Carol has received numerous awards, including the Russian Nebolsin Medal and the Earl Award which is awarded for Religious Futurists.

Her books include *Sophia Sutras*, the *New Dictionary of Spiritual Thought*, and the *Adventure in Meditation Series*, which won the Athena Award for Mentoring Excellence three years in a row. Her recent book, *Remember to Remember*, focuses on the culture and beliefs of the Mayans.

Mary's Message to the World
Annie Kirkwood
228 pp., paperback, 5.5 x 8.5, $14.95
Also available on CD: $49.95

Reincarnation for Christians
Evidence from Early Christian and Jewish Mystical Traditions
John W. Sweeley, Th.D.
294 pp., 6x9, paperback, $22.00

The Fifth Gospel
New Evidence from the Tibetan, Sanskrit, Arabic, Persian and Urdu Sources About the Historical Life of Jesus Christ After the Crucifixion
Fida Hassnain & Dahan Levi
344 pp., 6 x 9, paperback, $19.95

Buddha's Map
His Original Teachings on Awakening, Ease, and Insight in the Heart of Meditation
Doug Kraft
364 pp., 6 x 9, paperback, $22.00

Dreamwork Around the World and Across Time
An Anthology
Leland E. Shields, M.S., M.A.
316 pp., 6x9, paperback, $19.95, hardcover, $29.95

Consciousness Is All
Now Life Is Completely New
Peter Francis Dziuban
340 pp., 6 x 9, paperback, $22.00, hardcover, $34.95,

On the Tip Edge of a Miracle
Dreams, Visions and Prophecies for the Future
Dennison & Teddi Tsosie
304 pp., paper back, 6x9, $22.00

Initiation
Boys Are Born, Men Are Trained
Jeffrey Prather
266 pp., 5.5 x 8.5, paperback, $17.95

Esoteric Healing
A Practical Guide Based on the Teachings of the Tibetan in the Works of Alice A. Bailey
Alan Hopking
384 pp., 6x9, paperback, $25.00; hardcover, $35.00

Heal Your Cancer
Emotional and Spiritual Pathways
Bruno Cortis, M.D.
66 pp., 7 color photos, 5.25 x 8., paperback, $13.00

A Guide to the Dolphin Divination Cards
A guide for the use and personal interpretation of the Dolphin Divination Cards
Nancy Clemens
388 pp., 6x9, paperback, $22.00

Dolphin Divination Cards
Nancy Clemens
108 round cards, boxed, $13.00
Words of counsel and affirmation